Amatory Pleasures

Other Books by Julie Peakman

Peg Plunkett, Memoirs of a Whore (Quercus, 2014)
The Pleasure's All Mine. A History of Sexual Perversion (Reaktion, 2013)
Mighty Lewd Books, The Development of Pornography in Eighteenth-century England (Palgrave, 2003; reissued in paperback 2012)
Emma Hamilton. A biography (Haus, 2005)
Lascivious Bodies. A Sexual History of the Eighteenth Century (Atlantic, 2004)
(ed.) *A Cultural History of Sexuality* (Berg, 2011), 6 volumes
(ed.) *Sexual Perversions 1650–1890* (Palgrave, 2009)
(ed.) *Whore's Biographies in the Long Eighteenth Century* (Pickering & Chatto, 2007–8), 8 volumes

Amatory Pleasures

Explorations in Eighteenth-Century Sexual Culture

JULIE PEAKMAN

Bloomsbury Academic
An imprint of Bloomsbury Publishing Plc

B L O O M S B U R Y
LONDON · OXFORD · NEW YORK · NEW DELHI · SYDNEY

Bloomsbury Academic
An imprint of Bloomsbury Publishing Plc

50 Bedford Square   1385 Broadway
London   New York
WC1B 3DP   NY 10018
UK   USA

www.bloomsbury.com

BLOOMSBURY and the Diana logo are trademarks of Bloomsbury Publishing Plc

First published 2016

© Julie Peakman, 2016

Julie Peakman has asserted her right under the Copyright, Designs and Patents Act, 1988, to be identified as Author of this work.

All rights reserved. No part of this publication may be reproduced or transmitted in any form or by any means, electronic or mechanical, including photocopying, recording, or any information storage or retrieval system, without prior permission in writing from the publishers.

No responsibility for loss caused to any individual or organization acting on or refraining from action as a result of the material in this publication can be accepted by Bloomsbury or the author.

British Library Cataloguing-in-Publication Data
A catalogue record for this book is available from the British Library.

ISBN: HB: 978-1-4742-2643-1
PB: 978-1-4742-2644-8
ePDF: 978-1-4742-2646-2
ePub: 978-1-4742-2645-5

Library of Congress Cataloging-in-Publication Data
Names: Peakman, Julie, 1957- author.
Title: Amatory pleasures : explorations in eighteenth-century sexual culture / Julie Peakman.
Description: London; New York : Bloomsbury Academic, 2016. | Includes bibliographical references and index.
Identifiers: LCCN 2015047998 (print) | LCCN 2016004159 (ebook) | ISBN 9781474226431 (hardback) | ISBN 9781474226448 (paperback) | ISBN 9781474226462 (ePDF) | ISBN 9781474226455 (ePub)
Subjects: LCSH: Sex—History—18th century. | Sex customs—History—18th century. | Sex in literature—History—18th century. | BISAC: HISTORY / Modern / 18th Century. | HISTORY / Social History. | HISTORY / Europe / Great Britain.
Classification: LCC HQ16. P43 2016 (print) | LCC HQ16 (ebook) | DDC 306.709/033—dc23
LC record available at http://lccn.loc.gov/2015047998

Cover design: Catherine Wood
Cover image © Useless Resistance, Jean-Honoré Fragonard

Typeset by RefineCatch Limited, Bungay, Suffolk

For Jad

Let the world run its course of capricious delight
I none of its vanities prize;
More substantial the joys I experience each night,
From a touch 'twixt my charmer's white thighs.

If aught can entice me, if aught can allure.
My slumbering passions to rise,
Or aught kindle up my desires – be sure
'Tis of these snowy white thighs.

The arse of my love is delightful to see,
Its plumpness rejoiceth the eyes;
Her lily-white belly is heaven to me
But, ye gods! What are these to her thighs?

THERESA BERKELEY, VENUS SCHOOL-MISTRESS, OR BIRCHEN SPORTS *(C.1810)*

CONTENTS

Illustrations ix
Preface xi
Introduction xiii

PART ONE Norms and Anomalies 1

1 Continuities and Change in Sexual Behaviour and Attitudes from the Eighteenth Century 3
2 'Perversion of the Course of Nature': Sexual Variations in the Eighteenth Century 17
3 Blaming and Shaming in Eighteenth- and Early Nineteenth-century Print Culture 41

PART TWO Erotic Women: Fact and Fiction 59

4 Whore Biographies in the Eighteenth Century 61
5 Memoirs of Women of Pleasure: Autobiographies 79
6 Initiation, Defloration and Flagellation: Sexual Propensities in *Memoirs of a Woman of Pleasure* 101
7 'The Best Freind in the World': The Relationship Between Emma Hamilton and Queen Maria Carolina of Naples 113

PART THREE Exploring Bodies 131

8 Bodily Anxieties in Enlightenment Sex Literature 133

9 Medicine, the Body and the Botanical
   Sexual Metaphor in Erotica 145
10 The Eighteenth-century Erotic Garden 159

Notes 173
Index 215

ILLUSTRATIONS

1.1 A merry crowd with a fiddler playing a tune celebrates a marriage as the groom kisses the bride (n.d.). Wellcome Library, London.   5
1.2 An unhappy arranged marriage. Wellcome Library, London.   7
1.3 William Hogarth, *The Harlot's Progress*, Plate II, 1732. Wellcome Library, London.   8
1.4 Slave auction notice, 1769. From the Collection of Karen Halttunen, American Antiquarian Society.   9
2.1 Frontispiece to William Derham, *Physico-Theology, Or a Demonstration of the being and attitudes of God from his works of creation*, 1713. Wikimedia Commons.   19
2.2 Marquis de Sade, *La Nouvelle Justine*, Dutch edition, 1797. Wellcome Library, London.   30
2.3 Marquis de Sade, frontispiece to *La Nouvelle Justine*, 1791. Wellcome Library, London.   31
3.1 Frontispiece, *The Life and Death of John Atherton*, 1641. British Library, London.   46
3.2 Frontispiece, *A Correct Account of the Horrible Occurrence ... Bishop of Clogher*, 1822. British Library, London.   47
3.3 Frontispiece, *A New Collection of Trials for Adultery*, 1799. British Library, London.   48
3.4 Frontispiece, *A New Collection of Trials for Adultery*, 1799. British Library, London.   50
3.5 William Hogarth, *Marriage a la mode: Drunk and disorderly*. Wellcome Library, London.   53
4.1 Sally Salisbury wounding the Honourable Mr F----. Wellcome Library, London.   64
4.2 Nancy Dawson dancing the hornpipe. British Library, London.   66
4.3 Fanny Murray by Henry Morland. Wikimedia Commons.   67
4.4 Portrait of Beau Richard Nash. Wellcome Library, London.   68
4.5 A portrait of Miss Kitty Fisher. Mezzotint by C. Tomkins after Sir J. Reynolds. Wellcome Library, London.   70
4.6 William Hogarth, *The Harlot's Progress*, Plate 1. Wellcome Library, London.   73
5.1 Mrs Margaret Leeson (Peg Plunkett). Wikimedia Commons.   83
5.2 Harriette Wilson. Author's collection.   84

6.1 *Memoirs of a Woman of Pleasure*, London 1766 edition. British Library, London. 102
6.2 *Memoirs of a Woman of Pleasure*, London 1749 edition. British Library, London. 104
7.1 Emma Hamilton as Circe, by George Romney, c.1782. Wikimedia Commons. 114
7.2 William Hamilton. Wikimedia Commons. 116
7.3 Horatio Nelson. National Maritime Museum, Greenwich, London, Greenwich Hospital Collection. 119
7.4 Emma Hamilton in an attitude towards a mimosa plant, causing it to demonstrate sensibility. Stipple engraving, 1789. Wellcome Library, London. 123
7.5 Death mask of Queen Maria Carolina. Author's collection. 128
8.1 *Tableau de l'Amour*, c.1776. Wikimedia Commons. 136
8.2 Frontispiece, *Aristotle's compleat master-piece . . . displaying the secrets of nature in the generation of man*, 12th edition. Wellcome Library, London. 137
8.3 Title page to *Aristotle's Compleat and Experienced Midwife . . .* showing midwives attending a woman in bed and a newly born child, 1733. Wellcome Library, London. 138
9.1 Thomas Rowlandson, *Death and the Apothecary*, a satire on quacks, c.1815. Wellcome Library, London. 155
9.2 Flora at play with cupid in Erasmus Darwin, *The Botanic Garden*, 1791. Wellcome Library, London. 157
10.1 William Hamilton's English garden, Caserta, near Naples. Wikimedia Commons. 162
10.2 Temple of Ancient Virtue, Stowe. Imagno/Getty Images. 163
10.3 Temple of Venus, Dashwood's estate, West Wycombe. Author's collection. 165

PREFACE

While engaging in my research over many years, I have been lucky enough to visit many libraries all over the world and been assisted by many librarians, too many to list, but special thanks go to 'my own' library, the British Library, where the bulk of my research was carried out. I would particularly like to thank Wellcome Images for allowing me permission to use pictures from their collection for free.

I would also like to thank Bloomsbury for wanting to bring my published essays into one book, and to all those people who helped in its publication. There have been many people who have guided me along my career, but specifically I would like to thank the people who assigned the initial publication of these essays; Roy Porter, Jean Bloch, Marie Mulvey-Roberts, Clare Mence and Jenny McCall, Mark Pollard, Eva Maria Stolberg, Patsy Fowler and Alan Jackson, Louise Duckling, Carolyn D. Williams and Angela Escott, Merry E. Wiesner-Hanks, John McNeil and Kenneth Pomeranz.

As always, my final thanks go to my partner Jad Adams whose support and suggestions after the reading of many drafts of various scripts have been unceasing.

Apart from unpublished Chapters 3 and 4 which are new or substantially rewritten material, the essays were first published in their original form as follows:

1. 'Continuities and Change in Sexual Behaviour and Attitudes from 1750' in *The Cambridge World History* (Cambridge University Press, 2015), Vol. 7, eds John McNeil and Kenneth Pomeranz.
2. Introduction to Julie Peakman (ed.), *Sexual Perversions 1650–1890* (Palgrave, 2009).
3. A new article based on a paper given at conference on *Blame, Shame & Culpability*, St Petersburg University Conference, Russia, May 2009.
4. A new article incorporating the introduction to *Whore Biographies 1700–1825*, Vol. 1 (Pickering & Chatto, 2006).
5. 'Memoirs of Women of Pleasure: The Whore Biography', *Women's Writing*, Vol. 11, No. 2 (2004).
6. 'Initiation, Defloration and Flagellation: Sexual Propensities in *Memoirs of a Woman of Pleasure*' in Patsy Fowler and Alan Jackson

(eds), *This Launch into the Wide World: Essays on Fanny Hill* (AMS Press, 2003).

7 '"The best freind [*sic*] in the world." The Relationship Between Emma Hamilton and the Queen of Naples' in Carolyn D. Williams, Angela Escott and Louise Duckling (eds), *Woman to Woman. Female Negotiations During the Long Eighteenth Century* (University of Delaware Press, 2010).

8 'Bodily Anxieties in Enlightenment Sex Literature', *Studies on Voltaire and the Eighteenth Century*, No. 1 (2005).

9 'Medicine, the Body and the Botanical Metaphor in Erotica' in Kurt Bayertz and Roy Porter (eds), *From Physico-Theology to Bio-Technology* (Rodopi B. V., 1998).

10 'The Eighteenth-century Erotic Garden' in Eva-Maria-Stolberg, *Auf der Suche Nach Eden. Eine Kulturgeschichte des Gartens* (Peter Lang, 2008).

INTRODUCTION

The purpose of this book is to bring together a collection of disparate articles under one cover in order to make them more easily accessible. The aim is to provide an overview of some of the more hidden aspects of eighteenth-century sexual culture and to shed light on the private lives of individuals and collectives, as well as examining their reading habits which both expressed and affected people's attitudes. While this book is intended to provide the new scholar with an insight into the complexities of this world, I also hope it is a readable book for any intelligent reader interested in the subject.

Although there has been a surge in the study of the history of sexuality over the last thirty years or so, debates continue to be aired as to how best to tackle the subject. Gender has to be understood in terms of class, wealth, race, politics, religion and education, as well as the public and private domains of people's worlds. The vast array of material available to us shows the way which cultural attitudes were dispersed – newspapers, poems, novels, pamphlets, trial reports, memoirs, medical manuals, erotica, even a subject we might have thought far apart from the world of sex, that of gardening. Obviously in such a short space, my intention is not to cover everything, but to present material which, hopefully, informs and enlightens.

Many eighteenth-century men and women married or cohabited, and remained happily monogamous; some had adulterous affairs. Some confined their sexual acts to those ratified by the Church and State as licit, others varied their sex lives with non-mainstream acts of sex. Sexual acts which avoided conception were discouraged by the Church, but sometimes seen as permissible forms of entertainment by the broader sections of the community. Other non-mainstream acts were deemed 'perverse' or even criminal. Discussion around these areas will be examined within these chapters showing how mainstream texts often displayed a misogynistic view of the world, while other books, pamphlets and images positively fêted sexual activities of both men and women in a flourishing celebration of all kinds of diverse amatory pleasures. Through the lens of a multidisciplinary approach, I explore society's understanding of those sexually active men and women who conformed, and of those who broke the codes of permissible sexual conduct.

In the first chapter I have started with a basic overview of sexual attitudes and behaviour in the long eighteenth century which were considered acceptable. I have taken a broad sweep of the world to show how patterns evolved throughout Europe and the East examining marriage patterns, fertility and how these were affected by industrialization, urbanization, commercialization, migration and various other factors affecting shifts in societies. Most of what follows focuses on British history, occasionally with input on other parts of Europe such as France and Italy.

Chapter 2 on sexual 'perversion' explores those who broke the rules of permitted sexual congress. Religion played its part in defining what was, and what was not, a perverse body or a perverse sexual act, and while arguments have been made for medicine replacing religion as the main authoritative voice around the body during the eighteenth century, this was an evolution and frequently conflicting ideas ran side by side, with both religious and scientific aspects coming into play.

People who digressed sexually were often taken to court, the trials talked about, printed and read by an eager readership as seen in Chapter 3. This material allowed for the exposé of sodomites and adulterers as well as the plights of seduced, raped or murdered women. It was an excuse to use sensationalism to blame perpetrators while arousing and tantalizing readers in a less explicit method than outright pornography, thereby gaining access to a more mainstream readership. Part of the ideology was to expose the perpetrators of immoral deeds and to ridicule them in an attempt to monitor their behaviour (although in reality, it was also a slick operation of printing scandalous material for profit).

The second part of the book explores the development of the image of the sexual women in fiction and in reality. Courtesans who had become household names in the eighteenth century were viewed in a similar light as celebrities of today, gossip around them used as fodder for publishers. When their lives did not produce enough material, hacks made up extra 'details' to add in to their mini-biographies of these popular women. The fact that these women were associated with wealthy titled men did no harm to the sales and produced a new sub-genre in literature in 'whore biographies' seen in Chapter 4. By the second half of the eighteenth century, the women themselves wanted to take advantage of the market and make their own profits by producing their own autobiographies examined in Chapter 5. Each of these women had been involved in what was viewed as a scandalous life and had ended up in debt, writing their memoirs as a way out of poverty. Published in serial or book form, the tales revealed the bad behavior of various lovers and adulterous husbands, while divulging sensational details about their love lives. However, these memoirs were also part of the blaming and shaming publishing milieu of topical literature.

Exploring the prostitute in fiction afforded more graphic possibilities as seen in John Cleland's *Memoirs of A Woman of Pleasure* (1748/9), or *Memoirs of Fanny Hill* (abridged in 1750) as the novel is more commonly known. For the first time, pornography was being molded into a novelistic form, allowing the reader to follow a story in explicit sexual detail. Chapter 6 shows how medical ideas about flagellation were assimilated into pornography, with a scene in the book exploring the subject. This theme was a reflection of the more obvious use of the whip in society on a day-to-day basis (seen in beating of servants, wives and children); again, reflections of a broader culture were incorporated into the sexual side of life.

Friendships were cemented between women involved in the nebulous field of prostitution, these attachments providing them with mutual support in an uncertain world ruled over by men. But these whores could often rise to great heights as seen in one of the women explored, Emma Hamilton in Chapter 7, which shifts us from the world of brothel keepers and courtesans into that of royalty and elite Neapolitan society, and explores her intimate friendship with the Queen of Naples.

The third section of this book examines the new emerging interests of medicine, botany and gardening and exemplifies how different topics fed into, and off, each other. For example, we can see in Chapter 8 how sex manuals interacted with each other, taking bits and pieces from old medical texts and mashing them into new sexual advice books. New developments made by botanists such as Carl Linnaeus threw up new ways of looking at sex, with writers of erotica making analogies with botany. Chapter 9 shows how botanical metaphors fed into medicine and ideas about the body, and these in turn were taken up in erotica. Chapter 10 shows how the new connections forged between sex and botany were reflected in the development of the gentleman's erotic garden, a subject made real in landscaped estates and in fantasy in full-blown pornographic text.

An understanding of the readership of most of this material is helpful in establishing how these eighteenth-century writers and their audiences perceived sexuality, although this is not always easy to pinpoint. It has often been presumed that material of a sexual nature was bought mainly by affluent men because of its high price. Although the books were perhaps more readily purchased by the aristocracy and gentry, pamphlets and broadsheets were easily obtainable for those less well-off, so knowledge of the cases covered all classes. It is also often assumed that no women read this material due to its immodest content. In fact, it is more probable that there was a shared appreciation of such material by both sexes.[1] We know that it was read by the lower ranks; sellers and buyers of erotica included women;[2] some women even wrote roguish poems and titillating sex guides.[3] Second-hand sales, the loaning of erotica and the printing of cheaper pamphlets and chapbooks[4] would have brought the literature within the reach of many more.

As an end word to this preface, I concur with my old mentor Professor Roy Porter who stated many years ago in the introduction to one of his books: 'It be otiose to rehearse here all the theoretical positions being espoused, designed to demonstrate that sex and sexuality are not timeless, universal biological givens, but historical and cultural constructs.' For that, people can go elsewhere,[5] although I do touch on certain philosophies and frameworks which have informed my work. I also want to avoid self-indulgent over-theorizing or using convoluted language, as it rarely adds to our broader knowledge of a subject. Instead, this book aims to provide a general understanding in history of what was really going on in the world, and about the great variety of people's attitudes in the past, while recognizing that history is an interpretive subject and comes with its own inherent problems of interpretation.[6] Theories and conceptual analyses are, of course, important in their place, but straightforward language, stories of people, and the place and time of when, where and how things happened, I believe, are more important.

PART ONE
Norms and Anomalies

CHAPTER ONE

Continuities and Change in Sexual Behaviour and Attitudes from the Eighteenth Century

Global variations in sexual attitudes and practices depend to a large degree on elements such as religion, industrialization, urbanization, population growth and changes in technology; and on a more individual level, they depend on education, class, race, gender and age. The last two-and-a-half centuries have witnessed dramatic changes in societies which affected sexual behaviour around the world. However, only within the last sixty years or so would an effective separation between sex and procreation become possible; and only then would laws be enacted allowing a move towards greater sexual equality in Europe, the Americas, Asia and Oceania (the notable exceptions being Africa and the Muslim world). Generally speaking, on both a national and international scale, unprecedented social mobility, opening economic opportunities, and expanding urban markets saw major shifts in relationships of men and women from the beginning of the eighteenth century onwards, rapidly increasing during the twentieth century.

The study of the history of sexuality emerged around the 1970s and 1980s from feminist and women's history, and with the development of gender history to incorporate the examination of male sexualities. Early studies concentrated disproportionately on heterosexuality and on Western civilization, with a few notable exceptions.[1] More recently, historians have tended to examine specific areas of sexuality, such as the history of the body, the family, homosexuality, prostitution, pornography or sexual perversions at particular times in the past.[2] Scholars tend to fall into two camps, essentialists versus social constructionists.[3] Put simply, essentialists believe in an underlying truth of forms or essences; that these will be true and constant over time; and that certain phenomena are natural, inevitable and biologically determined. Social constructionists believe that reality is constructed socially, and that language and 'discourse' play an important meaning in the making and interpretation of history. The latter historians follow philosopher Michel Foucault, who focused on regulation, power and subjectivity in suggesting that the whole concept of sexuality is a creation of nineteenth-century bourgeois society.[4] Before then, he argues, there were sexual acts, but not sexual identities understood as an intrinsic aspect of the self. Other historians have criticized his assertions – if sexuality is a nineteenth-century social construction, how come prostitution, homosexuality and other sexual patterns can be identified in medieval Europe and earlier? The interplay between act and identity is therefore more complex than Foucault suggested.[5]

While it has been helpful to identify nuances in the past, it is essential to take a broader sweep if longer term trends are to be identified.[6] One longstanding premise throughout the world was that vaginal penetrative sexual intercourse between a man and a woman, later coined 'heterosexuality',[7] was 'normal' behaviour. The major belief systems including Christianity, Judaism, Hinduism, Islam, and Confucianism, reflected this understanding of sexuality as part of their code. Most deviant behaviours, including sodomy, bestiality and incest among others, were generally considered 'abnormal' or 'against nature' and thus were unacceptable – although there were exceptions to the rule. Marriage and reproduction were considered the natural path in an individual's life (Figure 1.1). Girls were expected to remain chaste until marriage, and young men were advised to control their sexual urges, although sexual activities among young men were generally tolerated. A premium was set on a girl's virginity and, without it, she could not expect to make a good marriage. Because of the 'purity' of a woman reflected her honour and that of her family, the higher up the social scale, the more important this virginity became. Generally, women had fewer protective laws, work opportunities and prospects of independence. This left them at a disadvantage when forging sexual relationships.

Historians of sexuality generally agree that in the West at least, the control of the regulation of sex shifted from the Church in the seventeenth century, to medicine in the eighteenth century, and to the State in the nineteenth century. Religious constructions of gender and sexuality were reinforced by science, politics and the law, all representing women as mentally and physically inferior to men, and homosexual men as inferior to heterosexual men.[8] However, I would argue that, on a global scale, religion has retained its influence on attitudes towards sexual matters in a large part of the world, including parts of the West, to today, and this influence can be seen in continued discrimination against women and homosexuals.[9]

This chapter will discuss three topics that played a part in the development of sexual culture in the eighteenth century. It will first examine sex and marriage during the eighteenth (and to some extent the nineteenth) century in three areas – Europe, the European colonies and East Asia – and then look at two more topics in greater detail: prostitution and homosexuality.

FIGURE 1.1 *A merry crowd with a fiddler playing a tune celebrates a marriage as the groom kisses the bride (n.d.). Wellcome Library, London.*

Sex and marriage in Europe

Although in post-Reformation Europe Catholics and Protestant had differing ideas about the relative merits of celibacy and marriage and the possibility of divorce, all Christian churches taught that sex was to take place within marriage in order to produce children, not simply for pleasure. Sex outside marriage was 'fornication' and a sin. Despite the importance placed on female chastity in Europe, young men and women (at least those among the lower classes) could meet each other with relative ease. Premarital sex was evident in both Protestant and Catholic countries and, within certain boundaries, it was regarded as an inescapable part of life. Young couples came together whenever they had the chance, at fairs, in church and at markets.[10] In some Protestant countries, they were sometimes allowed to sleep together in the same bed under their parents' roof. The young couple would remain semi- or fully-clothed, with a bolster or plank placed between them, a custom known as 'bundling'. In Switzerland and Germany, couples followed a pattern of courting called *kiltgang* whereby young men would visit via the window of young single women. Sexual activities were not supposed to include full intercourse, although this sometimes occurred and pregnancy resulted. This might not be a catastrophe for the woman, however, if a promise of marriage had been extracted from the young man, preferably in front of witnesses.[11]

Even in Spain, considered the exemplar of Catholic orthodoxy after the Catholic Reformation, local people often adapted church regulations and religion doctrine to suit their own needs. Although the majority of people abided by the church teaching, pre-marital sexual activity was sometimes tolerated by the immediate community.[12] Some couples who exchanged promises of betrothal had sex and cohabited, but did not always go on to marry, even if they had a child. Some took up with other partners when marriages failed, although divorce was forbidden by the Catholic Church. In Italy, premarital sexual activity seems to have been less common than in Spain, and more people followed the directives of the Church. Throughout Europe, premarital sex was rare for elite women.[13] Daughters within these classes tended to marry younger, binding them early in a bid to protect their virginity and increase the length of child-bearing years.

Since the 1970s, historians have debated how and when family structures changed in Europe to what is generally seen as the 'modern' family with companionate marriage based on love and sexual passion. Lawrence Stone has argued that in most of Europe, marriage was a contract between two families before 1600, but by the eighteenth century companionate marriage became more common. Edward Shorter similarly made claims about the modern family, pointing to what he saw as a growth of maternal affection in the middle classes and of sexual passion in the lower classes at the end of the eighteenth century. Other family historians have since nuanced these claims.[14] They have noted that although marriages were usually arranged by parents in Europe, young people generally agreed to them and were only rarely forced into marriages they did not want (Figure 1.2). Among the aristocracy, parental control over choice of partners was stronger, as these marriages were designed to tie two wealthy families together.

As cities developed in Europe, family ties became less strong and there was a loosening of control over sexual behaviour, especially in poorer families, although this happened at different times in different places for different reasons. Generally in Western Europe, by the eighteenth century, greater commercialization and increasing opportunities for wage labour led to young people having greater sexual freedom.[15] However in Russia, mobility was made possible by the abolition of serfdom in 1861, which

FIGURE 1.2 *An unhappy arranged marriage. Wellcome Library, London.*

reinforced the country's industrialization, and weakened traditional social constraints.[16]

Sexual relations in European colonies and empires

Empire building played an important part in the shift of sexual attitudes and practices with sex, gender and culture helping to shape the history of the European colonies.[17] Increased exploration, trade and travel led to sexual interactions between different groups, which ranged from violent rape to companionate marriage.[18] Christian missionaries preached self-control and monogamy, which affected local practices and attitudes. European settlers often criticized indigenous populations for their sexually loose morals; for example Native Americans were attacked for their 'impurity and immorality, even gross sensuality and unnatural vice'.[19] Yet along with new ideas about sexual restraint, European expansion also brought added promiscuity (Figure 1.3) as well as an increase in venereal disease.

For Europeans abroad, 'home' domestic arrangements were clung to steadfastly and would be to a large extent transported to the colonies. For

FIGURE 1.3 *William Hogarth,* The Harlot's Progress, *Plate II, 1732. Wellcome Library, London.*

example, Australian and New Zealand both shared the pattern of Victorian sexuality, although there was a lower average marriage age overseas than there was in Europe.[20] John D'Emilio has argued that American sexual history was reshaped by the changing economy and political situation from a family-centred reproductive sexual system in the colonial era to a romantic intimate nineteenth-century marriage, a similar picture to the one Stone depicted for Britain.[21] Just as in Britain, white middle-class authorities regulated sexual morality, and there was also a search for more emotional intimacy and greater physical pleasure, although women's sexuality was also viewed as dangerous. Such parallels with Britain tell only part of the story, however, as North America contained a diverse range of people from different areas of the world and invariably this meant different attitudes to sex. As Helen Horowitz has pointed out, in the nineteenth-century United States of America there was an earthly acceptance of desire, and sexual expression collided with the prohibitions broadcast from the pulpit, primarily made by evangelical Protestant Christians.[22]

Slavery was an important part of the story of colonization and had a dramatic impact on the sexual history of Africa and the European colonies

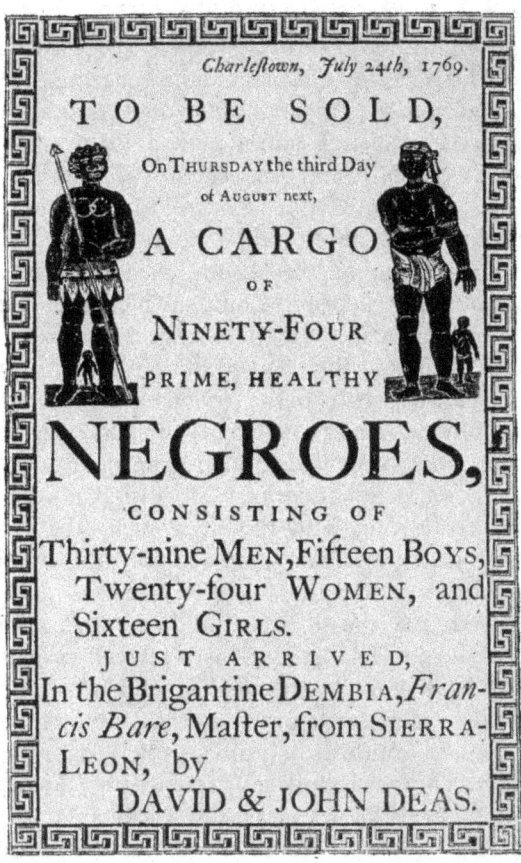

FIGURE 1.4 *Slave auction notice, 1769. From the Collection of Karen Halttunen, American Antiquarian Society.*

(Figure 1.4). While Peter Stearns has argued that patterns of sexual behaviour did not alter in Africa, he also points to the fact that West Africa saw an altered gender ratio as men were taken as slaves more often than women (over 65 per cent of slaves were male). This brought an increase in polygamy and complaints by men that women were harder to control.[23] In the Americas, with the importation of thousands of slaves, sexual interactions between plantation owners and their female slaves often meant enforced sexual subservience and abuse. It was often considered acceptable by planters to use female slaves for sex, either in rape or taken as mistresses.[24] Europeans tended to see non-white populations as 'bestial', and in reaction to their own highly imaginative sexualized images of the African man, white authorities issued new laws in attempts to control them.[25] As a result, in the United States, hundreds of black men were put on trial for rape in separate public courts established for them at the beginning of the eighteenth century, with little hope of being acquitted.[26]

Sweeping changes due to imperialism also affected South Asia. At the beginning of the eighteenth century, women in well-to-do Hindu and Muslim households tended to be segregated in separate quarters and spent their lives in the *andarmahal*, or inner sanctum of the house.[27] That continued, but the arrival of the British East Indian Company also had a further profound effect on sexual laws and practices. Initially, with an overwhelming amount of soldiers and so few white women in India, company authorities overlooked their employees taking Indian mistresses (*bibis*). Richard Hyam has indicated for example that 'the keeping of a mistress in British India became a well-established practice'.[28] Company men often had children with them, provided for them when they left them behind on their return to England, and sometimes sent their mixed race children to British boarding schools. However, increasingly from the second half of the eighteenth century in India (earlier in other colonies), voices of authority were set against inter-racial relationships. Fear of company men 'going native' fed into already entrenched attitudes of white superiority. In order to actively discourage British men from consorting with Indian women, 'the fishing fleet' was introduced to bring in single British women as potential wives for employees of the East India Company. Soon more women came to India – older spinsters and unwed governesses 'of the shrivelled and dry description', as one lady unkindly described them in 1779, as well as 'reformed' prostitutes.[29] Officers sometimes married back home in Britain and brought their wives with them, the couple setting up a mini-England within their Indian homes.

The pattern found in South Asia, of initial toleration for inter-racial and inter-cultural sexual relations followed by restrictions, can be found in many places in the colonial world. Laws against racial mixing were issued in North and South America, India, Southeast Asia and Africa in an attempt to draw firm lines between the races, although these were only selectively enforced.[30]

In some parts of the imperial world, along with men and women there were individuals understood to belong to a third gender. Though Europeans who encountered them focused on their sexuality, they were often distinguished from others by their work or religious roles, as well as their sexual activities. In South Asia, individuals known as *hijras* could perform blessings at weddings and dance at celebrations, although they also worked as prostitutes to survive. Among the Native Americans, 'two spirit people' (earlier called *berdaches*) acted as second wives, cooking and cleaning and playing domestic roles. Exactly how accepted they have been has been debated.[31]

Sex and marriage in East Asia

Just as sexual and marriage relations in Europe were influenced by Christianity, sexual relationships in East Asia during the Qing dynasty (1644 to 1912) were influenced to varying extents by Daoism, Buddhism and Confucianism, especially the latter. Marriages between families were arranged by parents, usually with introductions made through a matchmaker, even in poor rural villages.[32] The woman married 'out', taking up a role in her in-laws' home, and became subservient to her mother-in-law in a hierarchical system based on age and gender, in which filial piety and veneration of one's ancestors were central values. Married couples were not expected to be emotionally intimate, but were expected to produce children. Men were expected to find sexual fulfilment outside the home, with prostitutes or concubines, yet female virtue was central to morality.[33] Vivien Ng has argued that with the introduction of the new Qing Code of 1646 and a new rape law, a cult of chastity was promoted, which encouraged peasant women, and especially widows, to remain chaste. Women who had died defending themselves from rape, or wives who had resisted pressure to act as prostitutes, were honoured as martyrs. Even virtuous ex-prostitutes (*cong liangi*) could be canonized as part of the cult of chastity.[34] Matthew Sommer has argued, however, that a cult of chastity had already been thriving earlier, in the Ming dynasty. By the 1820s, with economic change, this cult declined, and chaste widows were viewed as objects of charity rather than heroic figures.[35]

During the commercial expansion and rapid urbanization of the eighteenth century, the volume of trade between Canton and Europe is reckoned to have doubled every eighteen years,[36] although foreign men were kept segregated in their own spaces. With the growth in population, people were shifting both physically and economically, migrating to work and moving up and down the social ladder. Female commoners might slide down the scale, and be sold into slavery; or move up it by becoming a concubine to a man of better status.[37] New regulations on sexuality emerged from growing concerns about social and demographic trends, which extended a more uniform standard of sexual morality, something akin to what would happen in Victorian society in Europe. Both men and women, higher and lower status, were now expected to conform to idealized marital roles. Elite men were in theory no longer exempt, but a general prohibition of extramarital intercourse was introduced, forbidding men the use of prostitutes or servant women for sex. In contrast to England, where 'mill girls' or women engaged in textile production were associated with promiscuity, in China, textile work was seen as a benefit to the family that would keep 'a check on female promiscuity'. Authorities showed particular concern over a surplus of young males at the bottom of the socio-economic scale, who threatened to disrupt family households. It was such young men who would suffer the brunt of the new laws; they were prosecuted for consensual sodomy, rape, pimping or selling their wives, and adultery with widows.

Until the middle of the nineteenth century, Japan remained relatively isolated from the rest of the trading world. Social relationships, based in part on Confucianism imported from China, were characterized in theory as several interlocking hierarchical systems: as 'five relations' (that of loyalty between ruler and minister; filiality between father and son; harmony between husband and wife; precedence between elder and younger siblings; and trust between friends) and, for women, 'three bonds' (that a woman was subject to her father, husband, and then son within her life cycle). Loyalty and obedience were at the core of the system, and the strength of the patriarchal family was understood to express itself in public morality. Within this structure, women were segregated in the home, most notably amongst elite families, but their model influenced the respectable middle classes. The lower classes had less opportunity to enforce strict rules regarding the etiquette and seclusion of women, as many women were obliged to work long hours in the fields or outside the home. As elsewhere in the world, women's status came primarily from being wives and daughters, not from their labour.[38] Polygamy was illegal, but second wives or concubines were taken, and their children were legally recognized.

Prostitution

The sale of sex has been an aspect of urban life since the world's earliest cities, but it has taken a variety of forms: unmarried women who had sex with their long-term partners, those who had casual sex with strangers, women 'kept' by richer men who were paid in gifts and rent, and professional sex workers who sold sex for money have all been labelled 'prostitutes'. In the cities of early modern Europe, classifications of those who sold sex were often dependent on the location of their work, from street-walking whores at the bottom, through to women who worked in city brothels, to those who made arrangements for men to visit them in luxurious apartments. Often women drifted into prostitution on a seasonal basis affected by employment opportunities. With fewer safety nets in cities, away from wider family support networks that had been afforded to women in the past, they sometimes used prostitution as a way of supplementing their low wages.[39] Most people who sold sex were female, although Randolph Trumbach has argued that before about 1700, men in Europe had used both women and boys as prostitutes, with the primary distinction that between the penetrator and the penetrated; after this, as the gender of one's partner became the primary marker of sexual identity, only men who identified as homosexual used male prostitutes.[40]

From the eighteenth century onwards, all over the world, prostitution was seen to be an ever-growing problem that needed regulating and containing.[41] Reactions towards prostitution were mixed, with some authorities bringing out new laws to prevent it, while others decided on a path of increased tolerance. In England, there was a notable shift in attitude towards the women who sold sex, with the image of the embittered whore gradually replaced in popular imagination by the penitent Magdalene.[42] Previously, prostitutes had been seen as innately lustful women who had chosen a life of selling sex rather than entering the profession through a lack of any other viable choice. Increasingly women were seen as having 'fallen' into prostitution through no fault of their own, either seduced by employers or duped by their lovers through a promise of marriage. This image of the redeemable prostitute was evident in literature and art,[43] and was turned into practical action. Philanthropists and religious bodies established Magdalene houses in various European cities, including London, Vienna and Paris, in order to 'rescue' women from a life of prostitution. Although in theory they were protective institutions, in reality Magdalene houses were more of a punitive system established for women who had transgressed society's idea of sexual morality; harsh regimes in such houses saw women and young girls subjected to fines and punishments for misbehaviour.[44] In France and Italy, fathers had their daughters incarcerated if they were considered to have behaved in a sexually immoral manner, by applying to the courts to have them committed to asylums. These punitive patterns continued from the eighteenth into the twentieth century, with female offenders, especially juveniles, institutionalized for sexual transgressions in the United States, Canada and many European countries. As one historian points out, 'places like convents, conservatories, poorhouses, houses of patience, insane asylums, and prisons were used … to manage women's destinies that were deviant compared to the common destiny of normality'.[45]

Western imperialism brought with it a huge rise in prostitution in every part of the world, both colony and metropole, and invariably venereal disease flourished alongside it.

With the increase in travel, business and migration for work between continents in the nineteenth century, the structure of the sex trade changed. Millions of Indians, Africans, Chinese, Pacific Islanders and others moved to provide labour for European colonial powers. Migrant communities were overwhelmingly male, and as a result, the demand for sexual service of women increased.[46]

Homosexuality

The debate between social constructionists and essentialists discussed above has been particularly extensive among historians of homosexuality. Mary McIntosh's crucial essay 'The Homosexual Role', published in 1968, was one of the first to identify the social construction of homosexuality from a sociologist's perspective, although it has often been overlooked. As Jeffrey Weeks has pointed out: 'There is a tendency to efface the theoretical origins of social constructionist approach to sexuality, with an accompanying tendency to privilege the contribution of Michel Foucault and his followers.'[47]

Social constructionists tend to see a significant change in the late nineteenth century, at which point the idea of permanent sexual orientations developed. Essentialists saw same-sex attraction as innate, or in a person's character or biology, and thus were willing to identify people who engaged in same-sex relations or had same-sex desires as 'homosexuals' even before the invention of the word. The Hungarian journalist and human rights advocate Karl-Maria Kertbeny is attributed to having first applied the term 'homosexual' to same-sex desire in 1869. However, historians have identified homosexual sub-cultures and identities prior to the nineteenth century and arguments have ensued as to when the homosexual identity was actually constructed.[48] Studies of homosexual sub-cultures have shown 'mollies' congregating in London taverns together, Portuguese transvestites dancing together, male pickups in the Pont-Neuf in Paris who mimicked women and used female nicknames, and 'warm brothers' who gathered in boy bordellos in Germany. Many of these men were married. Some were male prostitutes.[49] These have come to light mainly through exploration of trial records.

Similar debates emerged around the lesbian, about her 'construction', what terminology to use for which periods, and whether she can be said to have existed prior to the eighteenth century. Again historians have found ample evidence of both lesbians and lesbians' self-identity at various times in history, and have uncovered 'female husbands', 'female friendships' and 'lesbian-like' relationships.[50] Women who engaged in same-sex relationships were prosecuted more often for fraud – either because they married other women without revealing their true sex, or for taking a male sexual role by using a dildo rather than for the sex alone. Many societies remained silent on sexual acts between women, no doubt because women rarely sought out sex in public places, and were considered less important and therefore less noticed. What they did sexually between themselves held little threat to society, especially when compared to homosexual men.

Along with debates about whether 'homosexual' should be used across time, more recently, queer theorists and trans activists have also questioned the polarization between heterosexual and homosexual and introduced important questions about normative and non-normative sexualities. Historians of other parts of the world have also criticized the application of concepts and chronologies drawn from the West to other areas.

There has been less study of same-sex relations outside the West, but more is emerging. That on China, for example, has shown that although laws against consensual male homosexuality were in existence before the eighteenth century, new regulations were introduced in 1740 against homosexual rape. This law was justified as a way to curb rampant homosexuality,[51] but it has also been seen as a reflection of an increasing concern about the rogue and 'rootless male', a result of a growing mobile population, with more men than women. These laws aimed at punishing the consensual penetrated male, although desiring boys for sex was still considered understandable. Despite the laws, elite men would continue to patronize male prostitutes and cross-dressing actors.[52]

Meanwhile, although under Sharia law same-sex relations were condemned, France's colonies in North Africa, as well as other Islamic countries, conjured up images of an exotic availability of homosexuality in the minds of Europeans. "'Tis Common for Men there [Algiers] to fall in love with Boys, as 'tis here in England to be in Love with Women', commented one Joseph Pitts.[53] Tensions around homosexual desire and the exotic 'primitive' male also surfaced in other imperial territories, including Northern Australia in the late nineteenth century and early twentieth century.[54]

Religious strictures against homosexuality were transported across the Atlantic with European colonization. In North America, restrictions were placed on pre-marital sex, adultery and homosexuality. But urbanization would bring a lessening of oversight by the nineteenth century.[55]

On the European continent, in countries under the Napoleonic Code of 1804, sex acts between men were tolerated, but after 1848 (the so-called year of revolutions in central and western Europe), local statutes and laws covering public indecency meant that acts of sex between men were effectively criminalized. The threat of being perceived as a sodomite took on a more significant meaning in Britain during the nineteenth century, when a series of new laws came out which outlawed more acts of sexual behaviour.

Overall, shifting social and economic roles, such as mass migration to cities and increasing dependency on wage labour, led to changes in relationships between men and women. Some marginalized people, including women, indigenous people in colonial areas, slaves and homosexuals managed to manoeuvre themselves into positions where they had some degree of control over their own sexuality, or at least attained some protection from those in more powerful positions. A few even managed to achieve a degree of independence in the burgeoning cities around the world, although this was rare. There were huge changes in terms of economic growth, migration, industrialization and urbanization in the eighteenth and nineteenth centuries, but these often did little in terms of sexual or gender equality. Instead they brought increasing dangers, as many young women and men lost ties with family and communities with the move to the cities and became more vulnerable to sexual exploitation. Homosexual men continued to be persecuted for their activities and the majority of women remained in secondary economic and social positions.

CHAPTER TWO

'Perversion of the Course of Nature':

Sexual Variations in the Eighteenth Century

In 1677, a married woman from Cripplegate thought to be aged between 30 and 40 was sentenced to death for her crime. According to the summary of her case brought before the Old Bailey,

> not the fear of God before her eyes, *nor regarding the order of Nature*, on the 23rd of June last, to the disgrace of all womankind, did commit Buggery with a certain Mungril Dog, and wickedly, divellishly, and *against nature* had venereal and Carnal copulation with him.

Through several holes in the wall between her house and next door, her neighbours had been able to see her in acts of 'uncleanliness'. The dog was brought before the prisoner, and 'owned her by wagging his tail, and making motions as it were to kiss her, which 'twas sworn she did do when she made that horrid use of him'.[1] Only a few such bestiality cases were recorded in England in the seventeenth and eighteenth centuries,[2] but bestiality was always condemned as a heinous sin against nature. It was also considered a crime in the eyes of the law.

So why were such cases defined as 'against nature', and why were they considered criminal? After all, the perpetrator was not hurting anybody and, in this case at least, the dog seemed quite happy. Yet the legal system was only one of the aspects in the wider framework which made up sexual perversion in the early modern world. It emerged from a complicated interwoven understanding of nature, theology, the understanding of man's evil and the concept of sin. Within this structure, people's perception of the world at large was based around their comprehension of the social order of things – the natural order of the world was seen to be ordained by God and any act which upset this order was not merely deemed 'unnatural', but seen to be against God's will. Disruption to that social order was regarded with suspicion and dealt with by the Church, the State or the community. In other words, in England during the early modern period, the boundaries of acceptable sexual behaviour were set by religion, the law and tradition, the latter two aspects emanating from the rigid framework of the first. Outside of these boundaries, certain sexual behaviours or acts were deemed to be unnatural, and these acts made for 'perversion'.

The discussion on normative versus non-normative sexuality has been approached from many angles, usually from the premise that 'non-normal' has to emerge from its opposite, the 'normal', and that this normal is nearly always taken to be heterosexuality.[3] But can this observation be applied historically? Can sexual acts of behaviour considered perversions now be taken to be perversions in the past? The boundaries of acceptability in society have changed over time, as we can see in our attitudes towards homosexuality. The acceptability of male-on-male sex has shifted from being tolerated in Ancient Greece, to outlawed in the early modern period, to being acceptable again in present-day Britain. Although much ground has been covered in the study of homosexuality in current scholarship, discussions on sexual perversity have not abounded in academia and as a subject it is still fairly unchartered territory.[4] How far the understanding of the relationships between perversion and non-perversion were different from our current thinking varies depending on the type of perversion involved, although we can also find on-going similarities.

A finite definition of sexual perversion has proved near impossible, although some nineteenth-century sexologists and twentieth-century philosophers have tried.[5] However, most of them are of little relevance in connection with the period under discussion, as they fail to take account of the mutability of the concept, and the behaviours considered perverted in the twenty-first century are not necessarily the same as those so defined previously. If we are to understand sexual behaviour in history, it has to be within specific conceptual time-frames. How did the ordinary person differentiate between those sorts of sexual behaviour considered perversions in the early modern period, and those which were not? If we are to understand sexual perversion in the world of pre-sexology, we need to turn to contemporaneous influences for an explanation.

According to the *Oxford English Dictionary*, 'perversion' technically meant 'the actions of perverting or condition of being perverted, turning the wrong way; turning aside from truth or right; diversion to an improper use; corruption, distortion'. Yet there was also a conception of perversion as 'evil' or incorrect, a stray from religion or nature, notably in early modern

Britain. Wycliffe spoke of 'perversion of soule' as early as 1388; Caxton spoke of 'perverse' in 1484 meaning wickedness, calling it 'The deception and flatterye of the perverse and evyile folke'. More specifically, it can be applied in religious terms as 'change to error in religious belief (opposite of conversion)', as seen in its application to the Protestants who became 'perverted' or converted to the Catholic faith. This was then reflected in Protestant attacks on the 'perverse' sexual behaviour of Catholic nuns and priests. Apart from the religious sense, although closely connected with it, there was also a sense of perversion in nature. English clergyman and natural philosopher William Derham described the workings of nature in his book *Physico-Theology, Or a Demonstration of the being and attitudes of God from his works of creation* (1713) (Figure 2.1). A perversion of nature would mean a disruption or inversion of this perceived natural hierarchy. In the natural order of things, men were thought superior to women, and as such, were natural rulers. They were thought better equipped to make decisions; therefore, women should obey them. Women were considered naturally unruly, and in need of discipline by their husbands.

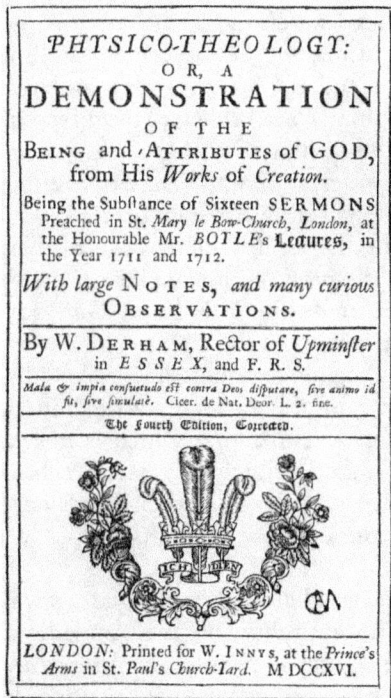

FIGURE 2.1 *Frontispiece to William Derham,* Physico-Theology, Or a Demonstration of the being and attitudes of God from his works of creation, *1713. Wikimedia Commons.*

Exceptions to this rule were found in the topsy-turvy world of theatre where unruly effeminate men and cross-dressing women could be found.[6]

The origins of the norms of the eighteenth century belonged to the realms of religious doctrine which had laid down the rules over two thousand years previously.[7] Religion was one of the main definers of 'good' and 'bad' behaviour, reinforced by communities under the guise of 'morality', and sanctioned by first the church courts, and then the magistrates' courts. Sex was considered licit only between a man and a woman within the realms of marriage – and then for procreative purposes. Although of course, not everyone adhered to this practice, this was the basic rule of permissible sex. All abnormal sex took place outside these confines, although not all the sexual acts outside of the rule were deemed perverted.

Understandings of perversion were closely bound up with the Bible and what it deemed unnatural or against God, this in turn producing social morality and the law, both methods of control. Although Foucault has been widely criticized in his survey of sexuality in history,[8] he at least recognized that the concept of perversion from the fourteenth century onwards served to inform legislation on moral correctness through the concept of sin and the confessional; or in his words, 'legal sanctions against minor perversions were multiplied ... a norm of sexual development was defined and all the possible deviations were carefully described'.[9] Although the use of the confessional did not apply in late seventeenth- and eighteenth-century Protestant Britain, the Judeo-Christian ethic and the concept of sin was deeply engrained. Originally, the Bible had been responsible for determining which crimes were unnatural, and theologians were therefore in charge of deciding what was perverse sexual behaviour. Same-sex behaviour was particularly castigated, as follows: Leviticus 20.13 stated 'If a man also lie with mankind, as he lieth with a woman, both of them have committed an abomination: they shall surely be put to death; their blood shall be upon them.' Romans 1.26 stated: 'For this cause God gave them up unto vile affections: for even their women did change the natural use into that which is against nature'; and again Romans 1.27, 'And likewise also the men, leaving the natural use of the woman, burned in their lust one toward another; men with men working that which is unseemly ....' There was, therefore, a definite understanding of sexual behaviour, pre-nineteenth-century sexology, which was considered either deviant or 'abnormal'. This behaviour was most commonly seen as that which was 'against nature' or 'unnatural'.[10]

As Thomas Laqueur has identified, 'perverted sex was the sign of perverted social relations'.[11] The morality of the immediate community would therefore act to induce shame on people deviating from what was considered unnatural or sinful behaviour and played a major role in the control of an individual's behaviour.[12] The community would also be a factor in delineating the 'good' sexual behaviour from the 'bad' and this would be manifest in a communal form of social control such as sexual slander, rough music and 'skimmington rides'. The unnaturalness of an act was based on the extent of how far it deviated from procreative sex between man and wife. The concept of what was natural or unnatural was not only part of the biblical interpretation but was an application to the world in general. The early modern world saw itself as based on nature, and the whole interpretation of the natural order of things was based around it.[13] As Pierre Hurteau sums up, 'Moral conduct was dictated by objective rules derived from natural law, which reflected the order of God's creation.'[14] This application of perversions as defined in the Bible, nature and morality was, in turn, incorporated into criminal law.

Sodomy as perversion 'against nature'

The phrase 'against nature' was most quickly applied in cases of sodomy. Although nowadays we take this to mean buggery between men, during the early modern period it covered three main types of act – that of anal intercourse between men; sexual intercourse with a beast, or bestiality; and all other types of immodest or 'unnatural' intercourse which might include anal sex between a man and a woman, or in fewer instances, penetration with a dildo of one woman by another. According to Jesuit Martin Bonacina (1585–1631), who wrote pages on the subject, sodomy meant anal intercourse between men and 'Emission of sperm was not required to apply, and penetration was sufficient'[15] for sodomy to have taken place, although this was not the case in British law. Since the buggery law of 1533, both penetration and ejaculation were necessary for a prosecution to be secured up until 1828 when the law changed to make conviction for sodomy easier and only proof of penetration was needed.[16] The law, however, was not always as consistent in the matter as it should have been, as shown by the case of the second Earl of Castlehaven in 1631 where only proof of ejaculation was needed for his conviction.[17] As seen in this case, political manoeuvrings could also influence action or non-action against a person or act.

Generally though, the concept of unnaturalness as stated in the Bible was reflected in criminal law. Men or women who were brought before the magistrates courts for committing sodomitical acts, were described as committing acts 'against nature'. When Thomas Burrows was brought before the Old Bailey on 4 December 1776 for sodomy, he was indicted 'for feloniously assaulting one William Brooks on the 28th of November, and that he feloniously, diabolically, and *against the order of nature*, had a venereal affair with the said William, and carnally knew him, and did commit and perpetrate with the said William that detestable and abominable crime (*among Christians* not to be named) called buggery'.[18] By the end of the century, the crime had become so disgraceful in public perception that the court decided to suppress reporting the crimes publicly, possibly thinking that the more the subject was aired, the more men might be likely to try it. On 15 February 1797, William Winklin was indicted for 'an unnatural crime' but the evidence on the trial 'being extremely indecent, the Court ordered the publication of it to be suppressed'.[19]

Theologians also considered 'sexual intercourse between two women' to be sodomy,[20] but the matter was made more complicated by the difficulty of determining exactly what it entailed. Although the Bible condemned women having sex with other women, various European cases were divided on their treatment. The Florentine inquisitional records between 1619 and 1623 show that the Church took relatively mild action against their two lesbian nuns, Bernedetta Carlini and Bartolomea Crivelli, and merely separated them, presumably to prevent any chance of a scandal. According to the Prussian Secret Archives, the case of Catherina Margaretha Linck and her female lover was taken much more seriously and Linck was beheaded in 1721. In the 1740s case of Catherine Vizzani, she was shot by an agent of her lover's uncle after she and her female lover had eloped, so the problem was resolved by the immediate community.[21] In each case therefore, different approaches were made to a perceived problem of lesbian sex. The law in Britain was somewhat tentative in attending to women having sex together. Indeed, it has been questioned whether the concept of lesbianism was taken seriously at all.[22]

Punishment tended to be inflicted only when a woman had been seen to be penetrated by another with the use of a dildo; in other words, if they were aping a man's position. This happened in cases where women had married other women pretending to be men. Mary Hamilton, who supposedly married a total of fourteen women, was sentenced in 1746 to a public whipping and imprisoned for six months. But culturally in England, lesbian behaviour tended to be considered less harshly than other sexual 'crimes'. Women aping men's roles were considered less of a threat than men aping women's, since it was considered peculiar for men to want to take up the socially inferior role of women (again, considered 'against nature'). Women tended to be convicted when implications of another non-sexual crime came up, most often fraud. In these cases, women had usually dressed as men in order to marry richer women and defraud them of their money. Typically, one such woman was convicted at Guildhall Westminster for having married three different women and defrauded them of their clothes and money, and was sent to the pillory at Charing Cross and imprisoned for six months.[23]

Although women together were treated less harshly than their male counterparts, their behaviour was still perceived as unnatural. In his book, *The Female Husband* (1746) based on Mary Hamilton, Henry Fielding described Hamilton's desires as 'unnatural affections';[24] John Cleland in his translation of *The True History and Adventures of Catherine Vizzani* (1755) perceived her to have committed 'so unnatural a Vice' in her behaviour with other women, while diarist Hester Thrale described Saphists as 'a Set of Monsters'.[25] This concept of the unnaturalness of sex between women (and hence its immorality) was therefore ingrained in society at large. Generally though, community reaction was less harsh regarding two women living together and they could easily escape serious repercussions as did the Llangollen Ladies, Sarah Ponsonby and Eleanor Butler, who lived together relatively unscathed.[26]

The last case of sodomy, that of bestiality, we might think would be considered the worst of crimes within this category, if we are to consider it as an act 'against nature', and for the eighteenth century, this holds true. The theological condemnation was again already present in the Bible: Leviticus 20.15 states, 'A man who has sexual intercourse with any beast shall be put to death, and you shall kill the beast.' Women who had committed sex with animals were condemned to the same treatment. Yet compared to cases of sodomy between men, relatively few people were brought to court for sex with animals in Britain. Christopher Saunders was indicted at the Old Bailey on 10 March 1776, for that 'he (*against the order of nature*) had a certain venereal affair with a certain beast called a cow, and feloniously and wickedly against the order of nature did carnally know the said beast called a cow, and with the said beast called a cow did feloniously and wickedly and *against the order of nature* commit and perpetrate the detestable and abominable crime, not to be named among Christians, called Buggery'.[27] As seen in the case of the woman from Cripplegate, women were also convicted of bestiality, but they were more often caught with dogs than with cattle. In both cases, the perpetrator was sentenced to death. From legal action taken against them, it would appear that sodomy between a person and an animal was taken more seriously than cases of sodomy between men, since men caught were usually sentenced to the pillory, a fine and a stint in prison (usually between six months and two years). The lack of bestiality cases in court indicates that such acts were either less detectable, or less common.

So why was it considered such a heinous act? From his study of bestiality in Sweden in the seventeenth and eighteenth centuries, Liliequist has found that it was an act which was considered not only against nature but potentially evil, and therefore frightening. Copulation with animals was associated with witchcraft and association with Satan and had greater implications for one's soul and the community.[28] In tracing the antecedents of perversion and its historical context, the conception of sin emerges as either an evil deposited on a person by connections with the devil or an inherent evil. The dichotomy of the correct and the perverse, the normal and the abnormal, becomes the parallel between good and evil. During the seventeenth century, French mathematician and philosopher Blaise Pascal in his *Pensées* ('Thoughts', 1660) examined the link between perversity, concupiscence and sin and its inescapability in moral life. He saw man's inherent perversity of desire as man's deviation from Good. Knowledge of the natural world was inextricably bound up with a positive knowledge of God. Guilt was part of the process of self-constraint, a parallel which Freud would find some 250 years later. Similarly, in Britain, witchcraft also figured in incest cases; in *Ravillac Redivivus, Being the Narrative of the late Tryal of Mr. James Mitchell* (1678), accusations against Major Thomas Weir were not merely of adultery, incest and bestiality but he was also accused of consorting with the devil, his crimes associated with magic and witchcraft.[29] Yet the act of bestiality continued to be classed with sodomy, at least in Sweden, right into the twentieth century. In his article, Rydström makes the case that bestiality, seen as the most problematic type of sodomy, was overtaken by homosexuality as the most cause for concern. This shift had taken place with the shift from rural living to city dwelling as 'older religious categories were replaced by new scientific ones, the "sinner" gave way to the "pervert"'.[30]

Although some people saw sexual deviations as acts of sin, sometimes the evil was considered to be inherent in a person. James Penney in his book, *The World of Perversion* offers us an example of the inherently evil person in the medieval sodomite Gilles de Rais. He left his personal and subjective testimony to his crimes, now preserved in the Nantes archives. Although he was famous as a nobleman and warrior who fought alongside Joan of Arc during the Hundred Years War, he was responsible for the kidnapping and torture of pre-adolescent boys whom he then decapitated and dismembered, all for his own sexual pleasure. As Penney correctly points out, the Church needed its heretics to reinforce its own dominance. There is little point having Good, if Evil cannot be detected and exposed. This example is useful in considerations of early modern thought on perversion as it so neatly aligned with the medieval notion of sexual perversion as moral and spiritual corruption. The Church saw his crimes enacted as a result of diabolical desire, an inversion of moral consciousness rather than a negation of moral law.[31] This was, in fact, seen as a form of radical evil, different from the concept of original sin.

Topsy-turvy world of dress

Cross-dressing was seen as a further perversion of the world, a topsy-turvy inversion of the sexes, although reasons as to why men and women cross-dressed, and reaction to it, were gendered. Again, the Bible had already laid down rules on the subject in Deuteronomy 22.5: 'The women shall not wear that which pertaineth unto a man, neither shall a man put on a woman's garment; for all that do so are abomination unto the Lord thy God.' Seventeenth-century theologian William Perkins was quick to point out: 'The use of attire, stands by the very ordinance of God: who Hath not sorted all men to all places, so he will have men to fitte themselves and their attire, to the qualitie of their proper places, to put a difference between themselves and others . . . By which it appeares, that many in these daies do greatly offend . . .'[32]

Although the Church was quite clear on the matter, the reaction of the public shows a clear distinction in the way they viewed known cases of sodomy and mere cross-dressing, for not all men or women who cross-dressed were condemned as sodomites. In the case of men, they are frequently associated with cross-dressing as part of their homosexuality, but for women reasons have often been given as a means of entrance into a man's world – for economic opportunities, or to go to war or sea.[33] Tales of women dressing up as men to go off to join the army and the navy were both plentiful and popular; as such, they were an accepted cultural tradition in which women were seen as hearty lasses, much in the style of the modern-day female Principal Boys in tights and boots. Rarely were these women thought to be lesbians or as having sex with each other, although some authors included lesbian innuendos to titillate the public,[34] but even then, these women were rarely portrayed as threatening.[35] In other cases, it also becomes obvious that women had been blamed for masculinizing themselves through their dress and mannerisms, and this was seen as distasteful by the public. Women who caused most concern were those seen to be penetrating their female lovers, or marrying them as men, as seen above. Both these actions were seen to be usurping the male role, and as such, attracted greater punishments. Penetration also connected to the act of sodomy thus making it a greater sin and potentially opening up the actions to broader condemnation.

Men who cross-dressed were most often associated with sodomites and, as such, more of a threat to social order. Examples of these can be seen in the men caught in Mother Clap's Molly House in the 1720s. Some of the men, called 'mollies', would dress in female clothes, especially during drag balls and what they called 'festival nights', and would act out female parts in role play involving marriages and giving birth to giant cheeses or wooden jointed dolls.[36] The crime was not so much the cross-dressing as the sodomitical acts taking place between the men, and the fact that they had reduced themselves to being women, thereby undermining their assertive masculine role. Their cross-dressing was considered a perversion in that it subverted the order of nature, by inverting the 'proper' gender roles in a hierarchy in which men dominated women.

Yet, men with airy ways might be thought fops, and would not necessarily have their sexual relationships scrutinized, particularly if aristocratic. Lord Hervey was one such eighteenth-century character who held good grace and an influential career at court while carrying on a relationship with his lover Stephen Fox, brother of the famous radical opposed to Pitt, Charles Fox. Effeminate men, although not always persecuted, frequently had slurs attached to their characters.[37]

Cross-dressing in recent sex studies has been connected with sexual arousal although most current day investigations into *heterosexual* (as opposed to homosexual) transvestites have found that the majority of men who cross-dress deny that they do it for sexual purposes. One study found that although the core groups denied this association – that dressing as women aroused them sexually – when tested in a controlled environment, heterosexual cross-dressers responded with penile tumescence (blood rushing to the penis causing erection) to written fantasies of cross-dressing. The conclusion of the study found that heterosexual cross-dressing *was* directly related to sexual fetishism.[38] This then adds to the dilemma of how to understand heterosexual male cross-dressers in the past, although so few cases have been uncovered and, as yet, we have little to examine.

In England, at least, there seemed to be ambivalence towards the subject of male cross-dressing. Although there was an antagonism towards sodomites who cross-dressed, those of status were less likely to be condemned. One case to cause a stir in London in the 1770s because of his cross-dressing was that of Frenchman Chevalier D'Eon; the *London Evening Post* for 11–14 May 1771 went as far as to declare 'that a celebrated Chevalier [D'Eon] has with a few weeks past, been discovered to be of a different sex'.[39]

D'Eon is difficult to fathom as, unlike the mollies, he claimed to be asexual, yet obviously took delight in silk dresses, offering detailed accounts of them in his memoirs.[40] D'Eon never mentions a lover of either sex, but does confess to living with a woman at the latter end of his life, although he claims it was a purely domestic arrangement. It was possibly the fact that D'Eon did not outwardly display signs of desiring either sex, and that he was living with a woman as a woman, which alleviated him from persecution by British authorities. The fact that he came from aristocratic backgrounds and had high social standing in society also meant that he was less liable for persecution than were unruly plebeians. Although he was not regarded as sexually perverted since his associations did not appear to be sexual, he *was* regarded as an oddity. His case was high profile, covered in the news, and he was the subject of various bets and raucous debates.

In her examination of the case of D'Eon, Lisa Cody has argued that there was a self-fashioning through bending gender. Vern and Bonnie Bullough in their examination of cross-dressing believe it 'allows an individual to express a different facet of his or her persona'.[41] For John Dollimore, this transgression can be seen as a quest for authenticity and individualism – in defying a progressive order, we can be true to ourselves. Transvestism is a mode of transgression which finds its expression in inversion. Dress is important not just in defining gender, but in defining class; but dress confusion could be seen by contemporaries as symptomatic of impending social collapse.[42]

If we examine dress fetishism more closely, in a broader sense rather than mere cross-dressing, we can do no better than to look at David Kunzle's definition in his book *Fashion and Fetishism*. He asserts 'Fetishism may be defined as the individual displacement of private erotic feeling onto a non-genital part of the body, or onto a particular article of clothing by association with a part of the body, or onto an article of clothing in conjunction with its effect on the body.'[43] In his book, *The Sex Life of the Foot and the Shoe* (1976), William Rossi describes a fetish as 'where the sexual desire chooses as its exclusive and sufficient object some part of the body (e.g. feet) or some article of clothing (e.g. shoes)'.[44] He asserts, 'The foot is an erotic organ and the shoe its sexual covering.'[45] He suggests that shoes became a subject of fetishism because of their importance for the female form. He explains, 'the voluptuous architecture of the body, owes much of its sensuous character to the foot, which was responsible for the upright posture and gait that altered the entire anatomy'.[46] The shoe has thus been connected to female sexuality in history in the Cinderella myths, with a small foot an example of perfection. Kunzle suggests that foot fetishism was a result of the need for male possession; he asserts, 'the expressed Chinese ideal of a foot small enough to fit inside a man's mouth probably reflect an oral-genital fantasy'; in the West, this was altered to a small foot should ideally fit into a man's hand.[47] What was seen to be a perversion in one country, however, would not necessarily be seen as such in another; although the British saw the type of foot obsession displayed by the Chinese as perverted, the Chinese obviously did not feel the same.[48]

In any case, the British displayed a liking for feet of their own. For many in the eighteenth century, a lady's pretty foot was something to be admired. Lord Jersey, beau to courtesan Harriette Wilson, carried her shoe in his pocket in the hope of finding her a new pair. She declared, 'His Lordship really loved me, and, above all, he loved my foot ... he used to go about town with one of my shoes in his pockets, as a pattern to guide him in his constant search after pretty shoes for me.'[49] Even more obsessive was that of a Marquis who wooed a friend of Irish brothel-keeper Mrs Margaret Leeson. Her friend related to her how the Marquis used to love to pick and wash her toes, yet declared that he 'never was even rude enough to give me a kiss'.[50] None of this foot fetishism seems to have been a matter of concern for eighteenth-century commentators, nor was it considered abnormal. Indeed, pretty feet appear to have been a source of joy amongst men and women alike. Why such a liking for pretty feet furnished eighteenth-century fashion is hard to say, except the possibility that as a part of the body seductively peeping out from under long dresses, feet carried mysterious appeal.

The word fetish carried different connotations in the eighteenth century. Fetishing was seen as 'to adorn oneself, dress up'.[51] Atkins, in his *Voyage to Guinea* (1735) commented, 'The women are fondest of what they call Fetishing, setting themselves out to attract the good Graces of the Men.' This fascination with dressing up would be displayed in eighteenth-century plays,[52] in memoirs,[53] in erotica and in gentlemen's magazines. In the erotic books and magazines such as *Exhibition of Female Flagellants* (1777) and *Bon Ton* magazine, the female dominatrix was depicted as a governess, or a mother figure. The wearing of both huge nose-gays and purple gloves is combined in an exploration of flagellation.[54] Far from being seen as abnormal, flagellation was recognized as a stimulant, a means to an end, an act which culminated in heterosexual 'normative' vaginal sexual intercourse between a man and a woman. The wearing of nose-gays and purple gloves in this erotica was seen as less of a fetishism than a signifier of female flagellants.

Pornography as perversion?

How far can we use pornography as evidence of perversion? Having looked at some of the perceptions of deviant sexual behaviour in religion and how morality and the law controlled it, I want to turn to the sphere of pornography to see if it can tell us more about thoughts on what was considered to be perverted, sinful, immoral or against the natural order. Although pornography can go some way in helping investigations of perversions in the past, and defining what was considered perverse or not, we have to be careful in its reading as in some cases pornography turns society's normal values on their head, and what is considered perverted in society is normalized in pornography. Although the type of acceptable behaviour (and the amount of its violation) might well have been contained by religious beliefs, the law and morality in real life (and it is impossible to gauge exactly how much systems of control worked since transgression occurred nonetheless), the range and scope of sexual perversity in pornography was limited only by the erotic imagination and this, to some extent, was dictated by class. Erotica was more easily obtained by the richer readers, so therefore they would have been more familiar with different types of fanciful sexual activities, having read about them. Aristocrats also had more time and money to indulge their fantasies, and therefore were often seen as more debauched. This did not necessarily mean their behaviour was considered perverted.

Increased privacy for many people during the eighteenth century meant that opportunities arose not only for private reading but for sexual experimentation. As Patricia Meyer Spacks has pointed out, 'eighteenth-century men and women simultaneously experienced heightened eagerness to penetrate the privacy of others ... as soon as privacy exists, it challenges the desire for knowledge'.[55] Personal curiosity and the need for novelty combined with this new privacy was reflected in pornographic developments as texts tried out more innovative methods of sex, some of them deviating from the sanctioned missionary position promulgated by the theologians. With new developments in printing techniques, pornography became increasingly available in eighteenth-century England. From the mid-century onwards, its textual style began to develop in terms of exploring sexual perversion.[56]

De Sade's pornography has been shown as the exemplar of perversion in various examinations of his works. Foucault highlights the point that central to the sex of de Sade is a lack of a norm, with a type of sex with laws known only unto itself. This, in itself, would serve as a contradiction of Foucault's theory – it would mean that de Sade's sexual world is therefore outside of Foucault's power mechanism. Leaving this aside, can we use de

Sade as an example of a catch-all European version of eighteenth-century perversions?

Marquis de Sade explored virtually every vice known to man – flagellation, blood lust, sadism, masochism, sodomy – in his work as well as in his personal life. In 1772, at the age of thirty-two, de Sade was sentenced to death at Aix for his cruelty and unnatural sexual practices. He later ended up, via the Bastille, in Charenton lunatic asylum where he was kept incarcerated until his death in 1844. He supposedly developed his taste for perversion in the army, and gave his life up to dissipation after the death of his sister-in-law who he idealized in his novel *Juliette*. One of his worst crimes was the forcible and indecent flagellation of 36-year-old Rosa Keller. He tied her to a bed and whipped her with a birch, made various incisions in her flesh with a small knife and dropped wax into the wounds. Some years later he took part in an orgy of prostitution and flagellation with several whores to whom he had administered an aphrodisiac. They complained to the court that it had been so powerful that it had made them quite ill. De Sade believed that 'every man wants to be a tyrant when he fornicates'.[57]

De Sade's contribution to sexual perversion came in the form of pornographic books such as *Les 120 Journées de Sodome* (1785), *Justine, ou les Malheureurs de la Vertu* (1791) (Figures 2.2 and 2.3), *Le Philosphie dans le Boudoir* (1795) and *Histoire de Juliette ou les Prospérités du vice* (1797). However, as Henry Spencer Ashbee, the notorious Victorian bibliographer of erotica stated, in de Sade's pornography, bloodthirstiness was usually connected with insulting virtue and making it ridiculous.[58] In eighteenth-century English pornography, this is not necessarily so, sometimes even the opposite. In *Female Flagellants*, for example, virtue is not mocked but exalted. According to Ashbee, de Sade's influence becomes evident in British erotica by the 1830s in such books as *The Inutility of Virtue* (1830), with similar sordidness and ridiculing of virtue seen in *The Seducing Cardinals* (1830). Humiliation is certainly an affect which increased in direct proportion with the violence. *The Experimental Lecture* by 'Colonel Spanker' (1836) contains the whole philosophy which was argued to exhaustion in de Sade – bloody orgies, vivisection and torture.

But how far de Sade was available in England, or indeed in English, is difficult to assess. A clumsy English translation of *Justine* was published in 1899 by Isidore Liseux imprinted by the Erotika Biblion Society for private distribution only – 50 copies were made for its members under the title *A Philosophical Romance*.[59] But translations were not available in England *en masse* until the Olympia Press publications in the 1950s, although a few select British readers and producers of pornography read him in the original. In any case, it is unlikely that de Sade had much influence on ordinary British people's view of perversion, even if the richer eighteenth-century libertine managed to obtain copies of his works. Even then, the perverse world of de Sade was not necessarily the same as the perverse world of the British pornographer.

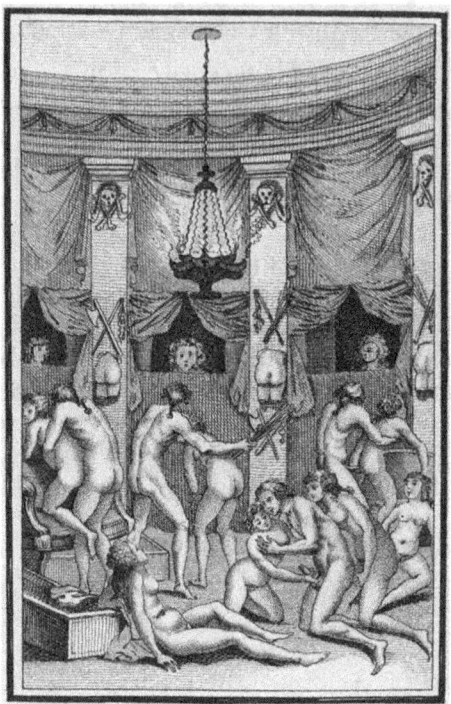

FIGURE 2.2 *Marquis de Sade*, La Nouvelle Justine, *Dutch edition, 1797. Wellcome Library, London.*

Theoretically speaking, pornography should have been seen as perverse as it was seen through transgressive eyes – the intention of most pornography is to break taboos. However, the trangressive nature of pornography had been overplayed, and the more important point about British eighteenth-century pornography was its incorporative, and even conservative, nature – how it fed on, and feeds back into, the normative cultural world around it. Thus what we learn from British pornography in particular is not necessary the perverse world itself, as in, say, de Sade, but what the normal world finds perverse. This can therefore act as a 'way in' to finding out what was considered sexual perversion in the eighteenth-century mind – or at least what the minds of the British writers and readers of pornography thought of as sexually perverse.

As forerunners of pornography, Britain looked to seventeenth-century French writers to begin the exploration of sex and its various derivations. Many of the story-lines were based on the introduction of young virgins to sex by an older woman, which would then lead to vaginal penetrative sex with a man.[60] Although lesbian interludes were seen as a normal part of a

FIGURE 2.3 *Marquis de Sade, frontispiece to* La Nouvelle Justine, *1791. Wellcome Library, London.*

woman's introduction to sex, the 'main' act would be heterosexual. Yet sex between women was not regarded as unusual or threatening but a natural progression in a young woman's sexual initiation. Although overspilling fluids (tears, blood, semen, female ejaculations) were frequently used in erotica to convey excess, they were often seen as normal manifestations of an otherwise wayward body.

Diderot, whose philosophical influence was arguably more profound on British people than de Sade during the eighteenth century, saw the body as central to understanding man and wrote constantly about the body and its image. His friendship and correspondence with John Wilkes after they had met at a Parisian salon showed his influences stretched to English libertines. Conlin has argued that, 'It was Diderot's analysis that sexual licence, if treated as a function of liberty, could erode civilisation and cause chaos.'[61] This would, if true, demonstrate an eighteenth-century belief that sex without constraints leads to the downfall of society. Yet Diderot delighted in descriptions of fleshy uncontrol and the precariousness of the body. In this way, he saw the body as acting directly, rather than merely being representative, as an external force in society. He rejected many of the constraints placed on the body and he thought that curbing its instinct was pointless.[62] This is evident in his writings on incest as discussed in *Supplément au Voyage de Bougainville* (1772); and in *La Religieuse* (1760) in which we see scenes of the main character noviciate Suzanne shedding copious tears and having nosebleeds while her Mother Superior foams at the mouth while she reaches a climax. Both narratives point to the impossibility of containing excess bodily fluids in relation to sexual outpourings as bodily transgressions. This bodily overflow was typically early modern manifestations of the body, seen in literature, medicine and erotica.[63] This all points to an eighteenth-century belief that the body would go its own way, despite any constraints placed upon it. It would follow that any act made outside of 'normal constraints' would be considered unavoidable. Thus certain acts of nymphomania, bestiality, even sodomy might be seen as outside the control of an individual which is why connections with the devil were often invoked, Satan having control of those sexually depraved bodies.

Sexual desire for children is another area of investigation which has recently opened up. Philippe Ariés argued that the invention of the notion of a separate childhood evolved only in the seventeenth century and with it came the theory of child innocence.[64] From this, it was recognized that children needed to be protected and laws evolved to deal with this issue. By the late Victorian period, there was the emergence of a definition of childhood as specifically a time in which sex with the person is forbidden, which in itself, attracted attention to the forbidden act. Furthermore, by the end of the nineteenth century, the question of the innocence of the child was subjected to sustained critique in sex abuse cases.[65] Running simultaneously with this was the emergence of a historically specific love of young girls which precluded sex and insisted on maintenance of 'innocence' up to and beyond the onset of sexual puberty.[66] Although much of the investigation has concentrated on the nineteenth century so far, George S. Rousseau has broadened out the debate in his recent collection in *Child Sexuality. From the Greeks to the Great War.*[67]

In pornography, although it was on the erotic horizon in the 1770s, as yet paedophilia was not part of the scene in terms of sexual perversion. Within the scenes, the potential for the lust for children was presented, but was never fully realized. From the way that the flagellator (who was nearly always female in eighteenth-century erotica) is revered in the narration, the sexual interest is centred on her, rather than on the children; if anything, the child would stand as substitute for the reader watching the scenario unfold. Only in the nineteenth century did pornography develop into full penetrative sex between guardians and their charges, sisters and brothers, and uncles and nephews and nieces as seen in *The Romance of Chastisement* (1866), *The Quintessence of Birch Discipline* ('1870', 1883)[68] and *The Romance of Lust* (1876). Not only are the later relationships made closer, but they are now between older men and young women. The 'gentler' form of lesbianism was overtaken by men's violent attacks on young girls, thus opening up a new world of sadism. By the nineteenth century, a pornographic technique, evident as early as John Cleland's *Memoirs of a Woman of Pleasure*, had been honed to perfection – gradations of sexual perversity followed on from each other in a logical progression, ending with the most perverse. Thus we can detect in the pornographic mind, what was perceived as the most perverted form of sex as it would be at the end of the book. Furthermore, as Lisa Sigel has pointed out, the scenes in nineteenth-century pornography became increasingly littered with swearwords which were used in a more cruel way; there was also a move from use of a word such as 'fuck' in bawdy terms, to its use as meaning polluted.[69]

Graphic stories of monks and nuns utilized the religious as sites of sexual perversion. The violent sexual flagellant theme had already infiltrated England in the form of French imports such as *Dom Bourge, ou Portiers Des Chartreux* (1741) and *Thérèse Philosophe* (1748). In reality though, in England, flagellation was never seen as a perversity, more of a divergence, and this was because it resulted, and even facilitated, vaginal copulation between a man and a woman. It had already been recognized as a cure for impotency. Flagellation assisted reproduction in that it encouraged erection which allowed for coition.

Flagellation as self-mortification had long been a favourite penance of the Catholics, and as such, was acceptable in the wider society. With the coming of Protestantism, both the confessional and self-flagellation were rejected as part of the Popish religion and instead, became butts of Protestant jokes. More seriously, Protestants saw the confessional as a potential area of seduction of their wives and daughters, a place where the usually vigilant father and husband had no control over his female kin. Wives and daughters were perceived as becoming religiously perverted while being sexually exploited by lecherous priests. In this context, religious perversion became closely linked to sexual corruption, particularly of the innocent.[70] This perception of Catholicism and its connection to sex was carried right thought to the nineteenth century. Rape scenes and necrophilia were also to feature in nineteenth-century pornography becoming more violent as the century went on. Furthermore, the perverting of the female form by applying negative attributes to them – in showing women to be nymphomaniacs, prostitutes and full of venereal disease – was often part of the pornographic tradition.[71]

Rape and necrophilia

Rape was essentially a crime against property, the woman being a chattel of her father and later, her husband. For this reason, until recently, married men could not be prosecuted for raping their wives. Although nowadays we talk loosely of rapists as perverts, was rape considered a perversion in the eighteenth and nineteenth centuries? As Joanna Bourke points out, perverts were only labelled as such in 1883, before that it was the acts rather then the person which was imbued with the crime. She also points out how rape myths abound in history at the expense of successful prosecutions of the crime.[72] The understanding of rape in the past has been further muddied, as rape has been seen as different things – as abduction, as seduction and as a means of exerting power. There is still no proper consensus on what rape entails. So how do we place rape in history?

Sylvana Tomaselli has argued that there is lack of a history of rape,[73] but more recently Barbara Baines has argued that the reluctance to acknowledge the reality of rape *is* the history of rape. She examines the literary world of rape in which 'Rape never primarily signifies the loss and suffering of the woman'.[74] In the past, women were not compensated for rape, rather their 'owners' were. In the Bible, Deuteronomy advises than when an unmarried virgin was raped, the offender had an option to pay the father of his victim fifty shekels or to marry her. During the medieval and Renaissance period, rape carried a meaning of abduction – 'the act of carrying away a person, especially a woman, by force',[75] as well as being seen as stealing another man's property.[76] By the late eighteenth century, this connection between woman as property and abduction would continue to be made in certain elopement cases; when the sister of courtesan Hariette Wilson, Sophia, ran off with Lord Deerhurst against her parents' wishes, the only avenue available to them was to sue him for loss of domestic services.[77]

An eighteenth-century understanding of seduction often meant 'accompanied with force', since any self-respecting maiden would not give up her maidenhead unless under pressure. As Anna Clark argues, violence was seen as an acceptable form of seduction.[78] Because of its public image, the British had a hard time seeing heterosexual rape as particularly perverse or 'against nature', although where it was proven it was treated harshly by the courts as a capital crime. But more recently, rape has been seen to be more connected with a widespread insidious misogyny rather than a sexual perversion *per se*; as Roy Porter sums up Susan Brownmiller's argument, rape 'is not a sickness of perverts, but the sickness of patriarchy'.[79]

The debased female body was conveyed in submissive terminology in mainstream literature and in pornography as part of this discourse – rape and violent seduction went hand in hand. Neither were considered perversions, but part of normative discourse. Violent seduction pervaded erotic fantasies in mainstream literature such as *Clarissa* (albeit off-side); as Laura Hinton points out, 'In *Clarissa*, it does not take great powers of speculation to see that what is at the bottom of the pit is the subjected female body.' The whole book centres around Clarissa's rape giving the overall feeling of a 'prettification of violence'.[80]

We can see how, from Ovid to Cleland, misogyny has pervaded the history of imagery of rape in pornographic texts, and more often than not seduction was seen as an attack. Rape featured in common defloration fantasies in pornographic literature blurring the boundaries between rape and seduction. The impression given is that women feign defence but want to be overcome; for example, in *The Petit Maître* (1749), women are conveyed as enjoying a struggle: 'This is the plain Reason, why most Women refuse to *surrender* upon Treaty, and why they delight so much in being storm'd.'[81]

Yet Roy Porter believes that, in reality, the silence on rape by social moralists of the day indicates that rape was not 'the scandal of the day'.[82] However, the realities and perception of eighteenth-century rape cases were muddled, and high-profile cases coloured the perceptions of the public's understanding of the rape law and the process of prosecution.[83] Few rapes were successfully prosecuted, because they were construed and understood in terms of seduction with pressure. There has been a history of difficulty in obtaining convictions for accused rapists; for example, between 1805 and 1818, only 76 men were convicted of rape. Despite rape being a capital offence only 47 out of these 76 men went to the gallows. There were not only difficulties in securing a conviction, but many rapes went unreported. During the same period, only 17 per cent of rapists were prosecuted, compared to 63 per cent conviction of all crimes overall; a much higher rate of men were acquitted for rape than other crimes.[84] Earlier statistics show a similar tale.[85] Seventeenth-century judge Mathew Hale is quoted as saying 'though rape is a detestable crime, it is an accusation easily made, and hard to be proved'.[86] Worse still, prosecutors, whether successful or not, had to pay the costs themselves, making the process virtually impossible for the poor single girl. Even men who had been convicted of rape did not necessarily have their reputation or career affected.

The rape of young children was taken extremely seriously and death sentences ensued in cases where prosecution was successful. In one unusual case, a woman was found guilty of assisting in a rape of under-age children. Alice Gray of the Parish of St Giles in the Fields, was found guilty of rape, 23 April 1707, after aiding and abetting Thomas Smith of raping ten-year-old Catherine Masters. The child, 'awaking about 2 a Clock in Morning, found a Man in Bed with them, that as she was endeavouring to get away, the Prisoner pull'd her back again, and held her down in the Bed, and stopt her Mouth, (that she could not cry out) while the Man gain'd the perfect knowledge of her Body'.[87] A further proof no doubt helped in securing a conviction in this case; after inspection, it was obvious not only had the child been abused, but Smith had given her the pox. Both Smith and Gray were sentenced to death. Pederasty in relation to men and boys would fit into the category of sodomy, and similarly attract a capital punishment.

Published reports of violence against children, beatings of domestic servants and molestation of dead bodies serves as a cultural witness to people's understanding of the subject matter. Sadomasochistic reports of abused children frequently circulated in penny dreadfuls during the early nineteenth century. Rape, murder and sodomy cases were similarly reported, as seen in Chapter 3. This interest in rape, violence and dead bodies found its sexual outlet in necrophilia. Traditionally necrophilia involves men lusting after female bodies rather than vice versa; as Elisabeth Bronfen's work states in her *Death, Feminity and the Aesthetic*, 'the feminine body as death turns the women into an object of sight', and the gaze on sex and death are invariably connected to women and her sexuality.[88] This connection has also been associated with male violence as Beverley Clack has pointed out: 'Any discussion of death is invariably associated with male violence and destruction.'[89] In this connection between women, sex and death, there has also been a development of a macabre exoticism created in the juxtaposition of love and death.[90] Lisa Downing has pointed out that definitions of necrophilia traditionally focus on the actual activities of the necrophile, obsessed with the act of intercourse with a corpse, 'the repeated focus of penetration of the corpse implicitly relegates necrophilia to the realms of male perversion'.[91] According to Dr Jonathan Rosman and Dr Phillip Resnick, who reviewed 122 cases of necrophilia in 1989, there are three basic types of 'true' necrophilia:[92] necrophilic homicide, which is murder to obtain a corpse; regular necrophilia, the use of corpses already dead for sexual pleasure; necrophilic fantasy, envisioning the acts but not acting on them. In his *Psychopathia Sexualis* (1894), Krafft-Ebing would call necrophilia a horrible manifestation of sadism.

As yet, little investigation has been undertaken into necrophilia in the eighteenth century[93] probably because of the difficulty in finding reports of such cases. We know about 36-year-old Samuel Pepys, who staged his own show for visiting cousins when he violated the corpse of Katherine of France, long since dead, even if it was only 'a fondle and a kiss'.[94] George Selwyn's love of dead bodies was evident, not only in his enthusiasm for watching public hangings, but in his excitement on visiting his dying friends. More serious medical non-fictional examinations of corpse profanation can be seen in Johan George Simonis's mention of it in *Brevis Delineato Empotentia Conjugalis* (1665) and in Martin Schurig's *Gynaecologia* (1730); both mention copulation with corpses,[95] but these are unusual for their time; also both were written in Latin and aimed at the medical profession.

Although real life cases are hard to uncover, an eighteenth-century interest in necrophilia was evident,[96] no doubt a reflection of a time when public hangings were a common spectacle, and medical dissections were increasingly on display, both in the surgeon's dissecting room and in art, as in Hogarth's 'The Reward of Cruelty'. Jonathan Sawday, Ruth Richardson and Timothy

Marshall have shown how dissection was inextricably linked to, and had an effect on, other areas of eighteenth-century life such as culture, art and literature.[97] Death and sex were increasingly juxtaposed in Gothic literature such as Horace Walpole's *Castle of Otranto* (1764) and Matthew Lewis's *The Monk* (1796). Necrophilia as the rape of dead bodies was in some ways an extension of the imagery which permeated eighteenth-century society in the image of seduction of the submissive female body – necrophilia was the height of this submission. Pornography also saw fictional depictions of girls being sedated, or raped while unconscious, linking scenes of rape to necrophilia as seen in *The Lascivious Hypocrite* ('1790').[98] Although this purports to be a translation of *La Tartufe Libertine*,[99] it has been substantially reworked and was probably published about forty years later than it states. The aggressiveness of the narration suggests sado-masochism as the protagonist Valentine St Geraud (a reference to the scandal of French priest Father Girard mentioned in Chapter 6) slips Eugenie a sleeping draught, renders her unconscious and rapes her. Thus we see a shift in the way these images were presented with these earlier loving scenes between couples, in which 'surrenders' were a common theme, being increasingly overtaken by scenarios which highlighted violence, brutal rape and pain.

We can perhaps see a retrospective connection between the sexologists and the time period covered by this book in Krafft-Ebing's definition of what sexual perversion *was not*; he believed that the purpose of sexual desire was procreation, and any form of desire that did not go towards that ultimate goal was a perversion.[100] Rape, for instance, was an aberrant act, but not a perversion, since pregnancy could result. Any sexual act which evaded procreation was seen to be perverse and anything which might result in procreation was deemed to be acceptable.

Creation of the perverse 'other'

The development of imperialism gave rise to a new measure for deviancy. European colonialists, eager to create and maintain a distance between themselves and their conquered peoples, registered their own sexuality as wholesome, human and natural but classed native sexuality as abhorrent, bestial or somehow perverse. Historians have classed this colonialist perception of natives as 'The Other', a perception of the native as a lower person or animalistic – in essence meaning a people other than British. This creation of 'The British' as the standard norm by which to judge foreigners helped to establish the perverted 'other'.[101]

Nationalism became part of the history of sexuality and, with the onslaught of respectability, came the need for self-control. Philippa Levine has examined how ingrained prejudices of the sexual practices of colonized people had a direct effect on how new colonial laws penetrated and reinforced the distinction between the colonized and the colonizer.[102] As

George L. Mosse declares, 'nationalism not only helped to control sexuality, to reinforce what society considered normal, but it also provided the means through which changing sexual attitudes could be absorbed and tamed into respectability'.[103]

Even before the eighteenth century, we see a belief in most travellers that the foreigners they encountered were bestial, savages, or at the very least below themselves in terms of human specimens.[104] Reaction against foreigners most often came in the form of attacks on their sexuality as perverse. As the British Empire stretched its rule, so did the notion of superiority of the British herald itself as never before. The encounters by soldiers, missionaries and explorers often give us our first views of the natives of other countries and with it came the biases and racism which infused sexual attitudes for the next three hundred years.

In conclusion, we can see that sexual perversion manifested itself both as a crime 'against nature' and through religion, and was reinforced through the moralist attitude of the local community and through legal attempts to control it. The acts which fit into that category had been defined in the Bible and were buttressed by centuries of theological interpretation, the worst being sodomy (whether with beasts, anal sex between a man and a woman, or sex between two men). Female cross-dressing was not generally regarded as perverse, although male cross-dressing was when it was associated with sodomy. Likewise, female-to-female penetration was regarded as against nature but less was mentioned about these activities, and they caused less concern. Flagellation was seen merely as curious diversions, while foot fetishism seems to have been a celebrated activity.

Apart from finding sexual perversion in the past by examining delineations of religion and in the classification 'against nature', another 'way in' to finding sexual perversion in history can be seen through the lens of pornography. What was considered 'against nature', or ideas about perversions in pornography in our time period, though, does not necessarily adhere to what we see as sexually perverse now. Therefore 'normality' is not a given, nor is it a concept set in time but it changes and mutates, it varies between classes and genders. Perversity can therefore be seen to be set against the norm, and in turn, this also changes in time. However, that change has been relatively slow and piecemeal. From the Restoration through the Enlightenment to the Victorian period we find a concept of perversity that was fairly constant and consistent, although this argument might be nuanced with further investigations. It included certain sexual acts considered deviant or divergent from what was perceived as 'normal' or natural – the further away from the perceived 'normal', the more perverse that sexual behaviour was seen to be.[105]

Although religion and ensuing moralities played a major part in influencing and overseeing people's sexual behaviour and the creation of perceptions of perversion, lofty values of the literary or moral world of eighteenth-century French (or even English) philosophers are unlikely to have deeply affected the perception of the ordinary person on the street (or in the field) of either his sexual perversion, or that of others. S/he was more likely to be indirectly influenced by the writings of the Church Fathers as they filtered down through lectures from the pulpit. Social control and community action also have played a large part in expunging deviant behaviour, but this effect declined as rural communities dispersed. As people redeployed into the cities, family networks broke down – spies were now the neighbours next door who resorted to the law for retribution.

Perceptions of behavioural types and acts were gradually recategorized as new scientific methods and appraisals came into view. The old religious connections of 'perversion' to sin, witchcraft and association with the devil were slowly being replaced with condemnation of deviant behaviour through medical and scientific models of classification or 'treatment'. Although these breakdowns and delinkings were taking place over the nineteenth century, only with the coming of the new sexologist models was sexual perversion defined as specific medical categories. Nonetheless, there was a continued link between an impressed knowledge of 'correct', or good way of doing things, and a 'bad' or incorrect way, with the old theological thinking of the individual moral consciousness being linked to the new ideas of the sexologists such as Richard von Krafft-Ebing and psychiatrists such as Sigmund Freud. In sexology and psychiatry, perversion continued to reinforce the notion of sexual normality through its inversion, but in a new language.

CHAPTER THREE

Blaming and Shaming in Eighteenth- and Early Nineteenth-century Print Culture

A culture of blaming and shaming emerged which attached itself to those who had committed crimes, misdemeanours or sexual indiscretions. All kinds of sexual offences were written about, and accounts of them were printed and distributed in the capital and countryside of England. This material was wide-ranging in terms of both subject matter and in its audience, and all classes had access; it acted as a precursor to the naming and shaming of today's blame culture seen in current British tabloids. But what was the content, why did it erupt when it did and what purpose did it serve?

The concept of blaming and shaming can be a way to understanding eighteenth-century print culture and the public reaction to it. If we turn to the exact meaning of 'blame', the *Oxford English Dictionary* states it is 'the action of censuring; expression of disapprobation; to find fault with; to censure (an action, a person *for* his action)'; in other words, accusing a person of wrongdoing. The definition of 'shame' is given as 'the painful feeling of humiliation or distress by the consciousness of wrong or foolish behaviour', which involves 'a loss of respect or esteem: dishonour'. It would seem that a person cannot be shamed unless they have already been 'blamed' for something, or at least had their wrong-doing pointed out. The perpetrator of wrong-doing does not necessarily feel bad about their deed, but the shaming of the community makes them uncomfortable. According to this framework, only within more 'sophisticated' societies would the concept of 'guilt' become more common.

Examining the reasons for the emergence of such materials, we need to look at the cultural shifts which had an impact on the way people viewed certain crimes and misdemeanours as they were crucial in realigning public opinion, and were part of the reason why these pamphlets became so popular. German sociologist Norbert Elias and French philosopher Michel Foucault both point to the modern state as promoters of 'civilized' or 'disciplined' behaviour.[1] In Elias's 'civilizing process' he argues that there has been a prolonged process of structural changes taking place in Western society since the Middle Ages up to modern times which has led to an increasing mutual dependence between people. This, in turn, has brought about psychological implications such as self-restraint and control that did not exist before. The rise of the middling sort held some influence over changing behaviours – they had more money to spend, indulged in luxuries and moved to more politeness of manners. They were also more literate and so read more.[2] Elias noted changes at table, in attitudes to natural bodily functions – from spitting to blowing one's nose – and changes in aggression. Overall, this related to a change in manners leading to a more 'polite' or 'civilized' behaviour.[3] Meanwhile, Foucault has argued for new formation of new authorities of power which asserted themselves over society and its problems.[4] Whereas Foucault's vision indicates a show of force from the modern state, Elias's theory relies on an increasingly individualization in life-styles and an internalization of the values of honour and shame resulting in guilt. In these frameworks, internalized guilt took over from regulation by shame and public dishonouring establishing the concept of 'guilt' in more 'sophisticated' societies. This, however, leaves no room for the ongoing power of blaming and shaming in public discourse, which we now recognize continued. As David Nash has pointed out, 'we rediscover that "shame" had it uses to a society that should arguably have outgrown it and its power'.[5] In reality, there is enough evidence to point to a persistence on the use of blaming and shaming in modern societies. Therefore, I believe Jürgen Habermas's theory is more useful in analysis of this material, particularly his suggestion that newspapers and print culture established a method of allowing public approbation and condemnation of bad behaviour.

The perceived shift from primitive public shaming to internalized personal guilt does not always stay within given chronologies. Human relationships and feeling have a more complex history than a straightforward movement from pre-industrial to industrialized societies. Opposing themes co-existed within the same time-frame in cultures. Community relationships with and beyond state mechanisms often had, and still have, a huge impact on society and behaviour. Norbert Elias's understanding of the filtering of ideas (the top-down and the bottom-up approaches) was influenced by anthropologists who saw honour and shame to be the basis of pre-industrial societies. As Marianna Muravyeva emphasizes, 'Shame has been consistently shown to be relatively successful as a strategy for upholding certain values, such as honour.'[6] Since reputation was closely tied up with a man or woman's honour, maintaining that reputation was paramount. This, of course, would only affect certain classes, since public reputation hardly mattered to some groups of people (although not all) at the bottom of society, whose main focus was on surviving at any cost. Status was important – if you had no reputation to lose, there were no consequences.

Turning to the material itself, we can see that topics ran from homosexuality to adultery and divorce. The sources examined below can be divided roughly into five main types of material; pamphlets which exposed those who had committed so-called 'crimes against nature' (for example, sodomy, bestiality or incest cases, all considered the 'worst of crimes'); cases of criminal conversation or adultery, considered less serious, but where the level of criticism varied depending on the characters involved and the circumstance in which they were presented; pamphlets which exposed sex scandals within the Catholic Church; rape and murder cases; and finally 'blaming and shaming' material such as whores' autobiographies, which are explored in Chapter 5 and are therefore not examined in this chapter.

In the first group – that of pamphlets on sodomitical behaviour, the earliest flurry of pamphlets concerned the case of Lord Audley, second Earl of Castlehaven. In 1631, he was accused not only of sodomy with his manservant but raping his wife and incest with his daughter. As previously noted in Chapter 2, the buggery law of 1533 insisted on proof of both penetration and ejaculation for a successful prosecution.[7] However, in the case of the Earl of Castlehaven, no penetration was proven and yet he was still sentenced to death by his peers. The threat was not so much as what he was doing inside his household, but the repercussions it may have outside it. In this case, Cynthia Herrup has argued that it was less to do with his sexual behaviour and more to do with the political manoeuvrings which influenced the action against Audley. It was also considered to involve a threat to bloodline inheritance, a fact which concerned Audley's fellow peers.[8] While political antagonism played its part in effectively calling into question Castlehaven's reputation in an attempt to dispose of an adversary, some of the problem lay in the fact that Castlehaven had failed to maintain control of his household.

However, by the time the case was reprinted in 1710 on the publication of *The Case of Sodomy in the Tryal of Mervin Lord Audley, Earl of Castlehaven* (given as 'printed from an original manuscript') some eighty years after the original, there can be little doubt that Castlehaven's case was published in order to pander to the interest in sodomy.[9] The well-known printer of pornography, Edmund Curll, was a man only too willing to take advantage of any public interest in scandalous exposés, and reprinted the pamphlets in a collection of prurient material.[10] Within the collection, he incorporated a package of other court cases involving sexual matters, including impotency, adultery and divorce.[11] While technology had made printing easier and helped bring down costs, increasing literacy meant more people were reading this material so there was an increase in demand. To a large extent, the emergence of this material followed the trajectory of the erotic book trade in general.[12]

Pamphlets on sodomy trials began to increase in number from around the 1720s and 1730s. These would run throughout the century and into the next and would vary in length and type of output from a one page hand bill such as that announcing the 'Final Commitment of Allison for a Detestable Crime' (c.1825) to large collections of all sorts of crimes as those of Curll's seen above.[13] Some of the pamphlets were summaries of the cases taken from trial reports with straightforward accounts of the alleged events from the perspectives of the defendant and the victim. Sexual attacks on youths were fairly common. A case heard at the Quarter Sessions on St Margaret's-Hill, Southwark was reported in a sixpenny pamphlet, *The Trial of Richard Branson* (1760). Branson, a clerk at the vinegar yard in the neighbourhood, was on trial for assaulting James Fawcett, a sixteen-year-old youth from Dulwich College 'with an Intent to commit Sodomy'.[14] He was found guilty, fined £100 and sentenced to a year in prison, which was a fairly average sentence for attempted sodomy.

Acceptance of guilt and atonement was a prevalent feature in *Some Particulars Relating to the Life of William Dillon Sheppard, Who was executed at St Michael's Hill Gallows, for Sodomy on Monday the 1st June, 1761*. The pamphlet had been printed at the 'request of the prisoner' and published by the 'authority of the sheriff' and was replete with religiously emotive language. Pious utterings about penitence peppered its pages and it was most probably written by the cleric who attended the prisoner. According to the author, the prisoner 'was never heard all this time to address himself to any but to the *Supreme Being,* to whom he seemed to pour out his very soul in tears and groanings which cannot be utter'd 'till his bodily strength would fail, as it frequently did, beneath the weight of his sorrow.'[15] Although Sheppard was arrested for having committed sodomy, he never admitted to this crime but *did* confess to having lived a previous debauched life, acknowledging, 'I have been heaping up sin, and heaping up wrath, and now it is come upon me'.[16] Despite the prisoner's denial of attempted sodomy on the youth, the accusation had shamed him into admitting other crimes of a debauched nature and supposedly ensured his ultimate repentance. Evidently, this was offered up as an example to all sodomites to steer clear of such temptations if they wanted to avoid the death penalty, as was Sheppard's fate.

While the perpetrators of sodomy had been blamed and shamed in earlier treatments, others were seeking complete exoneration for the defendants' actions. One of the more unusual cases can be seen in *The State of the Case of Captain Jones* (1772).[17] The text recorded a plea made on behalf of the captain by his solicitor in court at his trial and was one of the first incidents which promoted a fuller discussion of homosexuality.[18] Jones had been convicted at the Old Bailey for sodomizing a thirteen-year-old boy, and sentenced to death. Previously, pamphlets had been publicizing the indecent nature of sodomy, but here the public were finally given a chance to see a defence of an accused sodomite. It involved not simply a call for clemency, but was against punishment for sodomites unless there was solid evidence, not mere accusations. The solicitor declared: 'I say, that no Crime is to be punished but upon full Proof: And if you reply, That it never will be proved; I say again, That it ought never to be punished.'[19] Jones had allegedly attacked a boy, but there were no witnesses to the crime, nor did the boy show any tears or make any cries. The case was based 'on the simple Deposition of the Boy', a fact which the solicitor condemned particularly as it seemed the boy was complicit: 'That the Boy went twice to the Captain; that he suffered the first insult in silence, and that he charged him only on the Repetition of it, and that, three Weeks thereafter.' While the boy had said it was bashfulness which had kept him quiet the first time, why not the second, asked the solicitor for the defence. As he pointed out, 'the Boy went to the Captain a second Time, of his own Accord, or by the Advice of Somebody'. His defence summed up, 'If he went of his own Accord, he must necessarily raise a Suspicion that he consented to the Crime; and in this Case, his Testimony is not to be admitted. . . . If he went by the Advice of Somebody, I cannot conceive how that Somebody in consequence of the Advice given, certainly given with the View of obtaining an ocular, or at least an auricular Proof of the Captain's Crime, has not been able to obtain that Proof.'[20] The case prompted a flurry of letters to the newspapers including the *General Evening Post*, the *London Evening Post*, the *Morning Chronicle* and the *Public Ledger*. The plea was successful resulting in a royal pardon on condition that Jones left the country. Defence of the accused was now being included in the pamphlets as well as the shaming accusations.

Other attacks were mounted in the pamphlets for religious or political reasons, but separating out the two is sometimes more complicated than it first appears. In religion, there was a history of moral shaming in both the English Ecclesiastical courts and the Scottish kirk or church courts. Public punishments used the mechanisms of shame; fornicators were paraded through village squares in white sheets, whipped through towns in full view of onlookers, or manacled into the pillory to suffer the disapproval of the crowd, via an avalanche of rotten eggs, putrefying vegetables and dead cats and dogs. Now joining them from around the early eighteenth century, the pamphlets were being used to level attacks on the Church itself; criticisms were made against a particular set of dogmatic beliefs, or examples made of noteworthy members of the clergy; or by the British Protestants against the French Catholics. The attention was now turned away from the congregation and 'sinners' onto the church authorities.[21] The activities of some of the clerics were especially thought to be a subject worthy of exposure because they were held up as exemplars of virtue by the church and should have known better.

Dying speeches and verses were published after the case of John Atherton, Bishop of Waterford and Lismore in Ireland came to light (Figure 3.1). He was accused of buggery with his steward and tithe proctor, John Childe in

FIGURE 3.1 *Frontispiece*, The Life and Death of John Atherton, *1641. British Library, London.*

1640, and both men were hanged on Gallows Green. The subject matter of the anonymous pamphlet published in 1641 was again revisited in 1710, but this time the bishop was defended as the Protestant victim of a conspiracy by Catholic clergy who had resented his post.[22] While attacks and defence of homosexuality brought the subject into public debate, and attempts were being made to shift public opinion, when religious men were involved, it was considered particularly offensive because of their elevated religious position. Even then, defences were sometimes made pointing to the political motivations of the accusers. In this particular pamphlet, it was alleged that the attack was used as a method of disposing of an unwanted bishop by his Catholic detractors.

Indeed, sodomitical activities of the clergy were to figure highly when in 1822, Percy Jocelyn, Bishop of Clogher was caught with his breeches down penetrating a soldier he had picked up in a tavern. All was revealed in a sixpenny pamphlet describing the event and including a comic drawing seen in the frontispiece showing the two men (Figure 3.2). The Bishop was roundly condemned for his criminal activities, especially because of the exalted religious position he held, the author declaring, 'To hold the vicious up to odium and contempt should be at all times a particular care of the

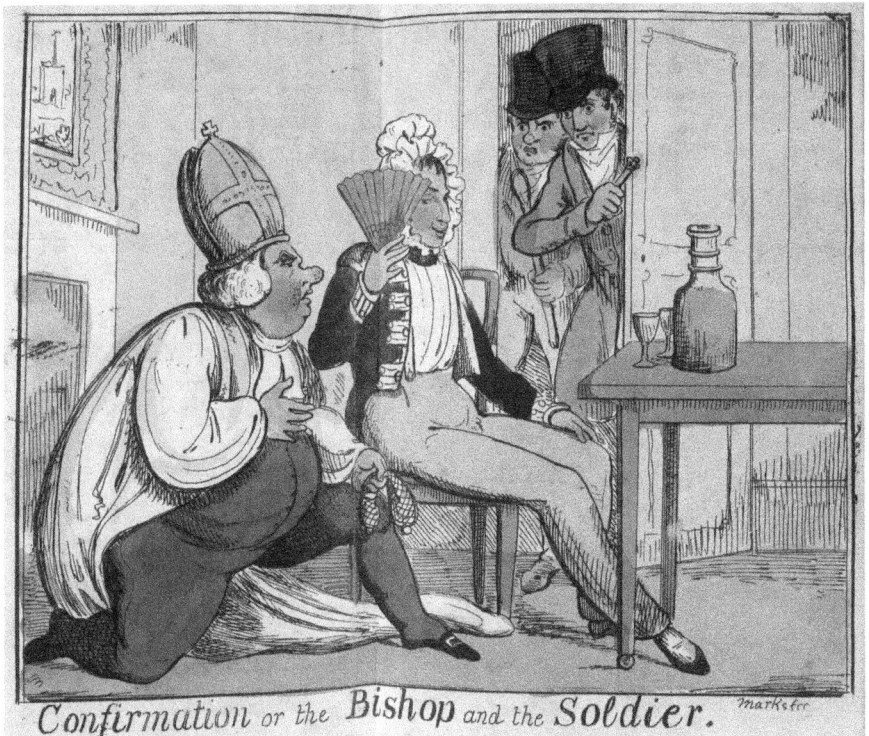

FIGURE 3.2 *Frontispiece*, A Correct Account of the Horrible Occurrence ... Bishop of Clogher, 1822. British Library, London.

Press; but when every powerful engine is exerted to veil vices of the privileged ranks, and to make appear that crime is peculiar to those who constitute what are called the lower classes, it become a sacred and imperative duty.'[23] The pamphlet's preface quoted a report printed in the *Observer* on 21 July 1822: 'On Friday night it appears that he was detected in a back room of the White Lion public-house, in St. Alban's place, St James's, in a situation with a private in the Foot Guards, to which we will not more minutely allude, but which led to his instant apprehension and removal with his companion to the watch house.' Next morning, both the Bishop and the soldier were pursued by an irate mob. The article contended with ingenious regret, but with much evidential glee, 'We cannot dismiss this article without observing that it is with great and unfeigned sorrow that we have to record this degradation of rank and dignity'.[24]

The source material in the second category of pamphlets, that of criminal conversation, was another subject picked up on by publishers as an easy way to profit from scandal. Between the 1530s and the Matrimonial Causes Act of 1857, the divorce laws were virtually unaltered from the medieval era, making it virtually impossible for people to obtain a divorce. Only the

FIGURE 3.3 *Frontispiece*, A New Collection of Trials for Adultery, *1799. British Library, London.*

wealthy had the resources to either take their case to Parliament or to buy their way to an annulment.[25] As court cases were recorded and published, tales of adultery of the rich and famous became eagerly sought after as a form of entertainment for the reading public (Figure 3.3). As one publisher suggested, 'these little stories will afford the curious not only instruction but an agreeable amusement ... They may be considered as a collection of dramatic pieces.'[26] Readers were eager to read about the disgraced aristocracy, so pamphlets relating to the proceedings of their criminal conversations meant certain remuneration for the publishers. Most enjoyable was the salacious detail provided in the often verbatim reports of the witnesses – sights gleaned from witnesses peeping through keyholes, examining stained bed-linen and hearing creaking beds in the day-time.

Similar to the sodomy pamphlets, from around the 1730s published trial reports of criminal conversation began to escalate and would continue through the century and into the next.²⁷ These cases were based on real court cases brought by cuckolded husbands against their wives on grounds of trespass, but many of them included fabrications. In contrast to the sodomy cases where witnesses were frequently passers-by or people who happened upon a site of assignation, nearly all of the criminal conversation cases involved witnesses who were members of the same household, usually the servants or domestic staff of the couple involved. Since servants lived in such close proximity to the family, it was virtually impossible for a woman to carry on an affair within her own household without servants becoming aware of it. Everyone from coachmen to nursery maids gave testimony in court, their declarations taken down in short-hand, and reported – often verbatim – by the on-looking reporters.

Wealth and status played a part in public perception of blaming and shaming. As with the clergy, those in more powerful positions were more likely to be the subject of amplified condemnation – and this was also true in adultery cases. Since it was the elite who could afford to bring about these litigations, it was they who were the main subjects of the criminal conversation pamphlets. Shaming was a very public activity and was recognized as a strategy for keeping unacceptable behaviour at bay, but popular concerns were not all equitable. Many of the population thought the cuckolded man was fair game, particularly a wealthy cuckold (Figure 3.4). One of the earliest cases in this type of pamphlet had been published in 1692 and related to the case of one of the most celebrated couples of their day, the Duke and Duchess of Norfolk. The duchess had committed the crime of adultery with Sir John Germain, 1st Baronet, thought to be an illegitimate half-brother of William III of England, and the case had been bought before the court on 14 January 1691. All the lurid details were available in a 22-page pamphlet entitled *His Grace, the Duke of Norfolk's Charge Against the Dutchess* [sic] (1692). The butler duly related in his testimony how he had seen Mr Germaine in bed with the Duchess who 'leapt out of the Bed, and put on a Morning Gown, and Germain hid himself in Bed'.²⁸ Another witness, Margaret Ellwood, saw them about 3 or 4 o'clock in the afternoon as she opened the door, 'my Lady upon the Stools in an ill Posture, Mr Germain's Breeches were down, he pulled them up and laid his hand on his Sword, saying God Damn you for a Whore, have you the Impudence to come back? My Lady bid him kick me down.' She found Germain's ruffles in her lady's bed with his name on them.²⁹ Readers would have enjoyed the explicitness of the evidence given by servant Ann Burton of when she was making her mistress's bed, she 'saw there were two Prints had laid ... she supposes the Bed was stained both by a Man and Woman'. The duke and duchess were divorced in 1700, due to the duchess's adulterous relationship, and she married her lover a year later, but the scandal would reverberate for years to come. While the public had much entertainment at the expense of the very public divorce, the exposé of the duchess's adulterous behaviour sullied the name of the Norfolk family.

FIGURE 3.4 *Frontispiece*, A New Collection of Trials for Adultery, *1799*. British Library, London.

Honour was not only class related, but also gender affected, as a man's honour tended to relate to his promise or given word and his honesty, but a woman's related to her sexual reputation. Laura Gowing has shown how early modern women were deeply concerned about their sexual honour and the implications that honour had for their spouses and their households; the litigations about sex were part of a confrontational process in struggles within neighbourhoods and the need for maintaining reputation. Similarly, Elizabeth Foyster has shown how a man's reputation relied on that of his womenfolk, since there was nothing worse for a man than the slur of cuckoldry, or an inability to control the sexual unruly females within his household.[30] However, this reliance by historians on the importance of *female* sexual reputation for both men and women's honour is being adjusted to show that men's sexual activities were also important in the upholding of their reputation.[31]

Some women disregarded the loss of their reputation in favour of love. In the instance of one particular woman involved in a divorce case, a Mrs Cibber, she would pursue her heart's desire despite public exposure. The exposé of the affair could be found in a cheap 12-page pamphlet, *The Tryals of the Two Causes between Theophilus Cibber Gent, plaintiff, and William Sloper, Esq., defendant* (1740), made accessible to those lower down the social scale for a mere 6d. The solicitor in the court was only too aware of the humour the case provided, as he indicated: 'this present Trial was to likely to afford so much Mirth and Entertainment to the Bystanders as the former, but yet that they should lay such an Evidence before the Jury, as should make it appear the Defendant did not keep her thus retired merely to look on'.[32] The defendant, actor-playwright Theophilus Sloper, had been brought to court for criminal conversation with Mrs Cibber in 1738 but the adultery case came up for another judgement the following year when, as the solicitor pointed out, 'it might reasonably have been expected the Defendant would have discontinued his Acquaintance with her [Mrs. Cibber], but it has unhappily proved otherwise. She has been secreted from her Husband in an obscure part of the World, *Kennington-Lane,* never went abroad, and had been there visited by the Defendant Mr Sloper.' The previous year's guilty verdict had been only for 'detaining' Mrs Cibber, not for adultery with her, but since Mrs Cibber had gone on to bear Sloper's child, the evidence of their intimacy was obvious. Initially, the three had been happily living together in a ménage à trois. Mrs Cibber would officially retire to her marital bed, then go to the arms of her lodger across the hall. Since Sloper paid for the rent and maintenance of all three of them, the situation had been acceptable. Only when Cibber became greedy did the case come to court when he sued Sloper for £5,000 damages for criminal conversation the first year, and a further £10,000 the following year. The jury's distain was seen in the small sums awarded to him of £10 and £500, but his wife had long since disappeared with her lover and their child.

Far from being meek inhabitants of an ideological straitjacket of gendered roles, eighteenth-century women did on occasion use opportunities to secure new forms of power and authority, in the process creating a kind of practical feminism, despite the relative paucity of eighteenth-century feminist rhetoric. In this instance, it can be shown that women also took responsibility for their sexual domain even at the expense of their reputation.

Both Elias's civilizing process and Habermas's public sphere argument have a relevant impact when we see how print material reflected flashpoints of non-acceptable behaviour, just as the methods of community punishment continued to be meted out in the pillory, rough music and skimmington rides. E. P. Thompson's framework marries community action and the wider official law. Despite the societies for the reformation of manners and the Evangelical push for the aristocrats to reform their own manners as an example to the lower orders, as Thompson noted, 'the process of social discipline was not uncontested'[33] and popular disturbances were still very much part of eighteenth-century society.[34] Public justice was being seen to be done. This was in effect trial by journalism, a new method specifically arising in the eighteenth century to mete out public justice.

While some cases merely provoked mirth of the public, others were intended to be taken more seriously. The deposition of the people involved often exposed not merely cuckolded husbands, but the exploitation of a friend's kindness. This sort of disloyalty against men who had offered trust to a friend was intended to outrage the public. Such tracts therefore tended to fall into two categories – the types of adultery which were amusing, and those which were a breach of honour between men.

One of the most shocking cases was that of Richard Lydell, a man who had had an affair with Lady Abergavenny under the nose of her husband, and in his house. Community approbation was apparent as servants and neighbours became directly involved in pursuit of the man involved with their master's wife. The pamphlet *The Whole Tryal of Richard Lydell Esq.* (1730) reported the testimony of servant Elizabeth Hopping who had been living in the house of the plaintiff Lord Abergavenny for six years at Sheffield House.[35] She 'took Notice of Mr Lydell's frequently kissing her Lady in the Dressing Room, thought the Familiarity was too great betwixt them, and unbefitting, gave Occasion to her to watch their Conversation; that she had seen her Lady's Bed rumbled after it had been made, when none but Mr Lydell and her Lady had been in the Room'.[36] On another occasion, 'knowing them to have been in the Dining Room, below Stairs, about nine in the Morning, was willing to see what they were doing, and placing herself in the Withdrawing-Room, she looked through the Key-hole into the Parlour, and opposite to the Place where she stood, she saw her Lady against the Door that went into the Hall, and Mr Lydell against her, that she saw her Lady's Petticoats up as high as her Gartering-Place, and that he had unbutton'd his Coat, but she could not see his Breeches down, because his Coat behind covered them; that she saw him do something that a Man ought not to do'.[37] It transpired that Lydell lived about seven miles from the home of Lord Abergavenny and was a good friend of his. While the servant had not dared to acquaint his Lordship with the fact that she had seen criminal conversation take place at least twice, she had told no-one except the laundry-maid Elizabeth Letchmere, who had also gone to witness the scene by peeping through the keyhole.

The fact that the maids saw it as their job to oversee the conduct of their employers is evident in many of these pamphlets. Whether they genuinely believed their employers should be setting a good example, or that they wanted to expose their behaviour as a result of some spitefulness or conflict between them, is hard to say. But given the close proximity of their living quarters to their employers, and given the nature of the job of waiting on the master and mistress of the house, they were in a prime position to witness any mischief they felt fit to report (Figure 3.5).

FIGURE 3.5 *William Hogarth*, Marriage a la mode: Drunk and disorderly. Wellcome Library, London.

Even friends and neighbours felt impelled to become involved and reports became longer to include complete stories. In this case, a Mr Matthews had suspected criminal conversation was taking place after he had unexpectedly come across the adulterous pair and 'he saw Mr Lydell upon the Couch, as if he were pulling up his Breeches'. By chance, he occupied an apartment under Mr Lydell's room and 'he heard a Woman coming into that White-Room that he heard the Voice of a Man, and presently heard the Bed crack'. On another occasion, he looked out and saw Mr Lydell coming out of the room, then went up the back stairs to find 'his Lady coming out very red, and in Disorder, and thought she had been in Mr Lydell's Room'.[38] After sharing his suspicions with Mr Osman, Lord Abergavenny's steward, and a Mr Day (a neighbour and relation), they all concluded that Lord Abergavenny should be advised of the affair. They had even told his mother so she might inform her son, but 'she was under a great deal of Concern about it, and desired some Body else might do it'. The extent to which other people might become involved is shown by the fact that three men were prepared to take on the burden of exposing Lydell themselves. The three men hid themselves in a closet next to Lydell's sleeping quarters and, when they heard the two voices above and heard the bed 'crack', they all went together into the

Chamber, crept to the bed-side, and quickly pulled back the curtains 'upon which Mr Lydell cry'd out, *O God!*' Matthews related how he 'saw her Ladyship in a very indecent Posture, and in a very great Surprize, she said, *Dear* Matthews *do not ruin me*'.[39] Unsurprisingly Lady Abergavenny was blamed for tempting Lydell, but £10,000 damages were awarded against him. Significantly, these pamphlets reveal much inside information about the perception of unsuitable sexual behaviour amongst supposedly reputable people. Whether blaming and shaming was intentional, it was obvious that the authors' focus of this material was on rousing public indignation, suitably inflamed by the pseudo-shocked tirades of the reporters. They also point to the willingness of witnesses to expose the perpetrators of adultery and their feeling that it was important to inform the injured party. The damages awarded to Lord Abergavenny were a huge amount at the time and reflected the importance that the jury held this betrayal of friendship.

Anti-Catholic tracts were rife, coming from both the Protestant British and French pornographers as a way to undermine the Church, and these tracts were used to expose the perversion (in the sense of both religious and sexual perversion) of Catholic priests. Celibacy had long been criticized by Protestants as an abnormal life for monks and priests, and these cases were used to support the argument. British antagonism against Catholics found their way into print in a third category of shaming pamphlets, seen in vitriolic attacks on the confessional and revelations about sexually philandering of Catholic priests. Of particular interest were exposés by prior clergy of the Popish Church. One example can be seen in *A Short History of Monastical Orders* written by Gabriel D'Emiliane (pseudonym of Antonio Gavin)[40] in his attack on the Gilbertines which, 'made up of both Sexes, did very soon bring forth Fruits worthy of itself; these holy Virgins having got almost all of them big Bellies. . . . These Nuns to conceal from the World their Infamous Practices, made away secretly their Children; and this was the Reason, why at the time of the Reformation, so many Bones of Young Children were found buried in their Cloisters, and thrown into places where they ease Nature.'[41] In the minds of the British Protestant, the monastical orders (as with all other Catholic clergy) were corrupt and debauched, supposed celibate men and women producing illegitimate children and then murdering them. While these scandals were seen by Protestants to be evidence of corrupt Catholic *religieux* at least they were confined within the monastic walls. But corruption within the Catholic confessional was seen to be even more abhorrent since it brought the Catholic clergy alone together with female penitents in an enclosed private space, places where innocent women might be despoiled. Penitents were encouraged to narrate detailed accounts of sexual thoughts, lusts and perversions of the body. Forfeiture of enjoyments, deprivations of the body through fasting, mortification of the flesh, and flagellation, were all suggested as penances. Hence, the confessional was seen as an area fraught with potential danger for womenfolk, places where wives and daughters might be molested by debauched priests.

Further sordid revelations were made in quasi-pornographic pamphlets, such as *The Case of Seduction Being an Account of the late Proceedings at Paris, as well* Ecclesiastical; *as* Civil *Against the Reverent Abbé Claudius Nicholas des Rues for committing rapes on 133 Virgins* (1725)[42] and *Tryal of Father John-Baptist Girard* (1732),[43] Curll was again among the first of the publishers who recognized the value in these stories and was, at least in part, responsible for supplying the public with this particular lascivious reading matter about debauched Catholic priests. Both cases were based on exposés of Catholic priests who had deviated from their virtuous path corrupting young virgins in their spiritual care. Both had been responsible for deflowering young penitents.

Printed trial reports were sometimes collected in composite volumes, which mixed adultery trials with those of rape and murder as in *A Collection of Remarkable Trials* published in Glasgow by Tom Tickle and sold by Mrs Tuz at the sign of the River Medway for the price of two shillings. This included the Lydell case and the Cibber case, as well as the infamous trial of Colonel Chartres for the rape of Anne Bond. Another case to instigate a flurry of pamphlets was the alleged abduction and rape of Elizabeth Canning. The most notable pieces were by authors John Hill and Henry Fielding. In John Hill's *The Story of Elizabeth Canning considered*, the pamphlet examined newspaper adverts as well as Fielding's pamphlet *A clear state of the case of Elizabeth Canning*. In the newspapers, Canning was described not as a woman, but as a child (she was in fact eighteen), influencing the feelings of those involved: 'Some few Days after that *first* of *January,* on which this *little Child,* as those who despairing to convince the Judgment [sic], attempt to Passions of Mankind, affect to call her, is said to have been carried away . . .'[44] It was thought that Canning had been abducted, as she was heard to shriek in a Hackney coach in Bishopsgate Street. Adverts were put in newspapers to try to find her and repeated in the pamphlet; taken from the *Daily Advertiser* of 6 January it reported, 'If the Coachman remembers any thing of the Affair, by giving an Account as above, he shall be handsomely rewarded for his Trouble.'[45] Hill asked the obvious questions: who heard her shriek and where were they when she was so forcibly taken away? What had become of the Hackney-coach side of the story? But he also asked questions which insinuate that she was not worth attacking – why should anyone forcibly take her when she was not pretty? Why should anyone rob her when she was so badly dressed? 'She is not handsome; so that the design could not be upon her Person; and certainly the Dress that is described so largely, could not tempt anyone to carry her off to rob her.'[46] After 28 days, Canning reappeared. According to Hill, she had concocted the whole story and then admitted in court to perjury. Hill blames Canning by raising questions about the validity of her story, asking why she went off with these people, and scoffs at her excuse as 'Unnatural, ridiculous, and absurd!' when she tells us 'she was tempted strongly: she was promised *fine Cloaths* if she would *go their Way*'.[47] Why did she not escape the first night, he inquires.[48] Notwithstanding the antagonistic overtones towards the victim, the pamphlets were now taking the turn of investigative journalism. Despite a public inquiry by the Mayor of London, requested due to Canning's admission of perjury and the suspicion of misinformation, the public remained on her side. The case was famous all over town.

Rape and/or murder pamphlets emerged which not only attempted to expose the criminal mind, but also allowed for the revelation of sordid details of female corpses. Only a year earlier than the Canning case there had been *An Account of a Barbarous Rape, and Bloody Murder committed on the body of Mary Carty, otherwise Venus* (1752). The title words 'otherwise Venus' seems to have been placed in the title to attract those reader looking for salacious detail as they would have recognized it as a word often found in titles of erotica. Similarly, another title to make use of sensationalism was the pamphlet *Horrible Rape and Murder!! The affecting case of Mary Ashford . . . who was diabolically ravished, murdered, and thrown into a pit . . . including the trial of A. Thornton, for the wilful murder of the said M. Ashford . . . To which is added copious elucidations . . . and a plan, etc.* (1817), even making use of a map to show exact details of the bloody event. Ashford's virginity became a focal point of interest: 'The evidence of a skilful surgeon will shew that, down to this violence, she had been a virgin.'[49] Her respectability and sexual morality was of vital importance to the prosecutor in seeking a conviction – if she had not been a virgin, it would have been more difficult to convict.

Earlier pamphlets from the late seventeenth century had focused on dying penitents, cases of conspiracy, high treason and murder, although witchcraft pamphlets were still published as late as the early eighteenth century.[50] There was an evident shift in the eighteenth century to a focus on sodomy and adultery cases. Although attacks on the Catholic clergy had been evident in the previous century, they increasingly contained a sexual element in blatant exposés. Rape and murder cases also became more prevalent, and by the early nineteenth century had become common. The reasons for the emergence of this type of material at this time are manifold, but involve a shift in cultural values and societal laws, combined with changes in technology making print material cheaper and easier to produce. While sodomy laws did not change until the nineteenth century, in the eighteenth century there was an increased fascination with it, a necessary precursor to legal changes. Similarly, divorce trials were increasingly reported as more cases came before the courts.

Essentially, eighteenth-century Britain was a period of anti-sodomy, anti-divorce and anti-Catholic sentiment. Anyone who transgressed the laws (sodomites, adulterers/divorcees and Catholics) was to be spurned. While the authors of the pamphlets purportedly related the cases in order to prevent such disruptive behaviour taking place, and feigned a reaction against it, at the same time there was a rising prurient interest from the reading public who wanted to know about these transgressors and their activities. The addition of rape and murder reports provided further grist to the publisher's mill.

The pamphlets were used to control both behaviour considered unacceptable in a community, and to police behaviour which was considered 'unnatural'; this involved denigration of men who had been violent to women or committed adultery, and condemnation of sodomites. They were also used as a caution to potential offenders, warning that a person could expect prison or the gallows, or at the very least, public humiliation for immoral behaviour. In other words, exposés were frequently used as a means to keep people within a community 'inside' it, and to ensure outsiders were kept 'outside', a means to ensure errant people were kept in their place.

In conclusion then, we can see that blaming and shaming in print was a new cultural phenomenon of the eighteenth century which included a broad-ranging type of material from pamphlets on sodomy to whore autobiographies. Although the material was diverse, the intention was essentially the same. The authors used their material to expose the culprits' bad behaviour and vindicate the victims or innocent parties involved. In this way, the public need for retribution and vindication could be harnessed to make a financial success for the publishing trade.

PART TWO

Erotic Women: Fact and Fiction

CHAPTER FOUR

Whore Biographies in the Eighteenth Century

Whore biography was another new genre of literature which had entered the market in the eighteenth century and related tales of both low-class prostitutes and higher-class courtesans. These stories described women's lives which were often a trajectory from one status to the other – the lower-class prostitute managing to escape poverty by rising to become mistress of rich noblemen; or those from the middling or upper echelons who chose to escape the confines of respectable boredom for a more exciting life as a kept woman. Prostitutes were part of the eighteenth-century cultural landscape, evident on the streets and at seaports, and in fiction.[1] A prostitute, particularly in eighteenth-century popular print culture, was typically seen as an elusive figure who constantly evaded and undermined the spectator's attempt to unmask her.[2] Yet in the biographies, intimate details would be revealed.

The very pleasure of reading biographies is the surprise of having the curtain drawn back to reveal secret lives, a theatrical spectacle of immorality, to which the reader thinks, perhaps guiltily, s/he should not be party. Relating tales about another person's life can be seen as a form of gossip, a form that can materialize as either idle chat or malicious scandal.[3] This tale-telling involves collusion between the biographer and their audience in the sharing of secrets. Biographies make public what otherwise would remain private.

Writings about whores can be traced back to ancient Greece. The term pornography, derived from the term *porni* (prostitute) and *graphein* (to write), was applied to art or literature depicting the life of prostitutes: in *Deipnosophistae*, Athenaeus mentions πορνηγράφος (pornographer) referring to one who writes about whores.[4] From the sixteenth century onwards, 'modern' writings on whores emerged as erotica in Italian literature with the emergence of Pietro Aretino's (1492–1556) *Sonette lussurioso* (1534), a text which accompanied Guilio Romano erotic drawings, engraved by Marcantonio Raimondi. English versions followed as seen in *The Crafty*

Whore (1658), taken in part from Aretino's *Ragionamenti* (1536) on the life of whores; *La Puttana Errante* (1660) translated as *The Accomplished Whore*; and *The Whore's Rhetorick* (1683) from Ferrante Pallavicino's *La Retorica delle Puttane* (1642). Seventeenth-century France led the whore's story in dialogue form between two whores as seen in *L'Académie des Dames* (1680), translated as *The School of Women* in 1682, and as *A Dialogue Between a Married Lady and a Maid*, printed in 1688 and again in 1740. By the middle of the eighteenth century, whore biographies would be honed into pornographic novels; most notable in England was John Cleland's *Memoirs of a Woman of Pleasure* (1748/49).[5]

The format was developed throughout the eighteenth century. In the first part of the century, the whore biography took the form of mainstream novels about promiscuous women. Daniel Defoe set a fictional trend with his novels *Moll Flanders* (1722) and *Roxana* (1724) with libertine literature taking up novelistic techniques in both French and British pornography such as *Histoire de Dom B., Portiers Des Chartreux* (1741), *Thérèse Philosophe* (1748) and *Memoirs of a Woman of Pleasure* (1749). In between both fictional types of material (the suggestive accounts in novels on the one hand, and the more graphic pornography on the other), lay another style of reading material which purported to be true – the new literary sub-genre of whore mini-biographies, influenced by the other literature mentioned above, while incorporating techniques from the rogues' biography.[6]

At the beginning of the eighteenth century, publishers realized that commentaries about whoredom together with revelations about real-life whores might prove just as well-liked as those on fictional whores in erotica. Writings about whores became immensely popular, and could be bought in various formats from short pamphlets for a few pence to more lengthy calf-bound versions for three guineas or more.[7] By the time writings about whores had crystallized into the whore biography, a literary style had developed that showed admiration for these effervescent women, although some material would also carry warnings to other young women against falling into the same way of life.[8] Generally, the revelations contained racy anecdotes, with descriptions of the women oscillating between luxury and debt. Readers were provided with a vivid impression of the flamboyant yet precarious lifestyles of courtesans, although the authors frequently stray from their subject matter, in order to gossip about the sex lives of other people. The protagonists are usually portrayed in a positive, sympathetic light as opposed to the derogatory comments exhibited by the moral reformers of the day. They are depicted not only as radiantly beautiful or saucily attractive, but as possessing forceful personalities, their suitors frequently finding them too wilful to control. Gaps (----) or asterisks (******) in the text are used as a literary ploy to engage the reader; in order to make sense of the text, the reader has to interpret the gaps and is thereby complicit in the 'naughtiness' of the story. Picking out the truths from the fiction poses problems in some cases, and there are few alternative extant sources from which to create the fuller picture; some of the lesser-known characters, who would have been recognized by the eighteenth-century audience, are now lost to us.

Stylistically, these whore biographies had moved away from the seventeenth-century whores' narratives of French erotica which had used dialogues to discuss whores' sexual activities, to describe the lives of whores in documentary-style biographies. Although little had been produced in the way of British pornography in the early decades of the eighteenth century, these mildly titillating mini-novelistic exposés of real-life whores were already being forged. They took the form of a sort of celebrity mini-biography, a collation of information and misinformation about the life of a popular courtesan from her poor beginnings (they were often from plebeian backgrounds or had been cast out from their families), to their introduction to their first seducer and their loss of virginity, through to their slide into prostitution. Frequently, the women found rich protectors who were well-known to the audience, making their stories yet more commercial. Early whores' biographies in books and pamphlets such as *The Life of the Late Celebrated Mrs Elizabeth Wisebourn* (1721), *The Genuine History of Mrs. Sarah Prydden, usually called Sally Salisbury and her Gallants* (1723)[9] and *View of the Beau Monde; Or Memoirs of the Celebrated Coquetilla* (1731) can therefore be seen as forerunners of later and more explicit pornographic British and French novels.

The Life of the Late Celebrated Mrs Elizabeth Wisebourn[10] is significant in that it was the first modern biography of a brothel-keeper, and started off a new genre while continuing older themes of sexual revelations of well-known characters combined with political attacks. The first edition of the book from 1721 sold for one shilling and three copies of the book are extant in the British Library.[11] Elizabeth Wisebourn (1653–c.1720) was a well-known bawd, and in 1679 could be found running a brothel near Drury Lane, a popular area for attracting clients from the theatre and night life of London society. In 1707, she began an affair with John Jacob Heidegger, an Italian opera producer and runner of masquerades who was to become her co-partner in her business. She died in November c.1720.[12] This book is also an example of how advertisements were used within the pages or spicy reading matter to promote quack cures for venereal disease, aimed at their libertine readers (men and women). The author of this biography took his pseudonym of 'Annodyne Tanner MD' from the well-known physician Dr Paul Chamberlen (1635–1717); 'The Anodyne Necklace' was supposedly a cure for venereal disease but in fact Chamberlain had nothing to do with the pamphlet. Nor was he a physician who treated venereal disease but belonged to the family of male midwives who introduced the forceps to the birthing chamber. The ploy was simply a means of puffing the book and advertising in Chamberlain's voice, 'I entirely approve of, advise, and recommend to the world, the use of two Anti-venereal Medicines; The one called by the name of the "Specific Remedy"; The other the "Diuretick Restorative Elixir for Broken and Empaired Consitutions", or for venereal disease.'[13] Although originally introduced as a quack treatment for children's teething problems, the anodyne (pain-killing) necklace also professed to cure venereal disease, sold for five shillings and appeared in many adverts around 1715 onwards.[14]

More usual were mini-biographies about well-known prostitutes. Wisebourne's protégé, Sally Salisbury (c.1690–1724), would become a celebrity, famous enough to have a squall of pamphlets written about her (Figure 4.1). *The Genuine History of Mrs. Sarah Prydden, usually called Sally*

FIGURE 4.1 *Sally Salisbury wounding the Honourable Mr F----. Wellcome Library, London.*

Salisbury and her Gallants, professed to tell 'the real story of her life' which sold at the pamphlet shops during 1723 for a shilling a copy; *Authentick Memoirs of the Life and Adventures of the Celebrated Sally Salisbury* (1723) sold for 2s. 6d.; broadsheets depicted her activities in *The Effigies, Parentage, Education, Life, Merry-Pranks and Conversation of the Celebrated Mrs Sally Salisbury* and *Sally Salisbury's Letter to Frank Rigg*; and songs were named after her such as 'Sally in our Alley' and 'four new songs' printed in *Sally Slisbury's [sic] Garland*.[15] Supposed personal anecdotes provided readers with a glimpse of a whore's personality. Renowned for her sharp retorts and her amusing asides, one biographer remarked of her, 'It must be confessed, that she can be very entertaining Company when she pleases; has a surprising Vivacity, and Redundancy of Thought, a Ready Turn of Wit, and is very sprightly at Reparteé'; another that she was considered 'a celebrated Wit, among a great variety of Noblemen that esteem'd her Smiles'.[16] With this skill, she made her way from a life of grinding poverty to become a sought-after plaything of rich men. Her lovers included Lord William Bentinck; Charles Fitzroy, Duke of Richmond; his half-brother, the Duke of Albans; Lord Bolingbroke and the Earl of Cardigan. She also claimed among them the Prince of Wales, later George II. Although the tales about her life frequently diverge, and parts were undoubtedly fabricated to fill in gaps or provide entertainment, there is sufficient agreed fact to create a composite version.[17] Her life came under increased scrutiny when she was arrested for stabbing her lover, the Hon. John Finch, son of the Earl of Nottingham, with a bread knife. Her actions were reported in *An Account of the Tryal of Salley [sic] Salisbury*: the pair had been drinking in the Three Tuns Tavern in Chandos Street, Covent Garden when Salisbury had become jealous of her sister for whom Finch had bought an opera ticket. The stabbing was recorded at her trial at the Old Bailey at which Salisbury was found guilty; 'Sarah Salisbury (whose Trial was publish'd at large on Monday last) fin'd a 100 l. to suffer a Years Imprisonment, and to find Sureties for her Behaviour two Years more'.[18] According to the pamphlet she died of fever in Newgate on 11 February 1723. All these accounts were published anonymously.[19]

Hacks continued to develop the genre in the second half of the century with biographies of Fanny Murray, Kitty Fisher, Nancy Dawson and Jane Douglas, seen in *Memoirs of the Celebrated Miss Frances Murray* (1758), *The Uncommon Adventures of Miss Kitty Fisher* (1759) and the *Celebrated Miss Nancy Dawson* (1760) (Figure 4.2). Publishers printed the usual gossip about the scandalous lives of these notorious women and found they could turn an easy profit, since readers were keen for any information they could find on their favourite celebrities. Music and songs were composed in the women's honour and jokes made with reference to their antics as seen in *While Some, in never Dying Verse. A Song Wrote by Mr. Boyce on Sight of Fanny Murray* (1755), *Kitty's Stream, Or the Noblemen Turned Fishermen* (1759), *Of All the Girls in Town* (1760), *The Meretriciad* (1761), *Nancy Dawson's Jests* (1761) and *Nancy Dawson's Variations* (c.1766).

FIGURE 4.2 *Nancy Dawson dancing the hornpipe. British Library, London.*

Writers of whores' biographies ran fictitious tales alongside facts, using gossip and divulging secrets as a means to bring their reader closer to their subject, but the 'facts' in different accounts sometimes conflicted. The life of Fanny Murray (1729–1778) (Figure 4.3) was portrayed in *Memoirs of the Celebrated Miss Fanny M* [Murray] (1758).[20] These memoirs state that Fanny was born in Bath, but elsewhere it was also claimed that she came from London; both that she sold flowers in Bath's Abbey Yard, and that she begged as a child on the steps of Covent Garden Theatre, London.[21] One biography, 'The Secret History, &c. of the Famous Miss F---y M—y' which had appeared in 1748 in *The Humours of Fleet-Street,* a collection of biographies of 'the most noted Ladies of Pleasure', asserted that she had been born into a well-connected family in Scotland.[22] The author named a titled man as her first 'seducer' thereby elevating her status and bumping down his reputation. Supposedly Jack Spencer (1707–1746), grandson to Sarah, Duchess of Marlborough, had raped her, but she was later taken up by Beau Richard Nash (1674–1761) (Figure 4.4), who introduced her to Bath's elite. At this time, the town was fast becoming the focal point of Georgian fashion – balls, promenades and concerts were all part of the social whirl; Nash was in charge of the Pump Rooms to where most of the *bon ton* flocked. One contemporary commented on Bath, 'Here is performed all the wanton dalliances imaginable; celebrated beauties, panting breasts and curious shapes, almost exposed to public view; languishing eyes, darting killing glances, tempting amorous postures, attended by soft Musick enough to provoke a vestal to forbidden pleasures.'[23]

At various stages Murray was mistress to John Wilkes, Sir William Stanhope and Sir John Montagu, fourth Earl of Sandwich, and became part of Sir Frances Dashwood's circle and an attendant at his Divan Club meetings, a club founded by Dashwood on 8 January 1744, at the Thatched

FIGURE 4.3 *Fanny Murray by Henry Morland. Wikimedia Commons.*

FIGURE 4.4 *Portrait of Beau Richard Nash. Wellcome Library, London.*

Tavern in St James' as a result of Dashwood's fascination with Turkey. Members included Lord Sandwich, Wilkes, Lord Duncannon, Dashwood's half-sister Mary Walcott, his wife Lady Ellys and the diarist Lady Wortley Montagu, wife of the British Ambassador living in Constantinople. They had their portraits painted in Turkish dress, and the paintings, including that of Murray, still hang at the Dashwood Estate in West Wycombe. Murray became so popular that songs were written especially for her, such as '"While Some, in never Dying Verse", A Song Wrote by Mr. Boyce on Sight of Fanny

Murray' (1755). Wilkes also famously wrote about her in the bawdy poem *Essay on Woman* (written c.1763):

Awake, my Fanny, leave all meaner things,
This morn shall prove what rapture swiving brings.
Let us (since Life can little more supply
Than just a few good Fucks and then we die . . .

Murray eventually married David Ross, the wealthy actor, with whom she lived in quiet retirement in assumed gentility until her death on 1 April 1778.

Some of the women became the muses of reputable artists of the day. Kitty Fisher (c.1741–1767) became famous enough to have her portrait painted by Joshua Reynolds and Nathaniel Hone as a result of operating as a high-class mistress to some of the country's elite (Figure 4.5). Her everyday adventures were reported in sketches and her activities mocked in satires,[24] and her biography told in *The Uncommon Adventures of Miss Kitty Fisher* (1759). Which particular affair first led Fisher to life as mistress to some of the richest men in Europe has been the subject of much contention,[25] but from around 1758 she reigned as one of the most celebrated figures of her day. Titled men among her conquests were Sir Thomas Medleycott; Thomas Bromley, second Baron Montfort; Admiral George Anson, Baron of Soberton; John Montagu, fourth Earl of Sandwich; and William Stanhope, second Earl of Harrington. Fisher was introduced to Casanova when he was in London and he said of her that she chatted like a magpie. He recalled a similar anecdote of Fisher to that told of Murray eating a £20 banknote in contempt of an offer made for her services, but with Fisher the value of the note had risen to 1,000 guineas, perhaps showing the different sums of money each could demand.

In 1760, Nancy Dawson was to become a subject of the whore's biography in *Genuine Memoirs of the Celebrated Miss Nancy Dawson*.[26] Her lovers included various army captains as well as royalty, attracting the attention of the Duke of Cumberland, Prince Henry Frederick. As with the other women, she had poems composed in tribute to her and songs sung about her as in 'Of All the Girls in our town. Nancy Dawson, a New Song' (1760).[27] Unlike some of the other courtesans, Dawson had started off working as a lowly performer in taverns and in puppet shows entertaining onlookers with her agility in acrobatics, as well as singing and dancing. She elevated herself to dancing at Sadler's Wells in Thomas Betterton's opera *The Prophetess* on 1 February 1758 and went on to work at Covent Garden Theatre where she became noticed when she danced the hornpipe in John Gay's *Beggars Opera* in 1760. Dawson wound down her theatrical roles, one of her last playing pantomime in *The Rites of Hecate* during December 1763. After her retirement little is mentioned about her. She died on 9 June 1767 and was buried in Bloomsbury's St George the Martyr's graveyard.[28]

Fewer pamphlets or books were written about brothel-keepers, although Jane Douglas managed to get herself into a whore's biography with *Genuine*

FIGURE 4.5 *A portrait of Miss Kitty Fisher. Mezzotint by C. Tomkins after Sir J. Reynolds. Wellcome Library, London.*

Memoirs of the Late Celebrated Jane Douglas (1761). The memoirs depict a somewhat ignoble picture of Douglas, portraying her as a mean-spirited, drunken and ill-tempered procuress, travelling all over the country and abroad to procure girls for her brothel in Covent Garden.[29] She died in June 1761, having suffered from dropsy, and was buried in Paddington churchyard.

While the names of some of those mentioned have endured, not much is remembered of nineteen-year-old Fanny Davies. She was brought to public attention after she was sentenced to death for stealing. According to an eight-page chapbook entitled *The Whole Life and Adventures of Miss Davies Commonly called The Beauty in Disguise. With a full, true, and particular Account of her robbing Mr. W. of Gosfield, in Essex, of Eleven Hundred Pounds in Cash and Bank notes, for which she now lays to take her trial at Chelmsford* (1785), Davies was tricked into entering a brothel at about 14 years of age, when 'one of the good natured Abbesses who took private rooms for gentlemen and ladies, took a fancy to her, and she was decoyed from her aunt's, and took our young adventurer home with her to the nunnery' (euphemism for brothel).[30] Her story was recounted in *The Female Amazon or A Genuine Account of the Most Remarkable Adventures and Complicated Intrigues displayed in the Life of the Celebrated and Notorious Miss Fanny Davies* by Mr Thompson (1786). Two other editions were brought out in 1786 and 1790 under a different title: *The Authentic Narrative of the Most Remarkable Adventures and Curious Intrigues, exhibited in the Life of Miss Fanny Davies.*

Because of Davies' low rank in the profession, and her reputation for stealing (a common side-line in prostitution), her life story comes across more in the flavour of rogue biography than of the other whore biographies of courtesans mentioned above. Although the tales relate her adventures under various wealthy keepers, this is alongside her connections with various swindlers, thieves and highwaymen. The crime for which she came to trial was robbing a man of all his money while dressing as a man and sharing a room with him in the Three Rabbits Tavern on the Rumford Road. At her trial at Chelmsford assizes on 6 March 1786, she admitted to stealing and she and her accomplices were sentenced to be 'hanged by the neck until they be dead'.[31] Although the death penalty was often applied to similar crimes, she was lucky enough to be reprieved and sentenced to 14 years' transportation. Davies had dressed as a man occasionally in order to make her life easier and to undertake her scams, a common trope found in other type of biographies of women.[32]

Irish women occasionally figure in whores' memoirs such as *Secret Memoirs of Miss Sally Dawson, Otherwise Mrs. Sally McClane; Otherwise Mrs Sarah Mayne, _____ Widow*. Based on the story of real-life courtesan Sally Dawson (1754–1805), who operated a brothel in Dublin, it carries the familiar themes as other whore biographies: Dawson was provided with a good education, with the best instructors in music and drawing; she had a fine figure, good complexion and could dance well – attributes credited to many of the other courtesans. Her first affair was allegedly with the third son of an earl, whose regiment was based nearby.[33] Fashionable people are mentioned to keep the reader interested. Casanova's well-known lover Madame Cornelys, famous for throwing popular musical concerts and balls at her mansion in Carlisle House in Soho Square during the 1760s, threw a masquerade which Dawson attended. Dawson allegedly encountered the Prince of Wales at a mercer's shop in town (he supposedly recognized her immediately as the 'Hibernian Paphian queen'), although there is no evidence that they met. Such mention of meetings with royalty, especially the Prince of Wales, was a common motif in whore biographies, as well as their autobiographies.[34] Dawson is depicted as a charitable figure, another familiar attribute ascribed to courtesans in the memoirs. The author points out her immorality, but highlights her generosity; 'though her life was masked by every kind dissipation, yet was it characterised the most genuine principals of charity, and repentance; and her last Will will do the greatest credit to her memory'. This particular memoir leans towards the more moralizing sort, warning young girls not to travel along the same path. Dawson died on 23 August 1805, at only 51. However, few hard facts remain about her, although Irish courtesan Peg Plunkett (see following chapter) refers to her friend, bawd and procuress Sally M'Clean (her alias given as McClane in the book's title page) who owns a brothel on Eustace-Street, Dublin, who was no doubt one and the same.

As a sub-genre, these books speak more about contemporary images of the whores that were being promoted rather than about the women themselves. Written by male hacks, these biographies are not recollections of the whores themselves, but those of the authors' and carry a male-oriented view of the women they are describing and of the world of prostitution.

Contemporary commentaries

Whore biographies need to be set in their contextual positon if they are to be properly interpreted and understood. Alongside these whore biographies ran various commentaries on whores – what to do with them, how to be rid of them and suggestions for suitable punishments for them. These commentaries came in the form of satires, proposals on and defences of prostitution, rallying between two extremes, seeing prostitutes as either a scourge on society or as a necessary fact of life. Within the discourse of the day, opposing images of the brazen whore and the seduced maiden permeated society: one was the personification of unbridled lust and sin, the other the embodiment of poverty and redeemable virtue, a vulnerable woman placed in a position outside her own control.[35] Many authors recognized that poverty was to blame while others blamed mercenary bawds or seductive young rakes for corrupting young innocent girls, as depicted in Hogarth's famous print in *The Harlot's Progress* Plate 1 (Figure 4.6).[36] The reactions to prostitutes and how they should be treated reflected contemporary attitudes to prostitution and women's sexual behaviour overall. Suggestions for tackling the problem ranged from the reasonable to the irrational, from proposals for the establishment of taxed legal brothels, to the setting up of rescue houses, known as Magdalene hospitals.[37] Early on in the century, Defoe published *Some Considerations on Streetwalkers* (1726) and clergyman Martin Madan would later undertake an exposé of the awfulness of a prostitute's life in *Thelyphthora; A Treatise on Female Ruin* (1789). John Campbell, under the alias M. Ludovicus, thought the establishment of foundling hospitals would prevent young girls falling into prostitution, but

FIGURE 4.6 *William Hogarth*, The Harlot's Progress, *Plate 1. Wellcome Library, London.*

magistrate John Fielding saw the large number of foundling children as being responsible for the high crime rate in London. He believed that boys became thieves and girls became prostitutes through economic necessity, prostitution being their only means of survival. Meanwhile Madan (somewhat facetiously) suggested polygamy as an answer to prostitution. Others continued to believe that it was the result of a woman's innate lasciviousness and wanton desires.[38]

Although written anonymously, English stationer and bookseller John Dunton (1659–1732) is thought to be the author of *The Shortest Way with Whores and Rogues*. It was written in response to Daniel Defoe's satirical pamphlet *The Shortest Way with the Dissenters* (1702),[39] both pamphlets fitting into a genre of satires which mocked bigots and raised social, religious and political issues of concern. It fitted into a publishing scene which allowed for duality, writing and publishing both dull sermons and lascivious frivolity. He played up to the moral movements of the day such as the Societies for the Reformation of Manners, which attacked prostitution and the prostitutes targeting them for prosecution and punishment.[40] Dunton also published *Proposals for a National Reformation of Manners* (1694), its appendix carrying a list of all the bawds and prostitutes (which may well have unwittingly acted as an advertisement). Realizing the commercial value of such books, he researched prostitutes for himself, going out on evening rambles to chat with them and then publishing his accounts in *The Night-Walker, or, Evening Rambles in Search after Lewd Women* (1696).

Bernard Mandeville, in his *A Modest Defence of Publick Stews*, recommended the establishment of a hundred public legal brothels in London in which 2,000 women should be placed (and a proportionate number elsewhere in the country) with regular medical inspections of the women paid by a tax on the brothel. Lewdness could then be exercised in its proper place, contained, and thereby removing the fear of spreading to other women and children. Although promoting the idea of licensed brothels, *A Modest Defence of Publick Stews* nonetheless reiterates society's view on the importance of female chastity. Debauching of virgins, although a common eighteenth-century practice, was not always condoned, but the deflowering of young virgins through promises of marriage was considered a particularly nasty seduction technique.

The extent of the problem of prostitution was contested by Saunders Welch who, in his *A Proposal To Render Effectual A Plan To Remove The Nuisance Of Common Prostitutes From The Street Of This Metropolis* (1758), estimated that there were approximately 3,000 prostitutes active in London in 1758; yet Baron von Uffenbach on his tour of England in 1710 had been told that there were 25,000 prostitutes in London alone.[41] In 1725, a certain 'German Gentleman' believed there were 107 brothels in and about Drury Lane. Yet the term prostitute incorporated a broad class of women, and the biographies reflect this assimilation including accounts of poor prostitutes, rich courtesans, actresses and bawds, as well as various noble ladies connected to sexual scandals. These women did not necessarily earn their living by full-time prostitution (although plenty of them did) and some had jobs as milliners, fruit sellers, domestic servants, shop-keepers, actresses and singers. While any woman consenting to sex outside of marriage was considered a whore – it was a flexible, negotiable position.[42] In his London Journal for 1762, Boswell describes five archetypes of the sexual underworld: the 'respectable' but adulterous married woman (in short supply); the more disreputable actresses of the theatre; the milliners, shirt and ruffle makers; high-class prostitutes retained in the brothels; and the common street whores. He observed London's prostitutes and the wide range of type 'from the splendid Madam at fifty guineas a night, down to the civil nymph ... who tramps along the Strand and will resign her engaging person to your honour for a pint of wine and a shilling'.[43] These women were not segregated from their community but worked within it, sharing lodgings and the streets with other workers; they were not geographically separate from the rest of the population, but they walked the same streets frequented the same taverns, gin-shops and parks as other Londoners.[44] Higher class courtesans meanwhile shared tables, masquerades and theatre boxes with the elite.

The position of the 'whore' was bound up with the eighteenth-century concept of 'The Ideal Woman' and the double standards of morality which allowed for men's sexual philanderings while condemning any sexual activities for women outside of marriage. Modesty, chastity and fidelity were the favoured characteristics which made up the 'Ideal Woman' whose life was to be centred around her husband. Under this prevailing morality, a woman's reputation was based on her chastity and once ruined, could never be recovered.[45] The Ideal Woman was passive, submissive and asexual, but simultaneously she was vulnerable to corruption through her sexuality; once she had been introduced to sex, a woman's passions were unleashed and she could become uncontrollable, both sexually and temperamentally.

Turning to the broader picture of sexuality which the books reflect, the eighteenth century was a time when heterosexual penetrative sex was promoted as both normal and ideal and it was considered proper that married couples should have sex with the main aim of procreation.[46] Pregnant unmarried women were ostracized or left to consider abortion as their best option for avoiding unwanted children. If working in the sex industry, any pregnancy would incapacitate, preventing them from working for a matter of months. Most courtesans would have sent their child immediately to a wet nurse and return to work as soon as they were physically healed. Medicines were advertised with warnings against consuming them when 'with child', an obvious hint as to their effects as an abortifacient; others professed cures for 'the most afflicting disorders to the sex' which might incorporate pregnancy as well as any amount of sexual diseases. Those more desperate committed infanticide despite laws demanding capital punishment for women caught disposing of their children.[47] Contemporaries continued to grapple with the problems of illegitimacy and what to do with unwanted offspring.

Ploys of seduction are explored in *Prostitutes of Quality Or adultery â-La-Mode being authentic and genuine memoirs of several persons of the highest quality* (1757), a series of fictional tales purporting to be genuine, which highlight the sordid side of men's quest for sex and women's attempts to defend themselves. It also highlights some of the very real problems for women operating in prostitution. Ruthless men were plentiful in eighteenth-century England, and images that portray sexual courtship as a battleground, with men fighting to gain access to a women's body, were commonplace in erotica.[48] Although sexual desire was thought to be best realized within the confines of marriage for both men and women, it was generally recognized that, for the unmarried, chastity was not always the best state; enforced celibacy might lead an honest man to make disastrous decisions when in the first flush of love, prompting an inappropriate choice of bride. A disastrous coupling might take place with a man marrying a woman below his status, or even worse, seducing a woman of good birth of whom he was not worthy, concerns expressed in seduction novellas. Yet debauching young maidens was nonetheless a particular ambition of many eighteenth-century libertines.

Sex with virgins was considered preferable because it elided the risk of venereal disease, and was even thought by some to cure a dose of the clap. The high demand for virgins therefore raised their price: a virgin could bring in from 10 to 50 guineas whereas a more experienced sexual partner might only fetch three, even at the top end of the market. Such was the demand that it was worthwhile for bawds to pass off their young charges as virgins, not just once but time and time again, as we see with Mother Wisebourn's continued efforts at revirginizing Sally Salisbury.

One of the side effects of prostitution was venereal disease,[49] and discussions on how to eradicate it abounded, with women in the biographies and commentaries frequently being blamed for giving venereal disease to men. The pox is frequently mentioned in the whores' biographies since it was one of the most prevalent diseases in London. Most people who were sexually active outside the home would have contacted one sort of venereal disease or another, the most fatal being syphilis. Frequently the clap (gonorrhoea) and the pox (syphilis) were seen as the same disease, the pox merely being a more advanced stage of the clap, although there is indication that some people differentiated between the two diseases. Treatments were few: mercury was applied or taken orally and would create a process known as 'salivation' where the poison would induce sweating in the patient. One letter from a physician to the *Gentleman's Magazine* in 1735 described the miserable condition of his patients with venereal disease: 'of this sort, the most unfortunate & pitiful object is a woman of the town who, if not quite abandon'd, gives loose to her passions on such occasions. The consideration of her past, present and future state, fills her with distraction, & involved her in endless evil, from which death only can deliver her.'[50] The women in these biographies therefore frequently found themselves 'clapped out' after only a couple of years 'on the town'.

The whores' biographies are generally set in London society (although some such as *View of the Beau Monde* and *Memoirs of the Celebrated Fanny Murray* include Bath, and Dawson mentions Dublin) and are full of descriptions of the places where these women operated, within a city full of contradictions: of poverty and wealth, of gaiety and misery, of liberation and suppression. The city was permissive and public in the sense that affairs which should have remained private were often played out in view of all to see, written up in gentlemen's magazines, reported in newspapers, and gossiped about in taverns. The locations mentioned would have been familiar to the London high-class courtesan and lower-class whore; Covent Garden, Ranelagh and Vauxhall Pleasure Gardens were all places where they worked and entertained. Covent Garden was full of brothels, some plush, some low-grade; playwright and poet John Gay declared that St Catherine's Street down to the Strand was full of street prostitutes plying their trade. Yet high-class courtesans would have worked from either their own houses or 'flash' houses (showy, fashionably smart, high-class brothels) run by well-known madams in St James or Pall Mall. The lower end of prostitution could be found in the East End, Wapping and Southwark and it was usually these women who were incarcerated for sexual misdemeanours or petty crimes. For lower-class whores, stealing frequently went hand in hand with prostitution, some women working in pairs – one emptying the client's pockets of his valuables while the other kept the client entertained. All sorts of people visited pleasure gardens; entrance to Vauxhall Gardens was only a shilling, and therefore more affordable, while Ranelagh at 2s. 6d. aimed to keep the lower classes out. Various women were reported as having got into scraps with each other when seen with another's beau while walking out; the *Universal Magazine* reported one such incident when a fellow courtesan of Kitty Fisher's spied her at Ranelagh Gardens and attacked her companion's periwig. All classes came together at one of the two London theatres, Covent Garden Theatre or Drury Lane Theatre, where the latest plays of Rich or Gay were performed. Well-known courtesans of the time, such as Nancy Dawson, Nancy Parsons and Kitty Fisher, all rubbed shoulders with gentry.

The poem *The Meretriciad* explored the theatrical world, focusing on actresses and others connected to the theatre. The world of brothels crossed over with that of the theatre in that many whores tried their luck in the theatre and many actresses became kept women. Well-practised in scintillating conversation and witty repartee, courtesans and actresses encouraged their suitors to make advances and took their expensive gifts while keeping them at arm's length for as long as possible to increase their own revenue. Invariably, some of these women gave in, then usually lost their source of income after their suitors became bored. Luckier ones managed to find rich men who would keep them on a longer term basis. Poor orange girls, such as Sally Salisbury and Fanny Murray, would take their cue from the actresses and look for a possible entrance into the world of courtesanship as a way out of their grinding poverty.

These biographies and commentaries on whoring provide us with a sense of the lives of eighteenth-century whores, as well as discussing conflicting contemporary opinions on the position of women. They show how, despite (and no doubt because of) their reputations, these women carved out a lifestyle for themselves in a society which ostracized those who operated outside a certain moral code; youthful fruit-sellers might rise to become the star of the season while high-class courtesans might fall into ill-kept seedy brothels once their looks had gone. At their heights, they shone brightly amongst the elite, brimming with gaiety, protected by noble clients; at worst, they ended up in debtors' prison, or in jail for vagrancy or disorderliness. For a courtesan, status rested on the ability to attract the wealthiest and most powerful of men – nobles and politicians, and high-ranking gentlemen. If she were popular enough, she could choose between suitors and refuse those who did not attract her. Once elevated, she needed to maintain an air of luxury and respectability while effusing sexuality; she needed her own house where possible, along with a coach and four horses, as well as a retinue of servants. It was essential for any woman 'on the town' to maintain a fashionable style of dress to enable her to attract the type of clientele she wanted and lower-class courtesans frequently relied on bawds for their board and lodgings as well as their expensive clothes. Bawds, such as Mothers Cresswell, Wisebourn and Needham, are usually portrayed in a poor light, blamed for procuring and then entrapping their girls through loans of money. To ensure financial stability, it was imperative for courtesans to seek settlements or annuities from the men they favoured. Where women did not take this precaution, they usually fell into debt. Few could maintain a high-class life style once they lost their looks and thereby their ability to find a protector.

Finally, a few words about the writers and readers of this material. Often authors remained anonymous, and the origins of the books could be directed at anyone of the hacks scribbling to scratch out a living for unscrupulous publishers. Readers were not merely elite men; women were known to read and appreciate erotica, and there is nothing to suggest they would not have enjoyed whore biographies. Although the more expensive versions of the tales might well have been outside the range of plebeian men and women, the lower classes could gain access to reading material in broadsheets, pamphlets and serializations, and through borrowing, reading aloud or sharing them in taverns and brothels.[51]

CHAPTER FIVE

Memoirs of Women of Pleasure: Autobiographies

These autobiographies stand out against the biographies examined in the previous chapter by the simple fact that they were written by the women themselves. In a world biased towards men, they spoke out for the right of women to pursue their own sexual pleasure and to have control over their own sexual behaviour. The autobiographies were to become popular because of the revelations about their scandalous affairs – they were drawing back the veil to reveal what had hitherto been covered, which notably included exposing the 'private' life of rich and cultivated men. Yet, despite the libertine and sexually 'free' image of eighteenth-century London, all women were constrained in both terms of economic opportunities and acceptable sexual activities, and continued to be considered as second-class citizens. The eighteenth-century notion of the ideal woman, as seen by contemporaries in both literature and commentaries, portrays women of the late eighteenth and early nineteenth centuries as characteristically void of personality. Alleged 'virtues' included charm, reserve and sexual passivity. However, the courtesans' memoirs show an alternative discourse on female sexuality at this time which relates to female assertiveness and independence which questions the double standard and existing sexual status quo.

These writers portrayed themselves as unruly and uncontrollable in an attempt to flaunt convention. As Markman Ellis and Ann Lewis have pointed out, 'While the gendered discourse on manners inscribed certain forms of behaviour as polite, domestic and feminine, the prostitute acted out of this expectation. It is this sense that sustains the heroic reading of the prostitute as a wild woman, a rebel against repressive social orthodoxy.'[1] However, this is only one aspect of the courtesan's image. While they may have acted outside the proscribed role of the 'Ideal Woman', they also simultaneously had to fit into it. If they were to retain a 'respectable' outward appearance, they had to obey the strict regulations of the double standard. If they failed in this attempt, they risked the chance of gaining a reputation of a common whore, thereby deterring richer clients. To this end, the authors of these autobiographies attempted to fit themselves into a certain ideological framework and invariably portray themselves as modest and sexually restrained.

Because of this desire to show themselves as 'good' women and simultaneously attract readers looking for sensationalism, an inherent contradiction exists in their writings. Thus, the two polarized images of Magdalene and Whore (or 'Ideal Woman versus the Harlot'), while well-established in history,[2] is too simplistic a story. A further contradiction emerges when we examine their portrayal of their life-styles. While they may well have attempted to carve out an independent life for themselves (and even succeeded), at other times, they were often reduced to staying in unsuccessful, sometimes violent, relationships, or relying on the goodwill of generous men.

Some women had already managed to carve out careers for themselves writing novels and poetry; others had written memoirs in order to vindicate themselves or to expose the bad behaviour of others. Divorcees and spurned actresses published both to make money and redress misbehaviour of men who had wronged them. Constantia Phillips wrote her memoirs, *An Apology for the Conduct of Mrs Teresia Constantia Phillips* (1749), in order to tell 'truths' about the corruption of the law, having been forced to drop her lawsuit trying to prove the validity of her marriage. She claimed the judge had been bribed by her husband to decide against her. In the same year Laetitia Pilkington published her memoirs, *Memoirs of Mrs Laetitia Pilkington,* and wrote with similar intent, in order to vindicate herself and to expose the 'proper colours' of her husband.[3] Yet Samuel Richardson notoriously condemned these women, declaring them a 'Set of Wretches wishing to perpetuate their infamy',[4] mainly because they had dared to speak out publicly. Their role was a precarious one as they balanced between exposing immorality but they were also having to attempt to restore their reputation as Good Women. In their memoirs, these women demanded the right to defend themselves and took women's writing in a new direction. Their memoirs were quickly followed by biographies and autobiographies of actresses such as Charlotte Charke (1755), Anne Bellamy (1785), Sophia Baddeley (1787), Anne Cately (1789), Mrs Billington (1792) and Mary Robinson (1802).

Recent theory of life-writing tends to concentrate on the nineteenth century onwards, so elaboration needs to be made if we are to discover what life-writing meant to the women in the eighteenth century. Some women obviously wrote for revenge as Norma Clarke points out about her subject, Laetitia Pilkington,[5] and the women under review here are no exception. For others, as Lynda M. Thompson has pointed out in her assessment of the 'scandalous memoirs' of Laetitia Pilkington and Constantia Phillips, while 'they were purportedly about picaresque sexual adventuring . . . one quickly discovers that they are less about sex or desire and more about eighteenth-century women's fraught and unequal relationship to money, property, law and "priceless" reputation.'[6] While sex was used as a sales advertisement for these books, it also disguised the women's serious assertions presented within their memoirs. These women defied convention by placing themselves in the public sphere and were unusual for their time in setting a new trend in women's literature.

These memoirists had some commonalities with diarists of the same period. Harriet Bogden, in her examination of *The Englishwoman's Diary*, which includes some eighteenth-century diarists, noted that although there was a wide diversity of diary styles, there was a recurrence of shared female attitudes and experiences, notably the problems of female roles in society and male power.[7] This particular theme can be seen in the following whores' autobiographies. However, the characteristics of the traditional female existence expressed in the diaries – that of reticence and self-devaluation – are missing in whore autobiographies. Instead they show defiance, self-aggrandisement and promotion of their own good natures. The other distinction is that diarists were unlikely to share any personal revelations, whereas for the female memoirists, it was their main aim. However, there *is* some overlap in the two, in the desire to illustrate their own charitable natures and the need to show themselves helping those worse off than themselves.

Some debate had taken place about when autobiography first developed. Elizabeth Bruss claims that the earliest mention of the word autobiography was probably at the beginning of the nineteenth century, suggesting the date as 1809, and prior to that, autobiographical works were called memoirs.[8] However, Felicity Nussbaum has suggested, 'Autobiography was first conceptualized as a genre towards the end of the eighteenth century';[9] and Laura Marcus pushes back the date to 1797, but has criticized the obsessive attempt to define autobiography, seeing it as an exercise undertaken mainly in order to allow for criticism of 'literary' autobiography, claiming that to try to pull all autobiography under a simple definition is near impossible.[10] Claire Brant has also refused to categorize women's writing of their own lives with other autobiographies at all, placing them within a gendered discourse of gossip, scandal and the mores on which reputation depended.[11] We can see nonetheless that writing about one's own life was being recognized during this period as a new phenomenon; as Isaac D'Israeli said in 1796, 'the art of writing lives had been but lately known'.[12] As yet, the market was still fluid in the eighteenth century; categories were only just emerging, and it is debatable whether autobiography existed as a singular practice at all. These writings have been referred to as 'prostitutes' narratives', 'scandalous memoirs' and 'courtesans' memoirs', but they are essentially all the same type of material.[13]

The memoirs fit into a corpus of erotic literature which ranges from bawdy poems to explicit pornography. The image of the libertine whore has reverberated throughout literature, but it was not merely a figment of the imagination of the male libertine or pornographer as has been suggested,[14] but in this instance was part of a wider image created by the female libertine herself. Within these texts, these female authors used sexuality to create their own social and economic space, writing up their own narrative to establish a separate niche for themselves. In their autobiographies, they explore their own identities, question society's attitudes and form their own conclusions as to their own femininity and sexuality. By analysing the writings of these women, we can retrieve the world of female sexuality as understood by the women themselves.

Through the examination of three autobiographies, memoirs of Mrs Margaret Leeson, Harriette Wilson and Julia Johnstone,[15] I will draw out their discussions on common topics which outline a definite separate narrative theme emerging in such works – one specific to this genre.

A helpful description of a courtesan is provided by Joanna Richardson in her book on the courtesans of nineteenth-century France, which fits well with the eighteenth-century English courtesan. 'A courtesan is less than a mistress, and more than a prostitute. She is less than a mistress because she sells herself for material benefits; she is more than a prostitute because she chooses her lovers. The courtesan is, in fact, a woman whose profession is love, and whose clients may be more or less distinguished.'[16] Courtesans operated within a certain social scene, outside of respectability, but connected to the affluent. The social status of these women, their life-styles and their working conditions were closely linked to the status of their clients. Many of them had annuities paid them by their seducers, and others had settlements made upon them, often as a result of surprising their lovers at moments of their intoxication.[17] A courtesan's success lay in obtaining a high-ranking protector, rather than becoming merely a brothel-keeper of superior quality, although some kept 'flash' houses, as they were sometimes known, at various times when finances demanded.

The first known brothel-keeper to write her memoirs was Margaret Leeson (c.1742–1797), alias Peg Plunkett (the name Leeson she took from one of her lovers, Sir Joseph Leeson III, 2nd Earl of Milltown) from Ireland (Figure 5.1).[18] She was a kept mistress, and on occasions kept a flourishing brothel in Dublin where she entertained most of the elite men of Dublin's high society, from Lord Lieutenants to lawyers and barristers. She led a colourful life, if somewhat overshadowed by her wheelings and dealings in attempts to keep abreast of her extravagant spending. After thirty years of the profession, with her career coming to an end, she decided to cash in her IOUs and retire, only to find them worthless. Ending up in debtor's prison, she published the *Memoirs of Mrs. Margaret Leeson* in three volumes between 1795 and 1797 in order to raise cash and revenge herself on all those who had not honoured their debts.

Harriette Wilson (Figure 5.2) was a well-known demi-rep amongst the *bon ton* of London. Mistress to some of the most well-known men of the

FIGURE 5.1 *Mrs Margaret Leeson (Peg Plunkett). Wikimedia Commons.*

time, including the dukes of Wellington, Aygyle, Beaufort and Grafton, her memoirs were published to an eagerly awaiting public in 1825. In the preface, *The Interesting Memoirs and Amorous Adventures of Harriette Wilson* declared the book was about 'one of the most celebrated women of the present day, interspersed with numerous anecdotes of illustrious persons; her first introduction into public life as the kept mistress of Lord Craven; her intrigues with the Hon. Frederick Lamb; her letters to the king; and how she became the kept mistress of the Duke of Argyle'. Again, they came out in a series of volumes, issued with warnings as to what could be expected

FIGURE 5.2 *Harriette Wilson. Author's collection.*

in the following volume, offering the opportunity for her intended victims to buy themselves out. According to her publisher's puffs, her memoirs went through at least 33 editions and were certainly popular and widely-read.

The third memoirs examined here are *Confessions of Julia Johnstone* 'written by herself, in contradiction to the fables of Harriet Wilson'. Julia Johnstone was Harriette Wilson's former friend and rival, and, much to her chagrin, not quite as popular as Harriette. She alleges to have written her memoirs in response to Harriette's. The introduction to her own memoirs dated March 1825 gives her reasons for publishing: 'Since the appearance of that scandalous work, "*Harriette Wilson's Memoirs*", I have suffered much by my own reflections and those of my friends: she has calumniated me whenever she has mentioned my name, and appears to delight in reducing all to her own disgusting level'.[19]

There are obvious problems inherent in the examination of this material: firstly, although we know the women were involved in the publication of the memoirs, we cannot be sure how much of the memoirs they actually wrote (although it has to be said, this is infrequently mentioned about male memoirs). They may have merely fed anecdotes to their publishers and the style and commentary may have been more of an expression by the publishers; but I think this is unlikely, not least because their personalities show through so clearly. Secondly, the memoirists were prone to wild exaggerations, for this is the very nature of this type of material. Finally, these women were perhaps unusual for their time in that they published their memoirs at all. Professional women plying their sex as their trade rarely published memoirs since confidentiality and discretion were part of implicit bargains of the transaction offered to their client. Publishing one's life story, including all the intrigues, would hardly be likely to have endeared a woman to her clientele and would certainly have finished off her business. However, since these women were at the end of their careers, they had little left to lose.

Common to all three memoirs (and to others in a varying degree) were the characterizations of the Wronged Daughter; the Educated Hostess; the Fallen Women; the Chaste Ideal; the Coquette; the Spit-Fire; the Temptress; and the Vengeful Whore. These images take the reader through the gamut of characteristics necessary for the life and survival of the courtesan, from their fall from virtue, their education, their first intrigues, their attitudes to sex, the wiles they played to attract and keep their men, the passions involved and finally through to the defence of themselves.

The 'fall' of the prostitute was a prevalent issue of topical concern, no less so for the prostitute herself. As seen in the previous chapter, the images of 'the seduced maiden' and 'the brazen whore' permeated eighteenth- and early nineteenth-century society.[20] Yet these courtesans fit themselves into the framework of female sexuality in quite a different way. Through the memoirs we can see how they evade blame for their fall, while accepting they might be naturally depraved because of their sexuality (an idea based on contemporary ideas of the essentiality of women's lascivious base nature).[21] Rather, they see themselves as victims of poor treatment by society at large, and a failure of their parents or male protectors in particular.

The Wronged Daughter: parental blame

In the memoirs, our heroines want to make clear the reasons for their venture into the *demi-monde* in order to distance themselves from responsibility. Early loss of a mother's tender care and tyrannical male family members are given as reasons for forcing the women from their homes, into another man's protection, and eventually entering the profession.

Margaret was still young when her mother was carried off with 'spotted fever'[22] and her father, desolate and afflicted with rheumatism, was left unable to manage his own affairs. She was about 15 when her father surrendered his financial affairs to her brother who took over with a vengeance, squandering the estate and turning into 'an harsh, unfeeling cruel tyrant'. Life for her and her sister became intolerable as he 'frequently horse-whipped and beat us in a most savage manner, so that our bodies were often covered with wheals [sic] and bruises'.²³ She added, '[H]e would banish the cold by warming me with his horsewhip' and 'he beat me with his horsewhip so vehemently that the sleeves of my riding habit, could not be got off my swelled arms till they were slit open'.²⁴ Later, having stayed over at a friend's home after a ball, she related how 'I no sooner entered the door, than my brother Christopher fell on me with his horse-whip, and beat me so cruelly that I vomited blood'.²⁵

Both Julia and Harriette cited cruelty of their father for their downfall. Harriette touched on some issues which might have encouraged her on the way to a life as a courtesan, but she declined to give us a definitive reason, and was even tantalizingly evasive. She opened her memoirs with 'I shall not say why and how I became, at the age of fifteen, the mistress of the Earl of Craven. Whether it was love, or the severity of my father, the depravity of my own heart, or the winning arts of the noble lord, which did induce me to leave my paternal roof, and place myself under his protection, does not now much signify.' The charms of Harriette's first lover, the Earl of Craven, were certainly not reason enough alone for her to have succumbed to his advances. 'He was, in fact, a dead bore, and had no peculiar interest for a child like myself, in short I soon found that I had made a bad speculation, by going from my father to Lord Craven. I was even more afraid of the latter, than I had been of the former.'²⁶ This statement hints at her father's despotic nature.

All three of her sisters, Amy, Sophia and Fanny, left home to live the life of a kept woman rather than stay in a 'respectable' home under such a repressive regime as they had. Harriette further hinted at her father's character in a later comment when speaking of the father of her lover, Lord Frederick: 'Lord Melburne [sic], his father was a good man, not one of your stiff-laced moralising fathers, who preach chastity and forbearance to their children', as presumably her own father had been.²⁷

Overbearing piety was also cited by Margaret as reason for her ruin; her sisters, due to their '*outrageous virtue*', would not forgive her first fault.

Julia also effectively dispensed with her family from the onset, blaming her fall on unsupportive parents:

> I shall dispose of my family very briefly – as they disposed of their Julia in her early days . . . my father I never saw – he died abroad in embarrassed circumstances it was a love match betwixt him and my mother – like all early love-matches, it proved unhappy. My father most cruelly – but, no matter – at least it is no matter to the public – and over a parent's errors, however greatly a child may have suffered from them, she is bound to draw the veil of Christian charity.²⁸

In Julia's case, she thought she was in love with her lover, Colonel Cotton. According to Harriette, looking back on their earlier life, it was certainly not for money; 'Cotton had not a shilling to spare for the support of Julia's children' and she was falling pregnant once every 11 months; 'She had often vainly applied to her parents, as well as to her uncle, Lord Carysfort, who only wrote to her with reproaches.'[29] At one stage, Julia was so penniless and in debt that she was at risk of being arrested, so Harriette begged her to make applications to some of her noble relations. In the case of Harriette and her sister, they were attracted to a new kind of independence: while General Madden, Amy's protector, was abroad, after the opera, she gave gay evening parties 'to half the fashionable men in town', yet it was thought by Harriette that 'poor Madden had not a shilling'.[30]

None of these women take responsibility for their fall from virtue, but place the blame squarely on the shoulders of their family. Yet they were, at the same time, creating a duel image of themselves, portraying themselves as victims of male tyranny whilst conveying assertive independence. Heroine-like displays of courage, escaping boundaries and asserting independence were all characteristics which would have been recognized by the eighteenth-century reader, and were conveyed in mainstream literature. Thus, the writers have managed to produce an image whereby the reader not only feels empathy, but also admiration for the courtesan.

The Educated Hostess: 'the art of pleasing'

A certain standard of knowledge was paramount for a courtesan and her education was a crucial element in her seduction technique. She should be well-informed, but not overly so: just enough to keep a man keenly entertained. Attracting clients involved displaying as many skills as she could to their best advantage. Public demonstrations of some (but not too much) learning about literature, music and dance for a courtesan was a means of advertising. It was through her education that she could retain her social status by appealing to men of the upper echelons of society. All of the women in these memoirs were educated to an acceptable standard of light entertainment and expert in the art of pleasing men. Julia grudgingly admits Harriette 'must have possessed the *knack of pleasing* to a high degree'.[31]

The women used their education to place themselves in the same location as a conventional woman of higher moral and social standing. As a child, Margaret lived in an elegant style 'with every amusement of music, dancing and rural diversions'[32] and was brought up with suitable skills to enable her to entertain her clients. Similarly, Harriette's background was certainly higher class as her education included convent attendance and she was allowed to develop her musical skills. What education she did not receive at school, she picked up from her paramours. Harriette's lover, Lord Lamb, introduced her to books; 'He sometimes passed an hour in reading to me. Till then, I had no idea of the gratification to be derived from books. In my convent in France, I had read only sacred dramas ... I was absolutely charmed by Shakespeare. Music, I always had a natural talent for. I played well on the piano-forte; that is, with taste and execution; though almost without study.'³³

Harriette's sister, Sophia, also obtained a higher standard of education than most young girls. According to Julia, 'she was some-time a day scholar at a seminary of high repute, under the patronage of Margravine of Anspach'. She had seven years' tuition and learnt rapidly

> all the light accomplishments, that qualify our sex to shine in the ball-room and musical *conversatione*, she acquired without an effort. She was nearly self-taught in the French and Italian languages, and had a pretty tolerable idea of the world's history, with a sovereign contempt for Monk Lewis, Mrs Radcliffe, and all the baneful tribe of novel and romance writers, in whom her sisters so much delighted.³⁴

Even though Julia's mother was not rich, she could still afford to send her daughter to a boarding school near Eton. From here she went on to a convent in the south of France where the Lady Abbess was lax in her educative principles: 'she had no religious prejudices, and paid no attention to her boarders – their morals and education were alike neglected'.³⁵ The imagery of boarding schools and convents as a hot-bed for vice was generally well known and part of popular culture, especially in the ballads, novels and pornography.³⁶ Julia goes on to apply herself and learn what she can, declaring, 'I learnt to read novels, dance with grace and elegance – to play tolerably on various instruments – and dream of love when I knew of it no more than the name'. Her education was finished with an 'Old Swiss governante [sic]' at the Royal Palace.

Limitations in education are pointed out and used as a weapon by the courtesans in attacks against each other. Referring to Harriette Wilson, Julia declared sarcastically, 'she was a perfect blue-stocking in her conversation; she scrawled over verses . . . spouted Shakespeare, and once wrote a farce, which she submitted to the critical judgement of the late John Kemble.'³⁷ This play was indeed staged but, according to Julia, was hissed off stage. Julia continued,

> The passion Harriette expresses for reading was only the affectation of a passion; she had no real taste for reading, and I have often written out quotations from Shakespeare, Milton, and others, for her to use in conversation; from want of knowledge she so often misapplied them, that her manner of expression caused her ignorance to be overlooked. I do not boast, when I say, that I found her very ill-informed, and with a bad ear for music; and, after as much pains as ever I took with my own children, I made her, if not learned, or talented, quite clever enough to pass in thoughtless company as a polite and decently informed girl.³⁸

Julia undermined Harriette's literacy and education, stating that it was all feigned. Implicit in Julia's attitude was an indication that, contrary to some condemnation on the subject of female education, the people in circles in which Julia and Harriet moved saw certain education for women as not just acceptable, but a necessary requirement.

All three women writers punctuate their dialogue with jibes and derisions of each other, while aggrandizing themselves and elevating their own educational achievements. Harriette mocked her sister Amy's attempts at seduction of one of her beaux: 'We found Amy in the act of turning over the leaves of Mr. Nugent's music book, and Mr. Nugent singing an Italian air, to his own accompaniment, ogling Amy to triple time.'[39] Yet she casually littered her dialogue with her own accomplishments, recalling a time 'when I went down to study Voltaire, and Roman history, by myself, for a week or two at Salt Hill'.[40] Education was thus presented not merely as part of a woman's own attributes, but its lack was highlighted as a means to denigrate others.

The Fallen Woman: her first lover

The courtesans provide descriptions of their first sexual encounters, with reasons as to why they were first enticed into sex. Their female sexuality was aroused at an early age. According to Margaret, her first amorous feelings were excited when she was fifteen. Despite being 'quite unexceptional', a certain Mr O'Reilly attracted her attention and made quite an impression: 'I began to feel emotions in my youthful breast, to which I had been hitherto a total stranger.' Once her passions had been stirred, she became aware of all the men around her. She believes this to be common to all women, 'But such is the female mind, that when it has once received an impression, though that it may be effaced, it becomes more susceptible to another.'[41] This statement indicates an acceptance of the common contemporary assumption that female base nature was lascivious.

Harriette blamed her sister Amy for leading the rest of her sisters astray. 'It was Amy, my eldest sister, who had been the first to set us a bad example. We were all virtuous girls, when Amy, one fine afternoon, left her father's house and sallied forth, like Don Quixote, in quest of adventures.'[42] But it was not only boredom and the search for a more exciting life which lured Amy away:

> The first person who addressed her was one Mr Trench, a certain short-sighted pedantic man, whom most people know about town. I believe she told him she was running away from her father. All I know for certain is, that when Fanny and I discovered her abode, we went to visit her, and when we asked her what on earth had induced her to throw herself away on an entire stranger whom she had never seen before, her answer was, 'I

refused him the whole of the first day; had I done so the second, he would have been in a fever'.[43]

Amy recognized the sexual tumult she created and was obviously aware of her allure to men. However, sexual frustration on her own part must also have some effect in making the move. She had accepted his offer virtually without hesitation, and with apparent disregard for the customary morals.

Julia's first affair was less in line with the image of the seduced victim as much as a willing partner in adultery. She had been sent to board with a Mrs Cotton and fell in love with the husband, Colonel Cotton. Her affair with this one man led to her downfall and she became an outcast from 'respectable' society. Extradition from public view was expected, as was Julia's ability to keep herself financially: 'A very retired cottage near town was hired by Cotton for Julia, who inherited a small fortune over which her parents had no control; and on that she had supported herself, in the closest retirement, for more than eight years.'[44] From a moral point of view, Julia saw her own situation with Colonel Cotton as an error, reluctantly admitting, 'I saw, in the fullest extent, the crime I was committing in living with my seducer',[45] a surprising stance since she had now been left little alternative.

Harriette recognized her downfall when falling in love for the first time with Ponsonby, as she declares, 'I am a poor fallen wretch'.[46] She burns with an infatuation so fervently that she makes herself ill: 'A slow, intermitting fever began to prey on my constitution.' She realizes the predicament into which she has fallen in following her heart's desire: 'It was now that I believed in all I had heard, as to the wretchedness of this life, and I wanted to reconcile myself to God.'[47] These women portray themselves as risking all for love.

All three women recognized the strength of their own sexual desire but attempted to place it out of their control. They all attempt to curry favour with the reader and to espouse their own virtues despite admitting 'falling' into vice; for this, they blame the lack of affection or care from their parents as contributing to their fall, and their lovers for not making honest women out of them.

The Chaste Ideal: sexual etiquette

The courtesans' attitudes to chastity, honour and morality were often contradictory. While on the one hand these women castigated the contemporary double standard of morality, of having one sexual code for men and another for women and societal demands for female chastity, on the other hand, they succumb to these attitudes themselves, often aspiring to the image of the perfect wife. They repudiate the premise that virtue lies in chastity alone, but simultaneously accept chastity as good, and sex as evil.

Margaret accepts chastity as an admired attribute in a woman while railing against the stupidity of the notion;

> Chastity I willingly acknowledge is one of the characteristic virtues of the female sex. But may I be allowed to ask – Is it the only one? Can the presence of that one, render all the others of no avail? Or can the absence of it, make a woman totally incapable of possessing one single good quality? How many females do we daily see, who on the mere retention of chastity, think themselves allowable in the constant exercise of every vice. One woman may indulge in frequent inebriation, she may ruin her husband, neglect, beggar, and set an evil example to all her children – but she arrogates herself the character of a *virtuous woman* – truly, because she is chaste.[48]

She also accepts the premise of one fall is all it takes into the route of prostitution: 'if the smallest breach is made in the mounds of Chastity, vice rushes in like a torrent'.

Extra-marital sex is seen as immoral. On contemplation of her first sexual encounter, with Mr Dardis a friend of her brother-in-law, she makes the equation of honour with chastity, reflecting her own double standard:

> Hope was at hand, that that impudence might be amended by his marrying me, which I did not doubt his honour would prompt him to do. Yet what reliance could I have on his honour, when I had so weakly given up my own.[49]

A man's honour was in keeping his word of marriage, a woman's was in retaining her virginity. The malfeasance of female sexuality was frequently accepted by these women and sexual incontinence seen as depraved: Harriette repeatedly mentioned depravity in the context of sex with men; when looking for her escape route from her first paramour, Lord Craven, she says: 'I was not depraved enough to determine, immediately, on a new choice, and yet I often thought about it.'[50] Depravity is seen by the courtesans as any behaviour outside of sexual continence.

All three women rail against the inhibiting double standard of morality. Julia bitterly complains,

> The world is very uncharitable! man may commit an hundred deviations from the path of rectitude yet he still can return, every one invites him; in sober truth, he gains an éclat by his failings, that establish him on the Ton, and make him envied, instead of pitied or despised. But woman, when she makes one false step, can retrieve it no more![51]

Julia echoes the dominant morality – once a woman has lost her virginity, she cannot regain her virtue or honour, while men are lauded for their numerous affairs. Here, Julia also sees the sexual female as 'the depraved victim of sensuality'. She sees female sexuality as synonymous with evil and equates abstention with virtue; 'If I could not rise to a level with the *good*, it was in my power to keep myself far *above* the evil.' In other words, she makes it plain that since she has already had sex once, she cannot regain her virginity (nor presumably her station in society) and therefore can never be wholly *good*, but she *can* prevent herself from sliding down the ladder of virtue, by not having sex too often or with too many people and thereby prevent her reputation from declining any further.[52]

Since a woman's honour was based on her virtue, the courtesans had difficulty in portraying themselves as honourable, a fact which creates internal conflicts in the narrative. Contradictory statements appear confusing but the contemporary reader would have understood this dilemma. A courtesan might have sex for a living but she has to pretend not to, or at least not have too many lovers or too much sex. She must establish herself as a woman of repute at the same time as a wild lover. Her weakness lies in the fact that she has to be known for her trade to attract clientele, yet at the same time maintain her reputation as a modest woman.

The Coquette: the deceitful heart

According to *The 1811 Dictionary of Vulgar Tongue*, a 'coquet' or 'coquette' is a 'jilt' or 'A tricking woman, who encourages the addresses of men whom she means to deceive and abandon'. Margaret, after being rejected by the man she loved, Lawless, in bitterness flings herself into the flirtatious role of the coquette:

> the ill usage of Lawless, had changed me to what I never was before. In short, I was become [*sic*] a compleat [*sic*] *Coquet*. I entertained every one who fluttered about me, I received every present that was offered, accepted every entertainment that was made for me; gave them all the hopes, yet yielded to none. I was disgusted with the man of my heart, therefore gave my heart to none. I looked upon all men as my lawful prey, and wished to punish the crimes of one on the whole sex.[53]

One of the tricks of the coquette was a display of false modesty. Harriette used blushing as a technique to encourage her men. On her initial meeting with the Marquis of Lorne (Argyle) in the park, he flirts with her enough to bring 'a deep blush into my cheek'[54] so proving her modesty to us, the reader. She shows herself to have feeling of misgiving exploring the residue of her previously virtuous path: 'I returned home, in unusual spirits: they were a little dampened, however, by the reflection that I had been doing wrong. I cannot, I reasoned with myself, I fear, become what the world calls a steady, prudent, virtuous woman. That time is past, even if I was ever fit for it.'

Similarly her sister Sophia, in seducing Colonel Berkeley, 'continued to hint, with proper delicacy and due modest blushes, that her living with him or not, must depend on what his intentions were'.[55]

Tom Sheridan, son of Richard Brinsley Sheridan, was attracted to Fanny, Harriet's younger sister, but saw through the practices of these experienced courtesans, declaring to Harriette, 'Fanny is the sweetest girl on earth; but you are all a race of finished coquettes, who delight in making fools of people.'[56] According to Julia, Argyle also saw through Harriette's feminine wiles, telling Julia one day, 'Tis a pity so beautiful a casket should hold within it no gem worth picking the lock to obtain. She is all hollow as sounding brass, or tinkling cymbals – she has no *heart* for anything but flattery, fine clothes, and love of admiration.' However, Harriette does not go out of her way to woo the man who pays for her, choosing to please herself, as Argyle described: 'She will try to please everyone, but him whom she ought to please most. She is one of those creatures, nature makes thousands of in a hurry; merely animates their frames with the breadth of life, and then throws them upon the world, ashamed of her handy work.'[57]

Abandonment of a paramour gives little grief to the coquette. Margaret admits that if she has no affectation for a man, she will leave him at once if she is attracted to someone else:

> My conduct, with respect to Mr. Leeson, will fully show, that neither pleasure, content, affluence nor gratitude, can bind a woman of a loose turn of mind, and changeable disposition, to the man who has formed an illicit connection with her. That he can have no confidence in an affection, however strong it may appear, that is not founded on Delicacy and Virtue.[58]

Nonetheless, it is part of the whores' narrative to portray themselves as honourable women; Harriette tries to show herself as a principled person: 'I will always adhere to good faith, as long as any thing like kindness or honourable principle is shown toward me: and, when I am ill used, I will leave my love rather than deceive him.' Despite Hariette's assertion, Julia condemns her for freely abandoning her paramours: 'her lovers she threw off as indifferently as her shoes – or trampled on them without compunction'.[59]

Harriette's sister, Amy, was head-strong in her quest for a paramour from the onset, not suffering any fools and suiting herself as she pleased. Julia exclaims:

> Amy was a perfect jilt, and a modern Messalina; she received and dismissed lovers daily, nay, hourly, if that be all. She had neither delicacy of feeling – her sole motive for action, for debasing herself, was to amass money: in dress she was very extravagant; in her household affairs mean and pitiful; and her door was continually beset by trades-people, dunning her for small sums, when she had probably a thousand guineas spread on

her toilet during morning visits of her admirers – to let them see she was not comeatable but by prompt and large payments.'⁶⁰

The Spit-Fire: 'wild' passions

The courtesans create a romantic illusion by depicting themselves as being governed by their passions, an inconstant temper which alludes to sexual abandonment. These women refuse to be dominated, and show themselves as hot-blooded spit-fires. Margaret admits, 'my temper was not of the most placid kind'.⁶¹ In one incident, when she found Mr Lawless drinking champagne with a Mrs Johnstone, she became incensed with rage: 'My jealousy was wound up to so high a pitch, that I screamed, trembled, and was quite beside myself. I snatched up the decanter, and was about to dash it in her face, when Mr. Lawless seized and held my hands, and prevented me from murder.'⁶² Her extreme expression of emotion also became evident in times of absolute despair. On finding out Lawless had left her and sailed to America she becomes insensible:

> Words cannot express the tortures of mind. I tore my hair, I beat my breasts, rent my cloaths, and became outrageously and raving mad – until nature, nearly exhausted by these violent passions, sunk spiritless and stupid, and the whole frame of my nerves were palsied. In this state I continued near a week, incapable to answer any question with propriety.⁶³

After his departure, Margaret could no longer admit any other to her bed, she was so devastated. She lamented, 'I was fated to taste the bitter cup of misery, and plunge in a whirl of those pleasures, which bring remorse and sorrow in their train.'⁶⁴

Commotion and disturbance are promoted in the memoirs thus reflecting their tumultuous life. Men rapping violently on doors, declarations of unending love, jealous outbursts and indignant whippings are presented as everyday life occurrences. At one such event, four young 'sparks' rushed into the house after being declined entrance while Margaret and Sally Hayes, her companion were dining. When asked to depart, Captain F____e gave such an impertinent answer as to induce Sally to discipline him; 'Sally Hayes seeing this behaviour, seized a horse-whip, with a long lash, which lay on the chimney-piece, whipped the Captain round, and round the table, which was pretty large; and then turned him and his comrades out and locked the street door.'⁶⁵

Anecdotes depicting the women as passionate and fiery pepper the pages. The word 'wild' is frequently used to convey a variety of strong emotions: Harriette uses 'wild' to describe both erratic or eccentric behaviour, as well as lust. She recognizes that her actions have been regulated by the impulses and feelings of her heart and she wonders if she might regret it: 'I thought of the youth I was passing away, in passions wild and ungovernable.'[66] Her nature is too passionate for her own good. Lorne, later Duke of Argyll, asks Harriette, '"Do you conceive yourself capable of loving any other person?" "Yes, provided he loved me in return, and that most passionately." "I fear me, Harriette, your love would be too hot to last long; it would blaze and expire in smoke – never burn like a taper on an alter, with pure, steady, and holy flame."'[67]

She describes the effect that seeing Ponsonby had on her; she felt a strong physical attraction: 'I came immediately in close contact with the stranger, whose person had been concealed by two large elms, and who might have been observing me for some time. I scarcely dared encourage the flattering idea. It made me wild.' Ponsonby says to Harriette, 'When we met, latterly, in the park, there was something so natural and unaffected, and wild, about your manner, that I began to forget your notoriety.'[68] Harriette writes to Ponsonby after he has left her, pining for him and attempting to get him back:

> I dreamed not of injuring anyone of my fellow creatures. In short, while I loved the world, and would fain have done them all good, I most respected Lady Ponsonby. This assertion may seem scarcely credible to young females, differently educated, or of less wild and childish dispositions.[69]

Wild behaviour included swearing and cussing. As Captain Sir Joseph Nourse commented to Julia,

> 'Your friend Harriette is very pretty, and would make an excellent sailor's wife, she swears such good round oaths.' She had indeed got a knack of swearing by her maker too often, and I had often cautioned her on the silly as well as immoral habit. She thought it gave her conversation a zest, as olives do wine. Lord Petersham once said, an oath came prettily from her lips; and she has practised swearing pretty much ever since.[70]

Despite already having a keeper, Harriette's sexual cravings overcome her when she meets Lieutenant Devall, has sex with him and becomes pregnant. Julia says of Harriette, 'her passions were as an impetuous torrent, which sweeps away all before it with resistless force, and leaves ruin and desolation on every side'.[71]

Amy, Harriette's sister, is represented as autonomous, refusing to buckle to her lover's will. Julia describes Amy, as 'a fine woman, with a Siddonian countenance, and a masculine spirit'. Yet Julia, always more conservative than the others, condemns this more unreigned behaviour, castigating Amy as unfeminine. She later adds, 'Miss Amy, was like her sister, without any fixed principal, except that of self interest; she was proud and avaricious.'[72]

However, pride and avariciousness in a courtesan also shows a consciousness of the need for autonomy, and a realization that money brings freedom from dependency. Amy showed shrewdness as she inveigled the first gentleman she lived with to settle an annuity on her of £100 per year for life, swearing never to leave him. When she does, she sends back a message with the footman, announcing, 'Tell the old fool I have done with him, and shall see him no more.'[73] Julia, on the other hand, was less capable of extracting money from her beaux.

These women depict themselves and each other as being capable of extreme emotions, their impulses dominating their lives. Once spurned by their true loves, they become victims of their own fiery natures.

The Temptress: jealous lovers

Descriptions of jealous lovers suggest the courtesan's own irresistibility, her allure capable of making men mad. Yet this passionate desire is destructive, capable of bringing about her own downfall. Jealousy on the part of Mr Lawless, Margaret's lover, frequently led to blows. Margaret tells of one incident of violence, of how she upbraids Mr Lawless for paying too much attention to another woman at a dinner party:

> When we got home, where we might make as much noise as we pleased, we became vociferous, in our contention till we were both nearly tired. I refused to go to bed, he insisted I should, which I still refused. He then cut the strings of my cloaths, and threw me into bed. I twisted from him and got under it; he, greatly enraged at my obstinacy, pulled me out, and in the struggle hurt me so much, that he was obliged to send for Surgeon Gleghorn, who found me so bad that he was forced to fetch in Mr. Cullum.[74]

She blames herself for his violence and warns 'women of spirit' that such rage, she calls 'spirit', degrades the sex below its real dignity and tends 'to disgust a man rather than recall his love'.

Harriette's exposés of male violence are seen in her descriptions of two passionate attacks made on her by her lovers, one made by Argyle and one by Lamb. These deliberately convey sexual overtones in her lover's breathlessness and passionate outburst.

> 'Gracious God!' said Argyle, 'how you torment me! If – ,' he proceeded after pausing, 'if you have ceased to love me – if – if you are disgusted.' I was silent. 'Do speak! pray, pray!' said he. His agitation astonished me. It almost stopped his breathing.[75]

Lamb near kills her in his passionate attack:

He talked for more than an hour, of Argyle, Lord Ponsonby, and his own former affection for me. He then became a little more practical than I liked; first taking hold of my hand, and next kissing me by force. I resisted all his attempt with mild firmness. At last he grew desperate, and proceeded to [be] very rough, I may say brutal, violence, to gratify his desires against my fixed determination. I was never very strong; but love gave me almost supernatural powers to repel this very tiger; and I contrived to pull his hair out by the roots ... he placed his hands on my throat, saying, while he nearly stopped my breath and occasioned me almost the pangs of suffocation, that I should not hurt him another instant. He spoke this in a smothered voice and I did in truth, believe my last moments had arrived.[76]

Fanny, Harriette's younger sister, was attacked by George Cooke, the tragedian, in a fit of jealous rage, after she had been entertaining his friends by singing for them. Julia describes the event:

One evening, when she had exerted her talents in this humiliating way, the company expressed their admiration so warmly that her keeper became jealous, and actually made an attempt to cut out her tongue, and probably would had he not been prevented by others more sober. He, however, made a scar on her upper lip and cheek, which diminished greatly the small remains of beauty she had left.

Alcohol was a mitigating circumstance in violent incidents involving courtesans and their lovers. Julia admitted that Fanny and Cooke 'both drank and lived hard, and neither valued the world's opinion a rush'.[77]

The Vengeful Whore

Revenge was the key which instigated the writing of all three memoirs. Margaret categorically points out the failings of the men with whom she has been involved: 'some have actually robbed me, others have borrowed my money, and to this hour have never paid me (*But I shall, in my next volume, lay before the public a list of all who are in debt to 'em, with the sum, an how long owing*).'[78] She was the epitome of the vengeful whore. Never did she let a person off without an even or winning score: 'I seldom failed of not only resenting any affront or ill-treatment given here, but have taken the pleasure of avenging myself of enemies, in proportion to the degree of the offence.'[79] Her memoirs are full of anecdotes dominated by the theme of revenge and as many references to the people she sued.

The memoirs are littered with lawsuits both taken against, and by the women, as they convey themselves as fearless advocates of revenge. A list of all the mentioned names prefaced Stockdale's publication of Harriette's

Memoirs, and Harriette made no secret of the fact that she was using it to obtain money in blackmail. The memoirs apparently had the desired effect, as various critics reacted to her scandalous text. One wrote, 'A more disgusting and gross prostitution of the press cannot be than the recent publication entitled "Memoirs of Harriette Wilson": it may very properly be called infamy exulting in its profligacy – or pollution seeking a retribution for the hire of its vice' and saw that 'the most material and serious consequences are the destructive operation of its effects on the minds of society'.[80] The author saw the book as so harmful that 'To guard the feelings of the subject in its civil and religious rights, and the morals of the nation, the press must be morally controlled.'

Revenge was exacted not only on debtors and men who had wronged them, but also on other women. Slighting one's sexual reputation was a commonly used form of retribution. Margaret took her revenge on the celebrated Miss Anne Cately when she openly confronted her in the street calling the actress 'a little street-walking, ballad-singer', informing her that she would hiss at her every time she came upon the stage. Although these women appeared to be carrying on a series of intrigues, the social protocol of the day demanded discretion.

Sexual activities should remain hidden and not be obviously aired or admitted. Any slight on a person's reputation, or indication of indiscretion, might affect a courtesan's business. A display of anger and denial by the victim was necessary if a woman was to salvage her reputation. Preferably the incident should take place in the public arena where as many people as possible are witness to the denial, or at least in a situation where gossip would circulate, so as to restore the reputation in question. Harriette Wilson adamantly denies her intrigues with Captain Nourse when Julia accuses her of the affair, retorting aggressively, 'I scorn your suspicions'. Julia shows herself a faithless and disloyal 'friend' to Harriette when she uses Harriette's sexual conduct against her. She informs the Marquis of Worcester of Harriette's dallying while he was abroad, knowing that Harriette would lose her income from him.[81] Harriette extracted her revenge by sending a certain Major Sibthorp over to Julia's house, intimating that his overtures to Julia would be welcomed. Julia, upset by this slight on her reputation, avenged herself by informing on Harriette to Beaufort, Harriette's keeper, thus depriving her of his income too.

One of the most surprising aspects of the biographies is how little sex is mentioned, considering the sales pitch of the memoirs, and the promise of lurid tales. Explicit details of carnal activities are non-existent. Men figure greatly, but in an amorous, flirtatious way rather than uninhibited descriptions of genitalia and sexual intercourse; actual sexual performances and position simply do not figure. *Allusions* to sexual activities however do. Lecherous men, seduction techniques, secret trysts, amatory advances and passionate machinations are all prevalent in order to stir and excite the emotions of the reader. All these are contrivances which had become more or less a literary convention in this genre in which certain themes emerge.

First, the memoirs show how these woman aspire to the conventional forms of femininity, seen through both descriptions of their education, and in evading blame for their fall into prostitution, while still affirming their assertiveness; secondly, they demonstrate how the women have attempted to maintain a certain outward code of sexual etiquette while railing against chastity; and finally we have seen how they use displays of violent tempers, high passions and generosity as evidence of their sensual, but considerate, natures. These courtesans could neither fit comfortably into the role of the conventional ideal woman, nor could they entirely forsake it. The image asserted by the female courtesan is therefore of a complex, and often contradictory nature. However, the memoirs provide us with an alternative discourse as to the image of female sexuality.

CHAPTER SIX

Initiation, Defloration and Flagellation: Sexual Propensities in *Memoirs of a Woman of Pleasure*

Then! then all my resolution deserted me; I skream'd out, and fainted away with the sharpness of the pain; and (as he told me afterwards) on his drawing out, when emission was over with him, my thighs were instantly in a stream of blood, that flow'd from the wounded torn passage.[1]

In John Cleland's *Memoirs of a Woman of Pleasure* (1749), Fanny Hill's introduction to sexual intercourse is both painful and bloody, and conveys the figure of the ravaged virgin. Such violent defloration was a representation of sexual initiation common to other erotica and pornography circulating in England in the eighteenth century.[2] Other sexual scenarios included predilections for tribadism (sex between women) and flagellation.

This chapter examines *Memoirs of a Woman of Pleasure* and compares it to other erotic works of the eighteenth century. It explores the configurations of the genre to trace the influences on these themes, and which of them proved popular enough to be honed into singular fetishist sub-genres. It examines the contemporary implications of these books within a gender historical context, in particular, looking at the image of the sexual woman, to see how sexual behaviour was depicted, and why certain predilections in erotica were prevalent. Overall, I argue that such descriptions did not emerge as isolated themes for the pornographic imagination as has previously been suggested,[3] but it reinforced popular representations which were already current.

FIGURE 6.1 Memoirs of a Woman of Pleasure, *London 1766 edition. British Library, London.*

There is no doubt that John Cleland's *Memoirs of a Woman of Pleasure* (*MWP*) was a defining moment in English erotica. In applying the form of the novel, Cleland became pivotal in transforming erotic writing. As Randolph Trumbach has pointed out, Cleland's fantasy of sex is accompanied by romantic love in that it is safe and comfortable, with the initial lovers reuniting in a finale of marriage.[4] Ruth Yeazell's assessment supports this notion, arguing that these stories do not resemble the whore biography so much as courtship fiction.[5] It has therefore been recognized that *MWP* (Figures 6.1 and 6.2) incorporated influences from mainstream literature, but how far does this book reflect contemporary sexual themes expressed in other erotic writings?

Ideas recurrent within the story of *MWP* were not necessarily new, the Italians and French having already developed their erotica in the sixteenth and seventeenth centuries respectively. English writers were slower to develop a highly charged sexualized writing style. During the late seventeenth and early eighteen centuries, they had tinkered with erotic imagery, toying with agricultural and botanical metaphors[6] and bawdy allegories,[7] but these were not enough to satisfy the increasing demand from a more sophisticated urban readership. Cleland surpassed the merely suggestive and whimsical, incorporating detailed descriptions of bodies and their libidinous activities into novelistic prose, creating a more detailed graphic and realistic style.[8] Within this process he gleaned images and erotic themes already circulating in French erotica, and in doing so, moved the English erotic genre forward.

Three prominent themes emerge as important in contributing to the development of erotica which are also evident in *MWP*. First was the theme of sexual initiation, with the introduction of an innocent young virgin to sex by another woman; second was the theme of defloration through sex with a man; and third, the theme of flagellation taking place between either two women, or between a man and a woman. These themes were not only part of the erotic imagination but echoed beliefs and opinions on sexual matters which circulated in the eighteenth-century culture, the latter two closely linked to blood taboo.

Sexual initiation of women by women

Tribadism, or sex between women, was often key in sexual initiation of female protagonists in pornography and introductions to sex did not necessarily involve men at all, either in factual or fictional reports. Frequently a young woman's first sexual experience came to her via another, more sexually experienced, woman usually through discussions which led on to experimentation, through kissing and mutual masturbation. Randolph Trumbach has suggested that Cleland knew that society had not yet constructed a lesbian role, and so his purpose was to show others that such behaviour existed.[9] However, it would appear that lesbian activities had already been widely aired through a variety of expositions including the anonymous *The Counterfeit Bridegroom* (1720), Henry Fielding's *The Female Husband* (1746) and various other books and pamphlets relating scenarios involving two women as sexual partners.[10] Since the public was already aware of the female-to-female roles, it is unlikely these scenes were iterated with didactic intent. Rather, the topic, as with other themes already current elsewhere, was incorporated into *MWP* with the intention to titillate and entertain readers already conversant with the subject. Moreover, in this erotica, tribadism was portrayed as a progression of natural sexual development, often initiated through conversation about size and shape of genitalia and dialogues about love-making.

In *MWP* Fanny's introduction to carnal knowledge is typical of other erotica in its portrayal of sexual initiation in that it included mutual female masturbation. She is introduced to sex by Phoebe, a whore in the brothel where she lives and with whom she shares a bed. Phoebe loses no time in corrupting the innocent Fanny who lies there 'tame and passive', allowing Phoebe to explore her body, 'her lascivious touches had lighted up a new fire that wanton'd through all my veins, but fix'd with violence in that centre appointed them by nature'.[11] Fanny describes herself as 'inflamed', 'transported' and 'out of myself' but seemingly unembarrassed by the affair. Phoebe artfully encourages Fanny's sexual curiosity by explaining to her 'the mysteries of Venus'.

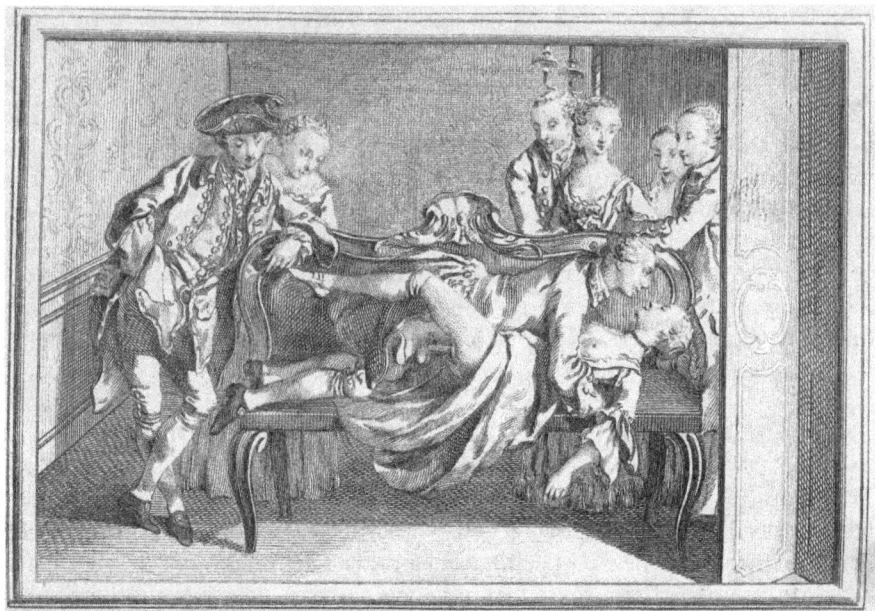

FIGURE 6.2 Memoirs of a Woman of Pleasure, *London 1749 edition. British Library, London.*

Initiation themes as seen in *MWP* had already been explored in earlier French erotica which had circulated in Britain from the seventeenth century. Such books as *L'Escole des Filles* (1655), *L'Académie des Dames* (1680) and *Venus dans la Cloître* (1683) were quickly followed by their English translations, under the titles *The School of Venus* (1725 and 1745) *A Dialogue Between a Married Lady and a Maid* (1688 and 1740) and *Venus in the Cloister, Or a Nun in her Smock* (1692 and 1725).[12] All three consisted of dialogue between an experienced woman and a virgin. This technique was inherited from the Italian Pietro Aretino and was to be widely used in eighteenth-century erotica.

In *L'Académie des Dames*, and its translation *A Dialogue between a Married Lady and a Maid* (1740),[13] there is no doubt that the women prefer relationships with men. The women exchange tales of love and sex in a form of verbal foreplay, with Octavia relating to the older Tullia the sexual action which has taken place between herself and her male lover. Notably, the English version of *L'Académie des Dames* excluded lesbian scenes, made the defloration scenes less aggressive, the sexual encounters less frequent and Tullia more passive. Furthermore, a section was inserted which was not contained in the original giving conduct advice for a wife, possibly reflecting the popularity of the English conduct manual, and indicating direction for interested female readers.¹⁴ *Venus dans La Cloître* moved away from the boudoir into the nunnery. This religious setting was to play an important role in a separate sub-genre of anti-Catholic erotic literature where tribadism was seen as a tendency which would arise if natural sexual desires were repressed. The slightly older woman was frequently seen to be the initial seducer of a younger woman in this erotica, and conveyed as the liberator of the younger woman's sexual energy. However, much older nuns, for example the mother superiors, were portrayed in a much more negative light, conveyed as vicious, twisted and bitter old crones, bent on the destruction of pure young virginal souls and bodies. Nuns were depicted as becoming more depraved the longer they were incarcerated within a religious order, indoctrinated with Catholicism and debauched through years of sexual repression. Furthermore, older seducing monks are seen as debauchers and oppressors, hell-bent on corrupting as many young nuns as possible. Thus, there exists both a gender and age disparity in depictions of sexually debauched *religieux*. This picture of older nuns and priests was used in French pornography to undermine the current regime, and as an attack on the Church prior to the French Revolution.[15]

Voyeurism and masturbation are usually introduced within the primary stages of sexual initiation. An example of this can be seen in *MWP* when Fanny watches the madam of the brothel having sex with a grenadier, the man with a 'great stomach', the woman with great pendulous breasts, 'navel-low' and 'flagging-soft', the scene causing her some excitement. Then, Phoebe takes her to a secret viewing place, where they can watch the activities of another couple through a crevice in the wall. Warming to the scene, Phoebe guides Fanny through the delights of her first orgasm. Similarly in *Venus in the Cloister*, the older nun seduces the younger 15-year-old novice, after she has watched her masturbating.[16]

Tribadism was perceived as merely a precursor to the ultimate goal of heterosexual sex. Generally, it is seen as a substitute for sex with men and classed as an inferior sexual activity. Unlike sodomy, tribadism was treated as a normal introduction to sex and appears not to have caused such a threat as male-to-male sexual activities. Sodomy in *MWP* is vehemently opposed, with Fanny attempting to have the two men she sees *in flagrante delicto* arrested. This echoes other contemporary erotica which generally refers to sodomitical acts as abhorrent, or as acts undertaken by foreigners. In *A New Description of Merryland* (1741),[17] the author dismisses the predilections of sodomites as a most disagreeable subject: 'I shall leave the Affair of the *Antipodes* to those who have a *Taste* that Way; only shall observe, there are some People who very preposterously (as I think) give the Preference to the PDX [podex].' Not only is sodomy disfavoured, but it is not considered an English trait. Foreigners were evidently thought to be more prone to sodomitical inclinations, as the author alleges that the Dutch and Italians have a partiality for this practice, 'although worryingly the vice seems to have crept nearer home'. Few erotic books of this period mentioned sodomy in favourable terms, although occasionally it was alluded to (but rarely graphically) if between a man and a woman. This was to change in the nineteenth century, when sodomitical accounts became much more prevalent in erotica.

Sexual initiation of women by men

Portrayals of the penetrative sexual act in pornography were soaked in sanguineous descriptions, and this interest in defloration was dependent, in part, on the excitement aroused by blood. It frequently involved violent descriptions with defloration conveyed as an 'attack', or 'assault' on the body of the woman, the taking of a woman's virginity seen as a battle to be won. Screams and entreaties were commonplace in erotic scenarios of initial heterosexual penetration, the picture completed with descriptions of open wounds of ripped flesh. In *MWP*, Fanny's lover is referred to as the 'murderer of my virginity'.[18] She faints away with the pain, 'my thighs were instantly all in a stream of blood, that flow'd from the wounded torn passage'.[19] The association between pain and pleasure is made by Fanny who declares, 'I arriv'd at excess of pleasure, through excess of pain.'[20] Later, though she has experienced intercourse frequently, when she succumbs to the charms of her benefactor's male servant, she bleeds after intercourse due to the size of his penis: 'the widen'd wounded passage refunded a stream of pearly liquids, which flow'd down my thighs, mix'd with streaks of blood, the mark of the ravage of that monstrous machine of his'.[21] The second part of *Fanny Hill* also displays a fascination with blood. A companion of Fanny's, Harriet, recounts her rape by a young male swimmer. Fearing him drowned, she falls into a swoon, only to regain consciousness at the pain caused by his penetration, causing 'streams of blood', leaving her 'in bleeding ruin'.[22] A friend of Fanny's, Louisa, even deflowers herself through masturbation, using her fingers, despite the pain.

The eighteenth-century interest in defloration[23] had already emerged in sexual instruction manuals which provided detailed discussions of female bleeding upon sexual initiation. One such book, *Rare Verities, The Cabinet of Venus Unlocked and her Secrets Laid Open* (1657), reprinted in the eighteenth century, described itself as a translation of Sinibaldus's *Geneanthropeiae* (1642) which in itself was a collection of ancient Greek and Roman physicians' and philosophers' sexual texts.[24] The problems associated with voiding great quantities of blood were disclosed in detail and women were warned of the potential frightful consequences of bleeding to death after initial intercourse:

> This membrane [the hymen] which is thus broken, yields a greater or smaller quantity of bloud, according to the largeness and fulness, or

smallness and emptiness of the veines. Some have immediately died by the greatness of the flux of bloud.[25]

Another similar anonymous sex guide, *Aristotle's Masterpiece* (1690), described defloration at some length and suggested a necessity for 'pain and bleeding' as did Venette's *The Mysteries of Conjugal Love Reveal'd* (1712)[26] in which visible signs of blood were taken as a crucial proof of virginity. Indeed, Venette advised unchaste brides to use dried lamb's blood inserted into the vagina on their wedding nights to act as a substitute for vaginal blood and thereby fool husbands into thinking his wife was a virgin. Similarly in *MWP*, Fanny fakes her virginity, using pig's blood she had hidden in the bedpost to mislead her clients into believing she has just lost her maidenhead.

> In each of the head bed-posts, just above where the bed-steads are inserted into them, there was a small drawer so artfully adapted to the moulding of the timber-work, that it might have escap'd even the most curious search, which drawers were easily open'd or shut, by the touch of a spring, and were fitted each with a shallow glass tumbler, full of a prepar'd fluid blood; in which lay soak'd, for ready use, a spunge; that requires no more than gently reaching a hand, taking it out, and properly squeezing between the thighs, when it yielded a great deal more of the red liquid than would save a girl's honour.[27]

The importance of maidenheads is echoed in other contemporary erotica. In *Dialogue between a Married Lady and a Maid* (1740), the translation of *L'Académie des Dames*,[28] a frank discussion takes place between the two women, Tullia and Octavia. Tullia relates the tale of her wedding night, when her husband checks for an intact hymen by inserting his fingers inside her 'and thrust it a little way up, till he met with a stop, and I complained he hurt me: This he did on Purpose, to be satisfied whether I was a Maid or not as afterwards he himself confessed.'[29] He is delighted to discover that his wife is a virgin, but the experience was painful for Tullia who tells her husband, 'I never can endure it, it will split me in two, you'll kill me, if all this must go into my Body'. Her mother congratulates her husband for his control and authority, the conquest seen as a victory, while the whole experience for Tullia is 'the battle of Love, where my virginity is to be the Prize of the Conqueror'.[30]

Men paid more money for virgins, so eighteenth-century prostitutes became knowledgeable on how to fake their virginity in order to increase their profits.[31] An account in *Nocturnal Revels* recorded the activities of Sir Francis Dashwood and his friends, all notorious English libertines, who formed a 'secret' gentleman's society to indulge in their passions of whoring and drinking.[32] Well-known brothel-keeper Charlotte Hayes supplied virgins for them; 'Twelve vestals for the Abbey. Something discreet and Cyprian for the friars.' Lord Sandwich, one of Sir Francis Dashwood's 'Knights', said of Hayes, 'She keeps the Stock Exchange supplied with real, immaculate maidenheads'.[33] With a little skilful preparation, she apparently passed off two young prostitutes, Kitty Young and Nancy Feathers, as virgins and supplied 'A Maid for Alderman Drybones' – Nell Blossom, who was about nineteen and had 'not been in company for four days and was prepared for a state of vestal ship last night' for which she received twenty guineas.[34] *Kitty's Attalantis* [sic] *for the Year 1766*, a register of sexually available women in London, reports of a Miss Ram____ who carried on intrigues at her family home for twelve months 'which she did with the greatest success, having sold her maidenhead, in that space of time, to fifty different people, when 'twas supposed, by her age, that her father's boy, who used to sweep the shop, got her real one, behind the counter'.[35]

An emphasis was placed on a man's ability to violate a maidenhead, and it was considered an indication of his prowess. The March 1793 issue of racy gentleman's magazine the *Bon Ton* writes that a condition of membership of the Adam and Eve Club was 'that every member must produce a similar certificate of having deflowered his virgin, or debauched his married woman, and the more of those feats he has achieved, the greater is his station in the assembly'.[36] Virginal blood was thought to be an indication of a woman's purity, and was tied up with her sexual reputation and her social standing. If a woman's chastity was under suspicion, midwives might well be called in to inspect her to ensure her hymen was intact.

Defloration and the conquering of virgins were prominent themes in both eighteenth-century erotica and everyday life, both closely linked to the exposure of blood and bound to the idea of family honour and masculine territorial rights. As such, writers recognized blood as a sexually exciting phenomenon, and the introduction of blood to erotic material rendered the content more sexually arousing.

Flagellation

MWP was one of the earliest English erotic novels which mentioned sexual flagellation. Mr Barville, a 23-year-old gentleman client who frequents the brothel where Fanny works, requests flagellatory services. Fanny experienced her first flogging by his hand:

> At last, he twigg'd me so smartly as to fetch blood in more than one lash: at sight of which he flung down the rod, flew to me, kissed away the starting drops, and, sucking the wounds, eased away a good deal of pain.[37]

Women being whipped, however, was less usual in much of the erotica; men tended to be the recipients, since flogging was thought to stimulate the flow of blood to the penis. A medical understanding of the use of flogging is in *A Treatise of the Use of Flogging in Venereal Affairs* (1718). John Henry Meibomius, a German physician wrote, 'there are persons who are stimulated to venery by strokes of the rod, and worked into a flame of lust by blows; and the part which distinguishes us to be men, should be raised by the charm of invigorating lashes'.[38] He advocated flogging as a medical cure for men who experienced difficulty obtaining an erection, this state usually being associated with older men. This idea was widespread during the eighteenth century, hence Fanny's surprise that her client, young Mr Barville, was so eager for the sport. Yet younger people do indeed appear to have indulged in the practice of sexual flagellation. In 1707, one case in the ex-Puritan town of Norwich involved a group of middle- and lower middle-class professional people playing such exotic games as voyeurism, group sex, wife-swapping, the trimming of pubic hair, and extensive flagellation.[39]

Flagellation scenarios had already been depicted in French erotica, a practice assimilated from the established penitential practice of Catholics priests and nuns. Transferring flagellation practices from religion into a sexual context allowed for the exploration of a new erotic form as seen in *Venus in the Cloister*, or *The Nun in her Smock* (1725). One nun uses 'the Discipline' to inflict bloody wounds thereby inducing sexual ecstasy in the recipient, an erotic appropriation of religious ecstasy. Sister Angelica, earnestly desiring a look at the bloody marks, pleads 'kneel down upon the Mattress, and hold down thy Head a little, that I may observe the Violence of thy Stripes!'[40]

Meanwhile, genuine cases of French priests' trials for seduction of young female penitents were reported back to England. The case of Father Girard, a priest who had seduced a young Catholic woman, Mary Cadière, was the focus of much gossip. A plethora of pamphlets detailed the priest's alleged debaucheries. One, entitled *Tryal of Father John-Baptist Girard* (1732),[41] explored both blood and whipping providing lurid depictions of their sexual encounters. When Father Girard became worried that the girl might be pregnant, he gave her a toxic in order to induce an abortion, 'the Effect of it was a great Flooding of Blood: That she not only inform'd him of it, but told him, she had something like a Piece of Flesh come from her; she shew'd him the Pot; which he carried to the Window, and examined with great Attention'.[42] However, the appeal in blood[43] displayed by English writers took a more light-hearted turn (see Chapter 6 for more on this pamphlet).

The backdrop for flagellation material in England shifted from French convents to English boarding schools. Faked correspondence on disciplining children was carried in various magazines throughout the eighteenth and nineteenth centuries, most expressly in the *Gentleman's Magazine* of the 1730s and the more risqué *Bon Ton* in the 1790s. One letter to the *Bon Ton*, in March 1792, disparaged the punishments taking place at a boarding-school near Parsons Green:

> ... whenever one of the Mademoiselles offend their Mistress so, as to deserve the calling of a third power, or, to speak more plainly, to need the application of any instrument with which nature has not already provided her, the young lady is conducted into a closet, set apart chiefly for that purpose, where they immediately proceed to action, after the following manner.[44]

Another letter in the *Bon Ton*, from March 1794, written by a 'Miss Birch' who kept a boarding school, declared

> [I] ... have been under the necessity to use the rod almost every day; and though I tickle my pupils very smartly, I assure you, that in an hour after the whipping they are as gay and as full of play, as if they had not felt the rod.

These letters were no doubt editorial hoaxes but both bogus and serious letters relating to the whipping of young girls would continue through the nineteenth century as seen in editions of the *Family Herald* and the *Englishwoman's Domestic Magazine* during the 1870s.

Erotic novels based wholly around the topic of flagellation were soon to follow suit. *Exhibition of Female Flagellants* ('1777')[45] provides anecdotes mainly about women flagellating other women and children. Flogging as a method of disciplining plays a major role in sexual initiation. The whippings are portrayed as creating a special type of bonding between the women. Indeed, the idea of a whipping society comprised of women seems to be a common theme in this erotica. Flirtilla, the protagonist, describes one particularly adept female flagellator, 'and there is not a lady who afterwards, of any society, or whipping academy, but was delighted with her manner'.[46] Conversely, Fanny Hill's experience of sexual initiation is unconnected with flagellation. Indeed, flagellation is perceived as only for the sexually adventurous. Mrs Cole, the brothel-keeper, chooses Fanny to entertain the flagellant since it is she who has the experience to cope with his needs.

Exhibition of Female Flagellants explores the theme of the blood-lusting Governess. One Miss L, another votary to birch-discipline, the daughter of a clergyman, opens a boarding school so as to give vent to her favourite passion, whipping sometimes a dozen girls a day. She takes her pleasures to the extreme: 'Her pleasure was to cut them, and generally whipped till the blood would come.'[47] Flogging of children was in fact a reality; Rousseau's penchant for a good whipping at the hands of his attractive governess is notorious.[48] Revelations of punishment of children at public schools are also well-known through the infamous tales of Dr Busby of Westminster and the lesser known Dr Wool of Rugby. Francis Fortescue Turville, a member of an eighteenth-century upper-class Catholic family, sent his two sons to boarding school where the master complained that one of them had 'practised indecencies in word and deed, which he admitted were common in his former school' and as a method of correction whipped the boy until he bled.[49]

According to *Venus Schoolmistress, or Birchen Sports* ('1788'),[50] allegedly written by Theresa Berkeley, flagellant *extraordinaire*, luxuriously fitted-up establishments exclusively devoted to flogging could be found in London with whipping parlours situated in the bawdy houses in or around Covent Garden. In the preface, 'Mary Wilson',[51] the editor, describes the customers: 'It is true that there are innumerable old generals, admirals, colonels, and captains, as well as bishops, judges, barristers, lords, commoners, and physicians, who periodically go to be whipped, merely because it warms their blood, and keeps up a little agreeable excitement in their systems long after the power of enjoying the opposite sex has failed them.'[52] According to the 'memoirs', sexual arousal came not only through whips and birches but an entire contraption called the 'Berkeley horse' was designed specifically for the purpose of flogging gentlemen clients. Such titillating revelations were to become commonplace in a genre of material wholly concerned with depictions of flagellation experiences.

Prior to *MWP*, English erotica was less obscene than its French counterpart. English writers were slower to establish a more pornographic style in descriptions of sexual activities and were holding to innuendoes and metaphors, creating titillating erotica through insinuation but without the emphasis on explicit detail. However, *MWP* was not an isolated erotic fiction but carried subject matter common to French erotica, notably themes of sexual initiation, defloration and flagellation. These themes were not merely those created for a fantastical erotic world, but permeated contemporary culture and reflected subjects prevalent in the external world. These sexual topics were made up from a hotchpotch of discussions from medicine, religion and culture. Cleland was particularly important in that he was the first British writer to pull together these motifs into a coherent novelistic structure geared to the enjoyment of readable sex.

By the end of the eighteenth century, British writers had progressed to include more explicit commentary on sexual action, no doubt thanks to Cleland's example. More importantly, although English erotica inherited many of the French erotic predilections, it was maturing to develop its own style in describing predilections. This can be seen in its pandering more specifically to the demands of a British audience, notably in the flourishing of the English boarding school setting in flagellation material from the 1770s onwards.

Within this erotica, a variety of images of women existed. In the sexual initiation scenes, women were portrayed as passive (and therefore innocent), yet becoming insatiable once having experienced sex. With the introduction of the dominant female flagellant, traditional roles were reversed creating a further *frisson* by playing on men's fear (and pleasure) of the woman in authority. Within these depictions, displays of blood – traditionally a taboo subject – are a means to sexual arousal and hence blood became an essential ingredient in many erotic works.

CHAPTER SEVEN

'The Best Freind in the World':

The Relationship Between Emma Hamilton and Queen Maria Carolina of Naples[1]

Gender was very much a political issue during the eighteenth century, and men were at the forefront of negotiations during wartime. Yet two women, Emma Hamilton and Maria Carolina, Queen of Naples, made a significant contribution to the diplomatic efforts being made during the Napoleonic War. Neither woman was sufficiently recognized for her contribution during a particularly dangerous time in Europe. This chapter aims to shed light on the little-known story of two of the most fascinating women in history.

Emma Hamilton (baptized c.1765–1815) (Figure 7.1) has always been a celebrated figure in British history but generally seen as an appendage to the life of Horatio Nelson (1758–1805), rather than as a successful person in her own right. She is usually thought of as the epitome of the classic 'rags-to-riches' tale of an eighteenth-century woman whose attractiveness to men enabled her to drag herself up from an impoverished background to become the wife of the British ambassador to Naples, Sir William Hamilton (1730–1803), and mistress to the most famous naval commander in history. Yet, as this chapter will show, important historical consequences also flowed from her friendship with a member of her own sex, Queen Maria Carolina of Naples (1753–1814). Emma was attacked by her contemporaries, and more recently by her biographers, for being a drunk, a whore and a pretentious socialite. She was perhaps all these things, but she was also a genuine friend to those who needed her. Emma has been described as 'at best a rather silly woman' who 'brought little dignity to her husband's career and ended by

FIGURE 7.1 *Emma Hamilton as Circe*, by George Romney, c.1782. Wikimedia Commons.

becoming rather ridiculous.'[2] Yet Emma's relationship with Maria Carolina gave her opportunities to prove her worth by providing valuable assistance to Britain in its war with France, and assisting the Neapolitan royal family to escape a potentially disastrous situation.

To arrive at this stage, Emma had to overcome her illegitimacy, her lack of education, and her torrid reputation as a whore. While Nelson and her husband Sir William were both commended for their actions in Naples, Emma has been denied adequate recognition for her contribution to Britain's eventual victory. Maria Carolina, too, has been overlooked, yet she played an important role, taking over from her boorish uneducated husband King Ferdinand IV (1751–1825), allying her country to the British at a pivotal time in the war, and avoiding the fate of her sister Marie Antoinette (1755–1793).

The cooperation between Emma and Maria Carolina was unusual for its period, and some features, particularly the disparity between their social backgrounds, may have been unique. Few women had managed to become involved in political action, particularly commoners. Elizabeth I (1533–1603) and Anne (1665–1714) managed to wield power as sovereign queens; and high-ranking noblewomen such as Georgiana, Duchess of Devonshire

(1757–1806) and Sarah, Duchess of Marlborough (1660–1744) tried to exert political influence; these, however, were exceptional cases. It was, after all, not a time when women were expected to express political opinions. It has been suggested that the idea of 'political culture' is perhaps more appropriate than 'politics' for feminist historians as a framework for women's involvement in 'dispensing patronage, influencing decision-makers and elections, petitioning, demonstrating, gift-giving, entertaining, haranguing, reporting seditious conduct, writing and disseminating ideas in print form'.[3] The language of politics used by women was frequently based on power and privilege.[4] Yet Emma and Queen Maria Carolina stand out as examples of women operating at the very heart of military activities during a pivotal time of war. Their letters went much further than mere rhetoric; they not only spoke in warm tones of sincere friendship but also contained orders for meting out punishment to rebels, and undertakings to assist Nelson in carrying out the planned retribution.

Although there have been some explorations into the importance of female friendships over the last few decades of feminist history, there have been relatively few in the context of British eighteenth-century history, and they have been mainly explorations of relationships between women writers, or as part of an investigation into lesbian relationships.[5] Fewer still have examined political friendships between women.[6] None of Emma's biographers attributes great importance to the friendship between Emma and the Queen, mostly concentrating on Emma's relationship with Nelson and Hamilton.[7] Yet the relationship between Emma and Maria Carolina offers insights not only into intimacy between a queen and a commoner, but also into the strong political influences these women exerted in a realm where women were less known for their involvement.

The trajectory of Emma's life up to 1805, when Nelson died, is generally charted in terms of her relationships with men, but, on closer examination, women appear to be of crucial importance, too. Emma's life began in obscurity: even the date of her birth is uncertain.[8] Her father died soon after her birth, and her mother returned to her own mother's cottage in Hawarden, near Chester. From then on, Emma was brought up by her mother and grandmother, both major influential figures in her life. It was probably because of these early relationships that later she would find it easy to form close ties with another older woman, Maria Carolina. Impoverished and uneducated, Emma was a prime target for seduction, and in 1781 a country gentleman, Sir Harry Fetherstonhaugh (1754–1846), whisked her off to his country estate at Uppark in Sussex. Nobody could have realized it at the time, but this was the point at which Emma's circuitous route to high favour in the Neapolitan court began. Before the year was out, she was pregnant and abandoned, a 'fallen woman' cast out from respectable society. Luckily, Charles Francis Greville (1749–1809), whom she had probably met through Sir Harry, was on hand to rescue her. He agreed not only to look after her on the condition that she handed over her child to be brought up elsewhere, but also to take on her mother as housekeeper. He became a major step in Emma's social rise, providing the basis of an education that would serve her well at court. His most valuable service, however, was to tire of her, and arrange for his uncle, Sir William Hamilton (1731–1803), to take her off his hands.

Emma first met Hamilton (Figure 7.2) when he visited his nephew at their house in Edgware Row in the spring of 1783 after he had returned from Naples to bury his first wife. At this time, Hamilton was British ambassador to the Court of Naples having first been engaged to the post in 1764. He was an amiable old soul, described as 'tall, with a dark complexion, an aquiline nose, and an air of intelligence, blended with distinction'.[9] Having tired of Emma, Greville urged Sir William to invite her to Naples for a trial visit, telling him, 'You will be able to have an experiment without any risk'; in other words, he could try her out sexually, and send her back if not required.[10] At first, Emma was unaware of Greville's intentions and thought he had simply sent her for a holiday. She quickly grasped the reality of the situation; she had been dumped by Greville and was supposed to succumb to Hamilton as his mistress.

Despite her lack of attraction to the much older Hamilton, ever-pragmatic, Emma decided to make the most of her current situation, and began to exploit the opportunities in front of her. Naples was a glorious town full of

FIGURE 7.2 *William Hamilton. Wikimedia Commons.*

opera, pomp and splendour and, as Hamilton's consort, she was surrounded by riches and glamour. She had a chance to mix with royalty as well as to socialize on a grand scale that she had previously only dreamt of. Hamilton provided her with her own apartment in his home, the Palazzo Sessa, overlooking Naples Bay. He did everything he could to make her happy, taking her to the opera, and holding regular concerts for guests. He also provided drawing and dancing lessons, as well as Italian language lessons which would increase her accessibility to the queen and ultimately allow her to speak to Maria Carolina in her own language.

Emma's status, however, remained insecure. In order to be fully recognized by polite society, she must be formally received by ladies of the highest rank at their own homes. The necessary degree of respectability could be achieved only by making Hamilton marry her. Sir William, however, hesitated; he admitted to his friend Sir Joseph Banks (1743–1820), 'I assure you that I approve of her so much that if I had been the person that made her first go astray, I wou'd glory in giving her a public reparation, and I would do it openly, for indeed she has infinite merit and no Princess cou'd do the honours of her Place with more care and dignity than she does those of my house.'[11]

At this stage, Emma was entertaining up to 50 guests a night, including nobles and visitors on their Grand Tour. She had made her place so well in Naples that Hamilton recognized he had found a potential life-time companion and finally married her, the couple returning to England for the ceremony. On her return to Naples she was officially received at court, and was presented to Queen Maria Carolina.

At this time, Naples was not just a city but a state which took up a third of (as yet) non-unified Italy, part of 'the Two Sicilies' ruled by Ferdinand, a younger son of the Spanish royal family. As the eldest daughter of Maria Theresa of Austria (1717–1780), Maria Carolina was a political asset; her sister, Marie Antoinette (1755–1793) was to marry the ill-fated King Louis XVI of France (1764–1793) and follow him to his death. Maria Carolina had been married to Ferdinand when she was only 15 and he 17 to cement a political union between Austria and Spain. Ferdinand had lacked a proper education in his youth and had grown into an uncouth, boorish young man, chiefly interested in hunting, drinking and whoring. As a result, the task of ruling of the country was left to his wife. Educated and astute, she rose to the challenge, taking over the every-day political decisions with efficiency and flair, and introducing the liberal reforms favoured by the most enlightened despots.

Emma, now formally recognized as wife to the British Ambassador, immediately made herself agreeable to the Queen, and the Queen, as it seems from Emma's letters, made herself equally accessible to Emma. In December that year, Emma wrote to her old friend George Romney (1734–1802), soon after her marriage: 'I have been received with open arms by all the Neapolitans of both sexes, by all the foreigners of every distinction. I have been presented to the Queen of Naples by her own desire, she as [sic] shewn me all sorts of kind and affectionate attentions; in short I am the happiest woman in the world.'[12]

No doubt Emma's affable nature worked its charms, and the Queen probably liked her unpretentiousness. Emma, in turn, devoted most of her time to the Queen and delighted in her newly-established position of confidante to royalty. Both would benefit from the friendship. Maria Carolina was politically shrewd enough to recognize that the new wife of the British Ambassador could act as a mediator between the Court of Naples and Britain. Emma, although politically unsophisticated, was cunning enough to see this as a chance to advance her prospects at court. They were also sincerely attached to each other. Sir William recognized Emma's efforts to compensate for her lowly beginnings and was very proud of her. Writing to Horace Walpole (1717–1797) on 17 April 1792, he remarked, 'Lady H. who has had a difficult part to act & has succeeded wonderfully, having gained by having no pretensions, the thorough approbation of all the English ladies. The Queen of Naples, as you may have heard, was very kind to her on our return and treats her like any travelling lady of distinction. . . . She goes on improving daily. . . . She really is an extraordinary being.'[13]

Life in Naples, however, was to alter radically as the Napoleonic Wars unfolded. By 1793, Britain had joined the alliance fighting revolutionary France, and Nelson's arrival marked a turning point in the lives of both Emma and Maria Carolina. Britain needed a stronghold in the area to protect it from the French. Reinforcements were urgently needed and Nelson (Figure 7.3) was under orders to recruit troops from Turin and Naples to help maintain the British occupation of Toulon. With those instructions, Nelson sailed into Naples on the *Agamemnon* on 10 September with his British fleet. Although Naples was officially neutral, Hamilton and Sir John Acton (1736–1811), the Neapolitan prime minister, had negotiated a secret treaty between Britain and Naples earlier that year in July and formed an Anglo-Neapolitan alliance. Nelson, seen as the saviour of Naples, was offered 6,000 troops and was provided with the provisions he so desperately needed for his crew. 'My poor fellows have not had a morsel of fresh meat or vegetables for near nineteen weeks', Nelson complained in a letter to his wife, 'and in that time I have only had my foot twice on the shore of Cadiz.'[14] He devoted much of his time to discussions with Hamilton, Acton and the King. On the fourth day of his visit, he made a dramatically abrupt departure, in pursuit of a French man-of-war, and did not return to Naples for five years. Despite the brevity of Nelson's stay, the first meeting between himself, Emma and Sir William, as well as with the royal family, must have had a great impact on all of them, as they were to keep up a correspondence thereafter.

Maria Carolina was now living in fear that Naples, like France, would become a republic. By June 1793, Naples had become so volatile that the royal family decided to move temporarily to their palace in Caserta, just outside of the city. Emma wrote to Greville, 'For political reasons we have lived eight months at Caserta, that is, making this our constant residence &

FIGURE 7.3 *Horatio Nelson. National Maritime Museum, Greenwich, London, Greenwich Hospital Collection.*

going twice a week to town to give dinners, balls etc and returning here at 2 or 3 o'clock in the morning.'[15]

Despite the turbulent situation, guests continued to drop in at the villa on a regular basis. The Hamiltons continued to give dinners for 50 or more and suppers for 300 people and kept up their routine of dining with the royal family at midday on most days. Emma would spend up to three hours most evenings talking with the Queen, tête-a-tête. Nonetheless, Emma retained her level head and resisted any temptation to presume on their intimacy in public; her discretion increased her popularity with the ministers' wives, and confirmed the Queen's favour. Emma wrote to Greville, 'I had been with the Queen the night before alone *en famille* laughing and singing etc. but at the drawing room I kept my distance, and pay'd the Queen as much respect as tho' I have never seen her before, which pleased her very much.'[16]

By now, Emma had become the Queen's closest confidante. In 1794, she wrote to Greville:

> She is everything one can wish – the best mother, wife, and freind [sic] in the world. I live constantly with her, and have done intimately so for 2 years, and I never have in all that time seen anything but goodness and sincerity in her & if you ever hear any lyes about her contradick them & if you shou'd see a cursed book written by a vile French dog with her character in it don't believe one word . . . if I was her daughter she cou'd not be kinder to me & I love her with all my soul.[17]

Their feelings were mutual and the Queen took every opportunity to show her concern for Emma. When Sir William lay ill of a bilious fever, she wrote a note to Emma telling her to 'put confidence in God . . . who never forsakes those who trust in Him', and confirmed her 'sincere friendship'.[18] Emma confirmed that, 'My ever dear Queen as been like a mother to me since Sir William as been ill: she writes to me four or five times a day, and offered to come and assist me; *this is friendship*.'[19] Hamilton indicated that the Queen was increasingly susceptible to Emma's influence: 'The Queen of Naples seems to have great pleasure in her society. She sends for her generally three or four times a week. . . . [I]n fact all goes well *chez nous*.'[20]

Emma was now well placed to enter into political manoeuvres. With the Queen's encouragement, she began to play a significant diplomatic role in Naples. When King Ferdinand's brother, Charles IV of Spain (1748–1819), wrote him a series of clandestine letters urging him to ally himself with France, as Spain was planning to do, the Queen 'borrowed' the letters, made copies and placed them in Emma's hands, along with confidential papers 'which may be used by your husband'.[21] These were hastily couriered to London to inform the government of the latest political developments. Emma reported to Greville on 19 April 1795:

> against my will, *owing to my situation here* I am got into politicks, and I wish to have news for my dear beloved queen whom I adore nor can I live without her, for she is to me a mother, friend & everything . . . [S]he is the first woman in the world, her talents are superior to every woman in the world and her heart is the most excellent and strictly good and upright.[22]

In February 1796, Emma wrote to Lord George Macartney (1737–1806) about political affairs in the Neapolitan court; the King was having some difficulty in deciding what to do, or whose side to take, while the Queen was doing everything in her power to prevail upon him to throw his allegiance behind the British. Emma reported, 'I have this moment received a letter from my adorable Queen. She is arrived with the King. She has much to do to persuade him; but he approves of all *our prospects*. She is worn out with fatigue. Tomorrow I will send you her letter.'[23]

The situation in France was increasingly dangerous and Naples was becoming affected; Emma, Sir William and the royal family were now in the thick of political unrest. By June 1796, Sir William was becoming increasingly concerned, conveying his doubts to Greville as to the safety of Naples: 'I must own to you that I think Italy is in great danger of being completely plunder'd and ruin'd unless some unforeseen accident shou'd operate in her favour, and that very soon.'[24] Emma relayed to Greville the intrigues in which she was involved, while emphasizing her role in the drama:

> We have not time to write to you as we have been 3 days and nights writing to send by this courier letters of consequence for our government. They ought to be grateful to Sir William & *myself in particular*, as my situation at this Court is *very extraordinary*, & what no person as yet arrived at; but one as no thanks, & I allmost sick of grandeur. We are tired to death with anxiety, and God knows where we shall soon be, and what will become of us, if things go on as they do now.[25]

Maria Carolina was quick to realize that any protection she might gain for herself and her family against the encroaching French lay solely with the British and made various gestures to signal her new allegiance. She asked Emma to say to the company, 'God save great George our King', and declared she loved the British prince as she did her son.[26] As the French attacked British ships in the Mediterranean, allies dropped off one by one, and the British began to recall their ships from the area. Nelson, annoyed at the withdrawal of British support, complained bitterly to the Hamiltons in October: 'Till this time, it has been usual for the allies of England to fall from her, but till now she never was known to desert her friends while she had the power of supporting them.'[27] Meanwhile Maria Carolina despaired; spies were everywhere and capital sentences were being handed out; all the prisons were full of traitors and massacres were occurring in the streets. The King and Queen demanded contributions from the monied Neapolitans as they poured their own jewels and money into the battle against the French.

Emma's relationship with Nelson, and the Queen's relationship with Emma, were integral to the dynamics of these political machinations. They affected the Queen's decisions and the movements of Nelson, Emma and the royal family. Emma's relationship with Nelson allowed the Queen to place her trust in him, while Emma acted as intermediary between the Queen and Nelson. News of Nelson's victory at the Battle of St Vincent on 14 February 1797 cheered his friends back in Naples. Maria Carolina now felt confident enough to backtrack on her harsh policies, releasing all her captives. She was cheered on by the Lazzaroni, but Emma was perturbed. She complained to Nelson, 'these pretty gentlemen *that had planned the death of their Majesties* are to be let out in society again. In short, I am afraid all is lost here; and I am grieved to the heart for our dear Queen, who deserves a better fate ... I hope you will not quit the Mediterranean without taking us ... I trust in God and you, that we shall destroy those monsters before we go from hence.'[28]

The Queen was well aware that all her hopes lay with the British fleet. Nelson, loyal to the core, was stirred by Emma's letter: 'the picture you draw of the lovely Queen of Naples and the Royal Family would rouse the indignation of the most unfeeling of the creation ... I am bound – by my oath of chivalry – to protect all who are persecuted and in distress.'[29]

In May 1798, Nelson's storm-damaged ship, the *Vanguard*, was anchored off Elba, in urgent need of harbour and restocking; he relied on the assistance of the King to allow him to dock in one of the Sicilian ports. Emma hastily dashed off a letter to Nelson after a meeting with the Queen, and reassured him, 'The Queen desires me to say everything that's kind, and bids me say with her whole heart and soul she wishes you victory.'[30] Nelson replied,

> I have kissed the Queen's letter. Pray say I hope for the honour of kissing her hand when no fears will intervene, assure her Majesty that no person has her felicity more than myself at heart and that the sufferings of her family will be a Tower of Strength on the days of Battle, fear not the event, God is with us, God Bless you and Sir William.[31]

Emma was playing a pivotal role in reinforcing the Queen's reliance on the British fleet. Without Emma, it is doubtful whether the Queen would have so easily been persuaded to form an alliance between Naples and Britain. Indeed, Emma was to add to her list of claims that it was due to her influence that the Queen, without the King's knowledge, had provided a letter instructing all governors of the islands to give Nelson the assistance he needed and allow him to dock at their ports. Nelson, with his ships restocked at Syracuse and his crew rested, was ready for battle again. He wrote to Hamilton, 'Pray, present my best respects to Lady Hamilton. Tell her I hope to be presented to her crowned with laurel and cypress.'[32] The royal family were delighted by the news that Nelson had won the Battle of the Nile at Aboukir Bay on 1 August; Nelson had, at least for now, protected them and made the capital safe. In gratitude, the Queen sent Nelson a letter of congratulation accompanied by casks of wine and a guinea for every man on board.

The *Vanguard* landed back in Naples victorious on 22 September 1798. Emma (Figure 7.4) had been faithful to Hamilton, now 68, for 12 years, but it was inevitable she would be attracted to Nelson, since they both aspired to adventure and glory. The trust Maria Carolina placed in Emma

FIGURE 7.4 *Emma Hamilton in an attitude towards a mimosa plant, causing it to demonstrate sensibility.* Stipple engraving, 1789. Wellcome Library, London.

allowed her to rely on Nelson; her political manoeuvrings were, to a large extent, influenced by Emma's relationship with him.

Staying in Naples was becoming increasingly dangerous for the royal family and Emma urged them to make plans for their escape. The threat came from both sides of the class divide: the nobility and bourgeoisie were considering allying with the French in the hope they would be allowed to retain their privileges and rights; and the poor were tempted by promise of the Liberty, Equality and Fraternity that France purportedly offered. Emma employed various strategies to induce the Queen to leave. She explained to Nelson, 'I translate from our papers for her to inspire her or them, I should say, with some of your spirit and energy – how delighted we British were to sit & speak of you.'[33] She outlined the hideous possibilities which might befall them all if the Queen did not make her move soon:

> I flatter myself I did much whilst the passions of the Queen were up and agitated, I got up, put out my left arm, like you, spoke the language of truth to her, painting the drooping situation of this fine country, her friends sacrificed & her husband, children, and herself led to the Block, and eternal dishonour to her memory, after for not having been active, doing her duty in fighting bravely to the last to save her country, her Religion from the hands of the rapacious murderers of her sister [Marie Antoinette] and the Royal Family of France, that she was sure of being lost if they were inactive and there was a chance of being saved if they made use of the day, and struck now while all minds are imprest with the Horrers their neighbours are suffering from these Robbers.[34]

The King and Queen could see that it was time to flee before they suffered the same fate as Marie Antoinette and her husband, Louis XVI. After holding a council meeting, the royal party agreed it was time to remove what valuables they could and make for Sicily. All details for their departure had to be made in the utmost secrecy to allay any potential hysteria from the mob. The slightest suspicion by the populace of the royals' impending disappearance would inevitably lead to looting and rioting. With increasing unrest in Naples, it became evident that the royal family and the Hamiltons had to evacuate and Emma, keen to play out her role, began organizing their escape under cover. She declared that if the Queen were to die at her post, she would remain with her to the last: 'I feil [sic] I owe it to her friendship uncommon to me.'[35] Promising unswerving loyalty, she scribbled a note on the envelope of her letter to Queen Maria Carolina, 'Emma will prove to Maria Carolina that an humble-born Englishwoman can serve a queen with zeal and true love even at the risk of her life.'[36] Although Emma's declaration might appear theatrical, she possessed a strong loyalty to the Queen. She also recognized that she was embarking on a quest which, if the situation turned out as planned, would elevate her to the status of a true heroine.

The escape was to be executed under cover during a soirée given in Nelson's honour by Selim III (1761–1808), Sultan of Turkey. Prior to the night of the escape, Emma carried messages back and forth in preparation between Nelson and the royal family. Despatches from Maria Carolina to Emma show a desperate Queen clinging to the hope that Emma and Nelson would be able to carry out the plan. At a time when she saw herself as 'the most unfortunate of women, mothers, Queens', she saw Emma as her 'sincerest friend'.[37] Both the Hamilton and royal households had to take as many valuables as possible through secret tunnels between the Embassy, the Palace and the shore. The royal family managed to smuggle out linen, silver, jewellery and other possessions, using Emma as courier. Nelson wrote to Lord St Vincent (1753–1823), 'Lady Hamilton from that time [December 14] to 21 every night received the jewels of the royal family and such clothes as might be necessary for the large party to embark.'[38] Emma was in constant fear of being caught and torn apart by the ferocious mob.

The intention was to board Nelson's ship, the *Vanguard* on 21 December, and set sail for Palermo. Ten of the royal family went down to the quay in the dark. Emma reported to Greville,

> On the 21st at ten at night, Lord Nelson, Sir Wm., Mother & self went out to pay a visit, sent all our servants away, & ordered them in 2 hours to come with the coach, & ordered supper at home. When they were gone, we sett off, walked to our boat, & after two hours ... to the *Vanguard*. Lord Nelson then went with armed boats to a secret passage adjoining to the pallace, got up the dark staircase that goes into the Queen's room and with a dark lantern, cutlasses, pistols etc, brought off every soul, ten in number, to the *Vanguard* at twelve o'clock. If we had remained to the next day, we shou'd have all been imprisoned.[39]

The ship finally sailed out of Naples Bay at 7 in the evening of 23 December, a worse night than Nelson had seen in 30 years. Emma was to write to Greville, 'all our sails were torn to pieces, and all the men ready with their axes to cut away the masts'.[40] Pitched fiercely about, everyone was violently seasick except for Emma and her mother, Mrs Cadogan. The sickest was the Queen's six-year-old son, Prince Carlo Alberto, who became gradually worse. Despite Emma's constant nursing, he convulsed and died in her arms on Christmas Day. Emma reported to Greville, she had 'not a soul to help me, as the few women her Majesty bought on board were incapable of helping her or the poor royal children'.[41] After landing, the Queen was inconsolable with grief at the funeral service. Emma lamented, 'My adorable Queen whom I love better than any person in the world is allso unwell, we weep together & now that is our onely [sic] comfort.'[42] The King and Queen moved into the Colli Palace, while Hamilton set up a temporary embassy at the Villa Bastioni.

Emma's role in the enterprise had been favourably reported back to England and she was praised for her courage in the escape and onward journey. *The Times* for 28 January 1799 announced, 'We are informed from a very respectable authority that the Queen owed her safety much to the address of Lady Hamilton, who assisted in her getting away.' Hamilton confirmed to Greville the central role Emma had played. He wrote, 'Emma has had a very principal part in this delicate business as she is, and has been for several years the real and only confidential friend of the Queen of

Naples.'[43] Even Lord St Vincent commended her 'magnanimous conduct'.[44] Yet these contemporary tributes were forgotten as time went by. Despite her impressive display of courage, resourcefulness and diplomatic skill, Emma's role at this time has been consistently played down, most probably because she was a woman, and, worse still, a woman of dubious sexual reputation.

The Queen had, by now, come to rely on Emma to a considerable extent. Emma, in turn, did not take her role lightly. Sir William praised Emma's political acumen in a letter to Greville: 'Emma makes a great figure in our political line, for she carries on the business with the Queen, whose abilities you know are great.'[45] But by June, Emma was sick with worry. She had been supporting her royal friends and her husband through illness. Nelson complained that she was 'fretting' her 'guts to fiddle-strings'[46] as a result of her concern for Maria Carolina. The Queen once again relied on Emma's relationship with Nelson to persuade him to consider retaking Naples. Emma offered to go with him (along with Sir William), ostensibly to act as translator; this was perhaps the time when they first consummated their love. Nelson's ships pulled into Naples Bay on 24 June. In a letter to Emma, Maria Carolina gave instructions that immediate and severe punishments should be inflicted on the rebels, including the women involved.[47] Meanwhile, Emma recognized the importance of her position, boasting in a letter to Greville, 'The Queen is not yet come. She sent me as her Deputy; for I am very popular, speak the Neapolitan language, and [am] considered, with Sir William, a friend of the people.'[48] But it was a sad time for Emma as she surveyed the destruction which had been wrought: 'I saw at a distance our despoil'd house in town & Villa Emma that had been plunder'd & Sir Wm's new apartment, a bomb burst in it but it made me so low-spirited I don't desire to go again.'[49] Fourteen days after the trio's arrival, the King joined them in Naples but would not come ashore, preferring to remain on the *Foudroyant*, while the Queen remained in Palermo.

After regaining some control of the situation in Naples, the party landed back in Palermo in triumph on 8 August, and here, too, Emma received recognition for her exploits, along with her husband and her lover. The streets were thronged with crowds welcoming them, cries of *Viva Nelson! Viva Miledi! Viva Hamilton!* ringing out in honour of the conquering heroes. In appreciation for their loyalty, the Queen showered the trio with presents; Emma and Sir William were given jewellery worth approximately £6,000 for their help during the ordeal; Emma received a fine gold chain with the Queen's miniature; Hamilton received a huge yellow diamond ring; Nelson was given a diamond-encrusted sword owned by Louis XIV. The British government at last rewarded his endeavours with £2,000 and a gift of £10,000 from the East India Company for defending their route as a result of the Battle of the Nile.

In April 1800, after more than three decades of serving his country, Hamilton was recalled to Britain. Nelson was also told to come home. By this time Emma was pregnant with Nelson's child. The trio finally set of to

England via Austria in summer, accompanying the royal party; this comprised not only Maria Carolina, but also three princesses, two princes and 50 of her retainers. By the time they reached Vienna, news of their imminent arrival had preceded them and celebrations were in place to welcome them. The court threw banquets on their behalf, concerts were arranged for them, and firework displays filled the skies.

Realization of the imminent separation from Emma distressed the Queen, a situation Hamilton had foreseen. Writing to Greville, he lamented, 'the Queen is really so fond of Emma that the parting will be serious business'.[50] Emma also acknowledged, 'I am miserable to leave my dearest friend. She cannot be consoled.'[51] Maria Carolina gave Emma a gift of a diamond necklace carrying tresses of the hair of the royal children made into initials, by which to remember her. Her gift to Sir William was a golden snuff box, with a lid inlaid with portraits of herself and the King. Emma was never to see her beloved Queen again. Emma went on to have at least two children by Nelson (and possibly a third, a twin who died), and continued to share her life with the two men she loved, the trio living together in the house which Nelson bought for them in Merton, South London. Maria Carolina continued in power until her husband abdicated in 1812 in favour of his son Francis (1777–1830), upon which the Queen was exiled to her homeland of Austria. She died in 1814 (Figure 7.5).

Although others may have neglected or forgotten Emma's achievements in these dangerous times, Emma herself was fully aware of their significance and value. Eventually, she would claim that her actions entitled her to a pension from the British government. She asserted that, due to her deliberate manipulation of her relationship with the Queen, Britain obtained vital information about the shifting alliances of Spain towards France, and its declaration of war against England:

> By unceasing cultivation of this influence [with the queen] and no less watchfullness to turn it to my country's good, it happened that I discovered a courier had brought the King of Naples a private letter from the King Of Spain. I prevailed on the Queen to take it from his pocket unseen. We found it to contain the King of Spain's resolution to withdraw from the Coalition, and join the French against England. My husband at this time lay dangerously ill. I prevailed on the Queen to allow my taking a copy, with which I immediately dispatch'd a messenger to Lord Grenville, taking all the necessary precautions; for his safe arrival then became very difficult, and altogether cost me about £400 paid out of my privy purse.[52]

Both Nelson and Hamilton recognized that, without Emma's help, Nelson might not have obtained his supplies and been unable to go on to conquer the French fleet. Nelson was to write seven years later, on the morning of Trafalgar:

The British fleet under my command could never have returned the second time to Egypt had not Lady Hamilton's influence with the Queen of Naples caused letters to be wrote to the Governor of Syracuse, that he was to encourage the fleet being supplied with everything, should they put into port in Sicily. We put into Syracuse and received every supply; went to Egypt and destroyed the French fleet.[53]

This is a remarkable instance, not merely of an eighteenth-century female friendship, but one which took place in the political realm and had a direct

FIGURE 7.5 *Death mask of Queen Maria Carolina. Author's collection.*

influence on international politics at the highest level. British military history might well have been different if Emma and Maria Carolina had not felt such strong affection for each other. Yet Emma also exploited the situation to fashion herself as a heroine: she grabbed every opportunity that life presented to her, finding herself a well-connected husband, educating herself, and setting herself up as confidante to the Queen; then she rose to the occasion when it was demanded of her by rescuing the royal family. But there can be little doubt that her actions were also those of a fiercely loyal friend. The Queen, for her part, helped Emma achieve acceptance into high society, something she would never achieve back in England.

PART THREE
Exploring Bodies

CHAPTER EIGHT

Bodily Anxieties in Enlightenment Sex Literature

At the same time as erotic fiction was being developed, sexual literature in the form of sexual advice manuals was readily available in both French and English. Within both sets of this material, discussions about the body raised concerns about its functions, its sexual potential and its fallibility. Some of these anxieties came about as a result of scientific developments emerging during the Enlightenment which were questioning assumptions about the body.

In this chapter, I will explore and compare two sources of writings about sex and portrayals of the body – as seen in French pornographic texts and their English translations – and will compare how the body in erotica was conveyed in dominant medical opinion. Within this exploration I will examine how anxieties about the body were expressed and show how erotica did not necessarily follow the line of newer scientific debate but frequently expressed popular doubts about current medical assertions about the body, preferring to maintain beliefs in ancient theories. Frequently, we can see preservation of old value systems rather than a rush to embrace new promulgations on sex and the workings of the body.

Descriptions of the erotic body and its fluids, often retained surprisingly conventional views. Although historians have highlighted the radical nature of pornographic material,[1] its conservative element is an issue which has not previously been examined. The analysis within this chapter therefore raises unasked questions about the nature of taboo in pornography. Is pornography always radical or subversive? If not, when not? Which traditional components are maintained and why?

Prevalent images in some pornography, although radical in some respects, continued to retain dominant contemporary attitudes towards men's and women's bodies, particularly in respect to genitalia and bodily fluids. This affected the way in which bodies were depicted, the display of fluids within any particular body depending on whether they were male or female. Dominant themes emerged, such as sexual initiation, defloration, an interest in body parts and bodily fluids, and these were used to express anxieties about authoritative assertions made through science. Although to some extent these themes have been explored in *Memoirs of A Woman of Pleasure*, discussed in Chapter 6, this chapter will explore the other literature in greater detail, notably that of medical texts, competing pornographic material and continuing older cultural beliefs.

For purposes of clarity, I have divided the chapter into subsections. First, a brief definition will be given of the erotic material under examination. Second, I will look at the popular medical theories around the workings of the body based on the humoral system in order to see how far theories on the early modern body fit with ideas promoted in erotica. Third, I will examine how the humoral theory was incorporated into writings about blood in erotica. I will argue that blood became eroticized as a result of ancient attitudes towards female blood, heat and desire. These notions were expressed in eighteenth-century descriptions of the female bloodied body and deflowered virgins, which would also be found in erotica. Finally, I will look at how genital secretions were viewed in both medical opinion and in erotica, with a concern about masturbation emerging in popular medical opinions around bodily fluids other than blood, particularly sperm and vaginal ejaculations. Within this material, both the male and female erotic body would provide grounds for concern; the female body for its very abundance of fluids and its 'incivility' and ungovernable qualities; the male for its potential weakness from excess expulsion of fluids. I will argue that these ideas were either appropriated or dispelled within erotica in attempts to create an 'uncivilized' erotic body.

Although definitions of 'erotica' and 'pornography' have been hotly debated, it needs to be stressed that the eighteenth-century discourse held no such distinctions. A broad base of erotica was pumping out of London printing houses, from expensive, calf-bound, gilt-edged pornographic novellas to cheap ephemera, such as single sheets of bawdy poems, but as yet, no clear separation of material existed.[2] In this chapter, 'erotica' is used as a classification for a broad base of material which speaks of sexual matters, either in blatant form or couched in euphemism; this would include pornography, bawdy poems, metaphorical erotica, obscene satires and parodies, quasi-medical material and legal material, clandestine and Grub Street publications of many sorts. I use the term 'pornographic' to describe material which contains graphic description of sexual organs and/or action (for example, detailed description of masturbation, anal, oral and penetrative sex), written with the prime intention of sexually exciting the reader.[3]

The humoral system

Balancing bodily fluids was an essential element in medical advice on keeping the body healthy, an idea passed down from ancient medicine and popular religious beliefs. These ideas originated from the fifth-century BC Hippocratic belief of a humoral system which was responsible for regulating the body, a philosophy incorporated into Galenic physiology in the second century AD. Four humours were thought to control and harmonize the body: phlegm (phlegmatic), yellow bile (choleric), blood (sanguine) and black bile (melancholy) based on natural elements of water, fire, air and earth. These were respectively responsible for the wet, hot, dry and cold balances in the body, with fluids such as blood, semen, milk, sweat and tears all interchangeable. These fluids could mutate into each other, for example, female bleeding from an assortment of openings could be taken as 'diverted menstruation', menstrual blood able to flow through ears, skin, gums, fingers, saliva glands and tear ducts.[4]

Ridding the body of unwanted excess fluids was effected through bodily processes of sustenance, excretion, menstruation and lactation which balanced out the humours. Within this framework, the body had a set of internal procedures characterized by corporeal fluidity, openness, and porous boundaries.[5] The taking in or dispersing of too much fluids, or their dispelling too frequent, could prove perilous, therefore any elimination of them should take place in a measured way. However, even when following the sensible prescriptions of Galenic medicine, sometimes the body's humours fell out of balance.

In women, excess menstrual discharge might cause harm, as would excess emission of semen in men. Such outwards dispersal of fluids were seen as a sign of personal weakness – a lack of control over one's own body equated with an absence of control over one's emotions. Women's bodies were thought particularly prone to this type of behaviour and the unrestrained fluid-secreting body was more often depicted as female.[6] Gail Kern Paster has shown how early modern female bodies were seen as embarrassing 'leaky vessels', with women lacking control over their own bodily fluids allowing their bodily fluids to seep out. Within this world of emitting bodies, Norbert Elias has suggested that a 'civilising process' was taking place, involving a progressive hiding of body parts and functions as a result of a lowering threshold of disgust.[7] In response, pornographic material which traditionally rejected the status quo and embraced taboo subjects, would revel in the display of bodily fluids.

Ancient myths, old folklore beliefs and quack notions about the body were expressed through enthusiastic discussions about blood in medical, pseudo-medical and erotic texts. Humoral notions about bodily fluids, including concerns about blood, were conveyed through a wide range of sexual advice literature. These books fed off, and into, each other. Parts of

FIGURE 8.1 Tableau de l'Amour, c.1776. Wikimedia Commons.

Sinibaldus's *Geneanthropeiae* (1642) were handed down from Ancient Greek and Roman medical texts and then passed on, and repeated in *Rare Verities, The Cabinet of Venus Unlocked and her Secrets Laid Open* (1657).[8] Venette then popularized the latter in his *Tableau de L'Amour Conjugal* (1686) (Figure 8.1), translated into English in 1703[9] as *Mysteries of Conjugal Love Reveal'd*. Other advice books were dissected and reinvented in *Aristotle's Masterpiece* (1684) (Figure 8.2), which was reprinted in various editions throughout the eighteenth century. The information within the text changed over the period, but remained popular (Figure 8.3).[10] The books had originally been written to instruct married couples on the best sexual method to produce children. However, publishers deduced that the popularity of the books might not be simply due to their heavily-loaded advice on conception, but as a result of the effects of sexual arousal on readers. As Roy Porter has pointed out, apprentices were caught masturbating over one guide.[11] Warnings placed by publishers therefore alerted the readers as to the type of material at hand, in reality acting as a signal to erotica.[12]

FIGURE 8.2 *Frontispiece,* Aristotle's compleat master-piece ... displaying the secrets of nature in the generation of man, *12th edition. Wellcome Library, London.*

FIGURE 8.3 *Title page to* Aristotle's Compleat and Experienced Midwife ... *showing midwives attending a woman in bed and a newly born child, 1733. Wellcome Library, London.*

Concerns about blood in medical texts and pornography

Sex advice manuals presented ideas about women and the processes of their bodies in the context of humoral medicine, but they raised particular anxieties about blood. *Rare Verities* expressed concern about the expulsion of large amounts of blood which were considered potentially dangerous; while loss of blood on initial intercourse sometimes occurred, it may also prove fatal.[13] In the chapter on the 'Retention of the Courses', the menses was blamed for many ailments, notably when the blood becomes blocked and could not escape the body. The author states, 'Obstructions do so inflame the womb and genitals, that as they cause a prurition, so likewise they are the origin of a thousand dangerous symptoms. The sign of this indisposition of body is too too [*sic*] visible to every ones eyes; to wit, a universal paleness.'[14] *Aristotle's Masterpiece* (1690) considered the problems of green sickness in young virgins and barrenness in women; symptoms included amenorrhoea, pallid skin, loss of appetite and changes in behaviour. Green sickness was seen in particular to affect young pubescent girls as the author mentions, 'The former of these ill conveniences is too apparent in Virgins, especially such as are of a Flegmatick Complexion, evidently shewing itself by discolouring in the Face, in making it look green, pale, or of a dusky yellow, which proceeds from raw undigested humours....'[15] The book deals with all aspects of virginity, what it is, and how it is violated. Doctors are generally in agreement that the hymen is broken after intercourse:

> most are of the opinion that the Virginity is altogether annihilated when this Duplication is fractured and dissipated by violence, and that when it is found perfect and intire, no penetration had been made. Also some learned Physicians are of opinion that there is no Hymen or Skin expanded containing blood in it, which divers imagine in the first Copulation, flows from the fractured expanse.[16]

Many physicians held to the belief that the expulsion of blood upon first intercourse was proof that the women was a virgin. This idea was expressed in *Rare Verties* and reiterated in *Conjugal Love Reveal'd* (1712); Venette highlighted the notion, but he also made it clear that the lack of blood was no clear indicator of loss of virginity.

Such beliefs expressed in sex manuals were often reflected in pornographic fiction. However, the protagonists often disagreed with medical opinion. In opposition to Venette's belief, evidence of a hymen was regarded as necessary evidence in proving a woman's virginity as seen in *L'Académie des Dames* when it is evident that the bridegroom feels it necessary to check for the intact hymen of his bride.[17] Her husband is pleased at the discovery that he has taken a virgin bride. Octavia's future husband also inspects her vagina before intercourse to ensure her maidenhead is intact, the sight of blood necessary evidence of her chastity. Her mother eagerly examines the bloodstains on the bed, and declares, 'Pluck off this Smock, which I will keep for a Relick since it is stained with thy Virgin's Blood.'[18] Erotica therefore followed popular belief in that the sign of blood after intercourse was thought to be proof of a chaste bride.

Erotica harnessed existing themes of defloration and used them as a means to expose blood in order to transgress moral boundaries of acceptability which deemed blood to be kept hidden. The violation of the hymen was closely linked to blood taboos which prohibited encroachment into the interior of a woman's body. To produce an element of excitement, the erotica therefore had to depict the 'break' into a woman's body to reveal her 'private' blood, particularly that associated with her sexual organs.

Concerns about sexual fluids: the physicians' debate

Sexual discharges raised similar concerns about those on blood, sometimes resulting in conflicting debate. Orgasm for both men and women was seen as a necessary process for conception, particularly important in the heating of sexual fluids. Cooling of the sperm would hamper this process and coldness was blamed for impotency. However, excess seminal fluid was also cause for concern culminating in debates about the moral and medical dangers of masturbation creating a moral panic about its consequential effects. This evolved from biblical implications of the sin of Onan, or what was seen as the 'unnatural' practice of allowing sperm to fall on the ground, thereby wasting seed intended for procreation.

Discussions about masturbation, or 'self-pollution' as it was then called, were entrenched with myths about its life-threatening potential. Samuel-Auguste Tissot (1728–1797) was perhaps the most well-known exponent on the subject, a Genevan physician with a pan-European reputation who counted both Voltaire and Rousseau amongst his friends. His book *Onanism: or, a Treatise upon the Disorders Produced by Masturbation* (1760) was a huge success in France and England, shown by its numerous editions and translations from the Latin into French, English, Dutch and German.[19] In his treatise, he declared, 'The human seed ... proceeds from all the humors of the body, and is the most essential part of them. This is proved by the weakness, the faintness which accompanies the loss of it in the act of coition, be the quantity ever so small. There are veins and nerves, which, from all the parts of the body, concur to their centre in the parts of generation.'[20] The terrible disorders which might ensue from masturbation included epilepsy, convulsions, boils, disorders and death. Patients' mini-biographies acted as warnings to readers as to the possible results of over-ejaculation and the wasting of one's sperm. The case of a clockmaker, L. D., was supplied with the intention of frightening them in order to act as a deterrent. His vice started when he was 17 years old, and he began to masturbate three times a day; 'The slightest irritation immediately cured an imperfect erection, which was instantly followed by an evacuation of this liquor, which daily augmented his weakness.'[21] Violent pains ensued and he grew weaker and weaker until he eventually died in June 1757. Unsurprisingly after witnessing such an event, Tissot asserted that all sexual activity could be potentially dangerous, as the sudden rush of blood to the head might incur insanity.[22] Women might find an equally detrimental effect of masturbation as Tissot pointed out:

> Women are more particularly exposed to hysterical fits, or shocking vapours; to incurable jaundices; to violent cramps in the stomach and back; to acute pains in the nose; to the *fluor albus*, the accretion whereof

is a continual source of the most smarting pain; to descents and ulcerations of the matrix, and to all the infirmities which these two disorders brings on; to the excretion and darting of the clitoris; to the *furor uterinus*, which at once deprives them of decency and reason, and puts them upon a level with the most lascivious brutes, till a desperate death snatches them from pain and infamy.[23]

Differences here are evident in the way masturbation might affect men and women. Excess expulsion of vaginal fluid was not the dangerous issue for women as excess expulsion for men of excess sperm. Rather it would affect their minds rather than their bodies. Part of the reasoning behind this supposition was that women were thought to be lacking in emotional control and suffered from wild imaginations. They were also particularly susceptible to external influences.[24] Hence, female masturbation was cause for alarm because of the peculiar frailties of the female mind. Consequently, depictions of insane young female onanists as unbridled nymphomaniacs became common.

Shortly after the publication of Tissot's *Onanism*, M. D. T. Bienville's book *Nymphomanie, ou Traité de la Fureur Utérine* (1771) was published, the English translation (*Nymphomania, or a Dissertation Concerning the Furor Uterinus*) becoming available in 1775.[25] It failed to receive the critical acclaim of *Onanism*, although his medical ideas echoed long-standing assumptions about women's bodies, and such ideas would continue into the next century. Many medical texts, novels and society in general expressed ideas about female insanity, and it was thought to be promoted by uncontrollable passions particularly associated with women. Bienville asserted that any female onanist (or woman who masturbated) was prone to falling into such an abandoned state. Her wild imagination was thought to be responsible for her increasing inability to control herself. She became unruly and ungovernable. He affirmed,

> it is then, that breaking down, without the least remorse, the barriers of modesty, they betray each shocking secret of their lascivious minds by proposals, to the expressions of which even ears not uncommonly chaste cannot listen without horror, and astonishment; and soon the excess of their lusts having exhausted all their powers of contending against it, they throw off the restraining, honourable yoke of delicacy, and, without a blush, openly sollicit in the most criminal, and abandoned language, the first-comers to gratify their insatiable desires.[26]

Physical changes also affected a woman's body as a result of her masturbation, as the clitoris became swollen and larger 'than in discreet women'.[27] A disorder in the uterus was blamed for causing a delirious melancholia which swept over them and, in turn, caused 'a maniacal *deliriumi*', in effect seen to be a disorder of the woman's brain. In this framework, a woman's sexuality was closed aligned with her imagination.[28] The reading of 'lascivious novels' was thought only to encourage this kind of behaviour.

Masturbation was thought to affect men and women differently, although equal concerns were given to them both. Medical opinions described a masturbating woman as sexually rapacious, abandoned and out of control, deranged and hysterical. Her afflictions would be those of the mind, leading to uncontrollable desires and deranged imaginings – a man may well become slightly melancholic, but a woman would become insane. However, an excessively masturbating man retained control of his reasoning faculties. His afflictions would show up physically in debilitation as a result of losing too much sperm thereby unbalancing his bodily humours and weakening himself. A woman's vaginal fluids were not considered important, with no 'vital force' and therefore dispensable. Unlike sperm, vaginal secretions played no part in this analysis.

Concerns about sexual secretions in erotica

Popular medical concerns over the loss of male body fluids, particularly semen, were shared by pornographic fiction, as was the *lack* of anxiety over female expulsion of vaginal secretions. Although men's health was portrayed as detrimentally affected by these emissions, women were seen to benefit from their orgasms. Indeed, in pornographic works, female ejaculations were positively fêted. Furthermore, contrary to scientific postulations, in erotica, female masturbation did not pose the threat suggested by medics. Women were portrayed as being able and willing to indulge at their leisure without physical or mental repercussions. This image of female insatiability in erotic prose therefore sometimes clashed with the medical image of nymphomania. Although women in erotica were frequently portrayed as sexually rapacious, they were rarely adversely affected. If anything, they were portrayed as full of *joie de vivre*. If they did become melancholic, it was due to a lack of sexual activity rather than too much.

Old-fashioned understandings about the mechanisms of sex persisted from the previous century into the eighteenth century and were incorporated into erotica. In *A Dialogue between a Married Lady and a Maid* (1740), the ancient medical notion of female ejaculation is reiterated in comparison between female and male genitalia. Readers are led to believe that the clitoris is the part responsible for the orgasm, ejaculating a liquid:

> Just before them, towards the upper Part of the C___t, is a Thing they call the *Clitoris*, which is a little like a Man's P____k, for it will swell and stand like his; and being rubbed gently, by his Member, will, with excessive Pleasure, send forth a Liquor, which when it comes away, leaves us in a Trance, as if we were dying, all our Senses being lost, and as it were summed up in that one Place.[29]

Mutual masturbation between women played a substantial role in sexual initiation, and the expulsion of vaginal fluids and female ejaculation were seen as natural occurrences. This joint sex act is introduced in *Histoire de Dom B. . . . . .portier de Chartreux* (1743)[30], as an experienced nun feigns fear of a thunderstorm in an attempt to seduce her fellow sister:

> I tried to comfort the Sister, who, in the meantime, had put her right thigh between mine, and the left under; while in this position she rubbed herself against my right thigh, thrusting her tongue into my mouth and smacking my buttocks with her hand. After she had done this for some time, I thought I felt my thighs wetted. She gave several deep sighs, which I imagined arose for her fear of the thunder.[31]

The scenarios in erotica depicted women as squirting fluids indiscriminately with no side effects; loss of vaginal fluids did not make them ill, as it did men. Books such as *The Uterine Furies of Marie-Antoinette, Wife of Louis XVI* (1791) and *The Private, Libertine, and Scandalous Life of Marie-Antoinette* (1791)[32] (both originally French) conveyed a lack of concern about any fluid loss in women, but incorporated connections between masturbation and tribadism as seen in Bienville's 'Uterine Furies'. Copious vaginal secretions were thereby depicted as an obvious sign of female sexual proclivity, and as such, a phenomenon to be enjoyed.

The male genitalia and its ejaculations were equally celebrated in *Dialogue between a Married Lady and a Maid*. Tullia explains to Octavia the amazing and enjoyable power of the male ejaculation, 'for it come out with that Force, that it leaps two Foot or more from 'em upon spending'.[33] The strength of an ejaculation is an obvious indication of a man's virility. However, in keeping with medical opinion of the day, men were weakened by sexual activity.

An examination of late seventeenth- and eighteenth-century French and English erotica shows that a form of writing existed which expressed older ideas rather than embracing new medical Enlightenment opinion. The traditional opinions contained certain attitudes about women and men and their bodily functions, particularly the evacuation of blood, sperm and vaginal secretions. Descriptions of these genital discharges were used to enhance erotic value and were exhibited graphically and in detail. While exposing the body and its fluids, erotica often incorporated medical opinions already prevalent elsewhere. Some themes present in sex manuals were echoed in realistic pornographic scenarios of sexual activities which discussed anxieties about menstrual blood, fears of seminal loss, and unrestrained female sexuality; these expulsions were connected to a lack of control over ones own body. However, in erotica, bodily fluids were expressed rather than contained. The more pornographic the descriptions, the more emissions were displayed in a reaction to the advocation of restraint and control in 'civilized' opinion.

A gendered view existed which prescribed one set of values for men, and another for women. Anxieties about the loss of sperm were related to sperm being seen as the vital force of life. Because it was of limited quantity, it was therefore to be preserved. Yet female sexual secretions were seen as copious, unlimited and expendable. Concern lay around not safe-guarding their expenditure but containing them. Erotica conveyed women as lacking in self-discipline, revelling in their own free-flowing emissions, and therefore irrational and inferior. Moreover, an abundance of vaginal mucus was seen as synonymous with an assertive sexuality, and as such was coveted yet perceived as threatening. A gendered perspective of blood was also apparent in erotica, where female blood was frequently displayed yet male blood was rarely exposed.

Because the civilized body was seen to be one in control of its fluids, the exposition of a female body gushing liquids had the effect of an ungovernable, or 'uncivilized' body. In erotica, this body was a humoral body intended to excite with its free-flowing juices. The fact that women were not in command of their own bodily fluids contributed to a definition of them as uncontrolled (and uncontrollable) and therefore ungovernable.

Exposure of blood and bodily fluids signified an underlying concern about female insatiability and ferocious sexual appetites. Women posed a threat in that they were capable of draining men of their fluids (and life force). Pornography portrayed a female body which continually escaped its confines whereby its very incivility would continue to excite and embarrass. Although the female body might have caused some concerns, nonetheless it was lauded for its sheer abandonment.

CHAPTER NINE

Medicine, the Body and the Botanical Sexual Metaphor in Erotica

Arbor Vitae, *or* the Tree of Life, *is a succulent Plant; consisting of one straight Stem, on the Top of which is a* Pistillum, *or* Apex. . . . *Its* Fruits, *contrary to most others, grow near the Root; they are usually no more than two in Number.*

ARBOR VITAE OR, THE NATURAL HISTORY OF THE TREE OF LIFE[1]

The Frutex Vulvaria *is a flat low Shrub, which always grows in a moist warm Valley, at the Foot of a little Hill, which is constantly water'd by a Spring, whose Water is impregnated with very saline Particles, which nevertheless agree wonderfully well with this* Shrub.

NATURAL HISTORY OF THE FRUTEX VULVARIA[2]

In 1732, two humorous pieces of erotica, *Arbor Vitae* and *The Natural History of the Frutex Vulvaria* were published, which contained detailed descriptions of the nature and functions of the male and female sexual organs. In this material, writers of erotica took up botanical metaphors for genitalia to openly question scientific ideas which were circulating during the early eighteenth century. In this erotica, the male tree or plant was a representation of the penis, and the shrub was a portrayal of the female genitalia. Although presented as titillating bawdy facetiae, these texts conveyed a certain set of attitudes towards the body and expose underlying assumptions about male and female sexual behaviour.

This ribald humour was written by way of a general homage to sexual activity, but it also challenged serious scientific assertions on generation, degeneration and venereal disease which were current among the medical elite. Scathing attacks were made on the *virtuosi* (or gentleman amateur collector and studier of the new sciences) and their new botanical notion of attaching gender to plants. The *virtuosi* were generally from a genteel background, having time and leisure to indulge in experiments or their promotion, and having the money to travel to establish a rare plant collection. Their frequent lack of knowledge of basic science together with their gullibility made them an easy target for the satirists. Mary Astell, in *Character of a Virtuoso* (1686), summed them up: 'He Trafficks to all places, and has his Correspondents in every part of the World; yet his Merchandizes serve not to promote our Luxury, nor increase our Trade, and neither enrich the Nation, nor himself.'

Little in the new developments escaped ridicule – from propositions being made in pre-formationism and epigenesism, to ovism and homunculism,[3] everything was a target for these satirists. In this whimsical erotica, they began to parody debates already taking place on scientific and medical issues, particularly the disputes as to which sex provided the primal force in generation. However, these writings were not merely skits on scientific theories of the day, but were public criticisms of the conflicting theories circulating in wider society, which also expressed concerns about male and female bodies. The Royal Society was to become the main butt of these satirical works, with quacks targeted as a side-line.

While this erotica does not show how far sexual behaviour was changing per se, it does show how older sexual beliefs and myths continued to shape shifting attitudes to eighteenth-century debates on anatomy and the physiology of sex. These discussions in erotica about the body surrounding procreation, disease and degeneration help to uncover further layers of cultural assumptions. They reveal just how far (or how little) new Enlightenment ideas influenced people's opinions and subsequently infiltrated popular bawdy material, and how these ideas were sifted and re-interpreted. Specifically, I will explore here two sets of gendered erotica containing botanical metaphors, to see how they conveyed a certain set of attitudes about sex, the body and sexual behaviour. However, caution needs to be exercised when examining this sort of material as satire inverts much of the meaning.

Although the eighteenth century is known as a licentious era, a new sexual anxiety emerged, which raised male concerns about women's bodies, an idea highlighted in this erotica.[4] Notions of female insatiability were prevalent in the wider culture,[5] as were speculations around nymphomania, hysteria and adolescent disorders. Popular bawdy material embodied these anxieties around the body, particularly male fears of cuckoldry, castration, impotence and the insatiability of women.[6] These concerns were also frequently voiced in erotica and ribald humour, the authors reflecting public apprehensions. Scientists' and medics' new assertions about the workings of the body were often disparaged, and frequently condemned. This meant that, in reality, there was no one coherent attitude to sex in the eighteenth century. Rather, the body was the subject of both scientifically professed fact, imagination and experience in daily life.

Historical context

Erotica emerged against a backdrop of a rapidly developing society with Enlightenment ideas being filtered through essays, fiction and coffee houses. Science served as a thin mask under which sex could be discussed,[7] and a plethora of quasi-medical erotica was already being published. The writers of such works were obviously quick to cash in on public eagerness to consume literature which combined sex, taboos and conjectures in science. Popular sex guides aimed at ordinary readers (as opposed to medical texts aimed at doctors or professions) proliferated and conveyed advice on sexual etiquette, fertility, pregnancy and warnings of venereal disease. Many such books regurgitated older scientific suppositions, particularly about the need for the emission of seed from both sexes to effect conception. Teachings dating back to Hippocrates, Aristotle and Galen, and medieval humoral medicine were incorporated into the material, which only added to the confusion. An example of this can be seen in the writings of Nicolas Venette, who wrote in *Conjugal Love Reveal'd* (1712):[8]

> It is also highly necessary, that in their mutual embraces they meet each other with equal ardour; for if the spirit flag on either part, they will fall short of what nature requires, and the woman must either miss of conception or else the children prove weak in their bodies, or defective in their understanding and therefore I do advise them, before they begin their conjugal embraces, to invigorate their mutual desires, and make their flames burn with a fierce ardour, by those ways that love teaches better than I can write.[9]

Venette viewed women as libidinous as men, and incorporated Hippocrates' argument that because of the 'intensity of pleasure involved', the seminal fluids were emitted from both male and female and were both equally necessary for conception. Similarly, John Maubray in *The Female Physician* (1724) stated that both sexes contributed to 'seminal matter'.[10] Both writers incorporated the premise that the pleasure of women was necessary for conception, thereby buttressing the idea that women needed an orgasm and ensuring women received sexual gratification.

Some physicians asserted that sexual intercourse was a cure for certain ailments. Dr Robert James (1705–1776), a friend of Dr Johnson, famous for his fever powder and pills, stated in *The Ladies Physical Dictionary* (second edition, 1740) that sperm was good for women's disorders: 'Venery both alleviates and removes various Disorders incident to Women: for the male

Semen, consisting of a fine elastic Lymph, rarefies and expands not only the eggs, but also, the Blood and Juices in the Vessels of the Uterus.' While too much sex might do harm to the male physique, 'too great a Retention of the Semen induces a Topor and languid State of the Body, and often lays a Foundation for terrible nervous Disorders'.[11] Not all medics agreed that sex was good for the body and some even believed it to be potentially life-threatening. Samuel Tissot (1728–1797), author of *Onanism or a Treatise upon the Disorders Produced by Masturbation* (1761) believed that all sexual activity was potentially dangerous, because of the rush of blood to the head posing a threat to one's sanity.[12] Sexual manuals frequently posited suppositions such as those advanced by John Marten in his book, *A Treatise of all Degrees and Symptoms of the Venereal Disease* (1708), which dismissed widespread myths that intercourse during the menses could excoriate a man's glans and prepuce, and even infect him with venereal disease. However, in *Gonosologium Novum* (1709), he continued to follow traditional beliefs about female insatiability, asserting that the penis 'is a Part in great Esteem among Women' and 'instantly inflames their Hearts with a Passion not presently assuag'd'.[13]

Erotica played with metaphors for procreation which abounded in the popular medical handbooks of the day.[14] In *The Midwives Book* (1671), Jane Sharp uses extended metaphors to expound theories of generation and descriptions of genitalia: 'The Cod as it were the purse for the stones to be kept in with the seminary Vessels; the stones' two whole kernels like the kernels of a woman's paps, their figures Oval, and therefore some call them Eggs ... they feel exquisitely ... those that have the hottest stones are most prone to venery ... The Yard is as it were the Plow wherewith the ground is tilled, and made fit for the production of Fruit.'[15] The 'Yard' is analogous to the 'Plow', which represents the 'active' male farmer inseminating the 'passive' female earth and deploys a device commonly used in the late seventeenth and early eighteenth century, incorporating terminology of the terrain. Similar connections, in which earth was associated with fertility, were being made in early erotica such as *Erotopolis, The Present State of Bettyland* (1684),[16] in which farmers tilling the soil serve as an analogy for sexual intercourse, the women being depicted as the soil and the landscape. The popularity of this such topographical erotica can be seen in the number of editions, reprints and reworkings available in the 1730s and 1740s, including *The New Description of Merryland* (1741), *Merryland Display'd* (1741) and *The Merryland Miscellany* (1742).

Techniques of describing sexual organs in a way which was inoffensive can be traced back to classical literature and is part of erotic folklore.[17] Sexual imagery in the form of botanical metaphors also had roots in biblical references.[18] However, although originally associated with fertility, in erotica, the tree of life is more related to virility and female sexuality, and fecundity is to be avoided wherever possible, as will be discussed below. In much contemporary erotica, pregnancy is seen as a nuisance interfering with the enjoyment of sex, and the elimination of 'tumours' (abortions) is advocated.

Potent images of the earth, its fruits and fertility were still widely circulating in the early eighteenth century. Despite the alleged meteoric shifts in ideas effected by the Scientific Revolution, perceptions of the world appear to have altered less radically than has commonly been supposed; the social, scientific, and sexual aspects of life were all intertwined,[19] and new ideas were grafted onto old traditional themes. The separation of medicine and botany had not yet taken place, and there was ready shuttling of information between studies of nature, botany and theories on generation.

Scientific developments

Images linking the earth and soil with the body were not the only naturalistic metaphors being used. Specific connections were also being made between the body, plants and nature in botany. Seventeenth-century scientists had already been drawing analogies between the ovule and the mammalian foetus of a mammal. R. J. Camerarius, in *Epistola de sexu plantarum* (1694) regarded seeds as 'the significance of male organs, since they are the receptacles in which the seed itself, that is the powder that is the most subtle part of the plant, is secreted and collected, to be afterwards supplied from them. It is equally evident, that the ovary with its style represents the female sexual organ in the plant.'[20]

This development of the botanical sexual metaphor in erotica was directly associated with new developments in botany in the late seventeenth and early eighteenth century, particularly in the work of Carl Linnaeus (1707–1778), who made significant innovations in the classification of plants, basing this entirely on the structure of their flower and fruit parts.[21] He used gender as the main principle in attempting to organize revolutionary views on nature, and gave rise to an emphasis on sexual difference in plant terminology.[22] In his descriptions of 'nuptials' of living plants and 'bridal beds' of flower petals, Linnaeus was defining the laws of nature in the same terms as the social and sexual relations between men and women.[23]

In his *Praeludia sponsaliorum plantarum* (1729), Linnaeus drew a comparison between the sexuality of plants and that of people, labelling the parts of the plant as parts of the male or female body: the filaments of the stamen were seen as the vas deferens, the anthers became testes; the stigma corresponded to the vagina, the seed to the eggs. Linnaeus' work was based on the difference between the male and female parts of flowers; and the correlation between plants, nature and the body can be seen directly through his sexualization of plants. Such terminology allowed for erotic interpretation,[24] particularly because of the phallic terms he used, as is seen in the translation of his *Systema naturae* (1735).[25] There, the descriptions of plants have distinctly sexual overtones; leaves are described as 'naked', 'erect', 'stemless', 'membranous', 'hairy', 'shrubby' and even 'pubescent', and the terminology is that used in the sexual anatomy of humans: for example, 'receptacle', 'fruits' and 'seeds'. Linnaeus' system achieved wide circulation and critics of the Linnaean system, which granted a sexual life to flowers, were quick to take up an attack on the notion as ridiculous. The very sexual nature of the language used by Linnaeus was open to ribald humour, an obvious target for lewd humorists, and gave sharp-witted satirists a chance to make an easy profit on bawdy parodies in the eroticization of botany.

Arbor Vitae

The botanical metaphor as seen in *Arbor Vitae* and *History of the Frutex Vulvaria* was a specific response to the new developments in botany which incorporated gendered terminology, and described a sexual life, for plants. This erotica not only drew upon an existing tradition in which male and female bodies were seen in agricultural terms but also reflected the content and style of popular medical handbooks.

The Natural History of Arbor Vitae purported to be a tale of the tree of life but is in fact a portrait of the male genitalia, and how to deal with its maladies. It considers the dimensions of a perfect penis: 'It is produced in most Countries, tho' it thrives more in some than others, where it also increases to a large Size. The Height here in *England*, rarely passes nine, or eleven Inches, and that chiefly in *Kent*.'[26] The functions and growth of the genitalia are also given due attention, with a description of male youth coming to full sexual development during adolescence: 'The Tree is of slow Growth, and requires Time to bring it to Perfection, rarely feeding to any purpose before the Fifteenth Year; when the Fruits coming to good Maturity, yield a viscous Juice or balmy Succus.'[27]

The author expresses the delights of a penis in its prime at the same time playing on the audience's fears of impotency. Friendly advice is offered to the reader in a double entendre which brings together the practices of gardeners splinting up older plants and flagellation as a means to stimulate the flagging libido, 'Birchen Twigs' being used for both: 'In the latter Season (winter), they are subject to become weak and flaccid, and want Support, for which Purpose some Gardeners have thought of splintering them up with *Birchen Twigs*, which has seem'd of some Service for the present, tho' the Plants have very soon come to the same, or a more drooping State than before.'[28]

'Birchen twigs' or whipping crops were frequently referred to in erotica and would have been recognized as instruments and aids used in sexual activities.[29] Flagellation was considered to be a medical cure for impotence, as it was thought to animate the blood supply and encourage erection. John Henry Meibomius' *A Treatise on the Use of Flogging in Venereal Affairs* (1718) was a serious medical work originally published in Latin, which advocated flogging to raise the blood as a cure for impotence. A translation of the work was republished by Edmund Curll, the notorious publisher of erotica, for which he was prosecuted, illustrating the fine line between medical and obscene literature.[30]

The writer of *Arbor Vitae* gives a further cure for removing the scrotum: 'Some *Virtuosi* have thought of improving their Trees for some Purposes, by taking off the *Nutmegs*', although how this was to help is not explained. It is possibly a reference to the assumed virility of the Italian opera-singing castrati, well-known for escorting women of fashion around town. Another suggestion was the practice of ligature around the penis to aid erection. This, however, was not without its hazards:

> The late ingenius Mr. *Motteux* thought of restoring a fine Plant he had in this condition, by tying it up with a *Tomex*, or Cord made of the Bark of the *Vitrex*, or *Hempen Tree*: But whether he made the Ligature too strait, or that Nature of the *Vitrex* is really in itself pernicious, he quite kill'd his Plant thereby; which makes this universally condemn'd as a dangerous Experiment.

The reference alludes to the recent scandal of Peter Anthony Motteux (1660–1718), a dramatist who wrote satirical plays with evocative titles such as *Love's a Jest*, *The Loves of Mars and Venus* and *The Temple of Love*. He also edited the *Gentleman's Journal or the Monthly Miscellany*. He had died in a house of ill fame in 1718 in Star Court, Butcher's Row near St Clement's church where he had gone with a woman named Mary Roberts after calling in at White's chocolate-house. Roberts alleged that he had been taken ill while still in the coach but the brothel-keeper and her daughter were committed to Newgate to await the inquest as there had been much speculation surrounding the incident.[31]

In *Arbor Vitae*, a good dose of sex is proffered as an aid for curing a wide variety of female disorders following a long tradition of such practical advice: 'The Virtues are so many, a large Volume might be wrote of them. The Juice, taken inwardly, cures the Green-sickness,[32] and other Infirmities of the like Sort, and it is a true Specific in most Disorders of the Fair Sex. It indeed often causes Tumours in the Umbilical Region.'[33] For a cure for syphilis, the author points to various infamous quacks and their remedies. One prominent figure is a certain Mr Humphrey Bowen, a 'judicious Botanist' who, in his book *La Quintyne*, cautions against the 'poisonous Species of *Vulvaria*', which are 'too often mistaken for the wholesome ones'. He 'has seen a tall thriving Tree, by the Contact only of this venomous Shrub become *porrose scabiose*, and covered with *fungous Excrescence's* not unlike the Fruits of the *Sylvestris*: . . . these venomous shrubs have spread the Poison through a whole Plantation'.[34] The spread of the disease is blamed on women here, reflecting the general public sentiment. Another, better-known, French physician, Dr Misaubin, was ironically lauded for his wonderful cures for venereal diseases, although in reality he had excited much ridicule in London society for his accent and manners.[35]

Women's bodies were portrayed as bodies with powerful desire, and alternatively might also be nurturing or corrupt.[36] Depictions of the body-politick through the notion of degeneration can be seen in *Arbor Vitae*, and in other contemporary erotica such as *Potent Ally* (1741) which refers to disease and places where whores can be found. It also includes political satire and reflects concerns about decay, decadence and dissolution, declaring, 'It must be confessed however, that *Corruption* has crept in some Boroughs, but these are generally of the *poorer Sort* ... the Corrupters themselves, however, anxious to conceal their wickedness, have made some Atonement, by their Readiness to *wipe off stains*, and rejecting the means of spreading Infection.'[37] Concerns surrounding size, function, degeneration and diseases are similarly expressed in the *Frutex Vulvaria*.

Natural history of the *Frutex Vulvaria*

The 'Flowering Shrub' of botanical terminology became a recognized metaphor for vagina and pubic hair, to be taken up in *Natural History of the Frutex Vulvaria* (1732), a counterpart to the Tree of Life. In this erotica, both nature and the female form were revered in florid sexual descriptions of plants and nature/woman. The *Frutex Vulvaria* is described as 'a flat low Shrub, which always grows on a moist warm Valley, at the foot of a little Hill, which is constantly water'd by a Spring whose Water is impregnated with very fine Particles, which nevertheless agree wonderfully well with this *Shrub*'. Unlike in contemporary views of nature held by scientists such as Linnaeus, the female was not relegated to an inferior position to the male, but was given equal admiration and held in similar esteem.

In *Frutex Vulvaria*, the proportions of the female genitalia were of major importance in consideration of its beauty, a small-sized vagina being one characteristic of the English woman which was obviously well-prized. Moreover, the English version is considered far superior to its European counterparts because of this very fact:

> Contrary to the *Arbor Vitae*, which is valued the more the larger it is in Size, the *Vulvaria* that is least is most esteem'd; for which Reason our *English* Shrubs are priz'd vastly more than those grown in *Italy*, *Spain*, or *Portugal*; and indeed, those that are above five inches in Diameter, are worth little or nothing.[38]

Despite this veneration of the female genitalia, attitudes to mercenary sex and venereal disease continued to apportion blame for the spread of disease to female prostitutes. Women were presumed to infect more men than vice versa, and the pox was thought more difficult to cure in a woman; we find 'more bad Symptoms in the *Shrub* than in the Tree, but are more difficult to be remedied, and will diffuse their Poison a great deal farther; since, for the one *Shrub* that the *Tree* can hurt, the *Shrub,* when infected, may spoil twenty *Trees*'.[39] The quack John Marten offered advice to men to withdraw as soon as possible to avoid catching the pox from women, warning that if 'the Man made long stay in the Women's Body, and through excessive Ecstasy, Heat and Satiety, welter and indulge himself in that Coition, (that) is much sooner way to attract the *Venom*, than quickly withdrawing'.[40] However, although women had frequently been castigated for their role in sexual degeneracy, in *Frutex Vulvaria*, men are seen to be as much to blame. Attacks on men were iterated in mocking criticism of the withering plants of the realm, while women were lauded for their attempts to stir the flailing members.

'Anxiety-making' and trading in fear of the pox was the hall-mark of quack doctors, and adverts for wonder treatments for venereal disease were even carried in such respectable magazines as *The Female Tatler*.[41] This proliferation of medical charlatans was highlighted by the writers of erotica, who attacked them, warning the reader about the side-effects of alleged medical 'cures'. They criticized the incorrect treatments given to women suffering venereal infections and vilified uneducated quacks for their misdiagnoses, at the same time linking women and plants together in the imagery of insect infestation: 'Some unskilful *Botanists*, who have not been apprised of the Nature of these Insects, have imagin'd that their Shrubs have been infected by the Contact of a poisonous *Arbor Vitae*, and have accordingly applied a Remedy proper only for that Disorder, which instead of doing any Good has quite spoil'd the *Shrub*.'[42] In this particular instance, the treatment of lice with preparations for the pox had a notable harmful effect, and was given as an example of the worthless medical treatment for venereal disorders and the widespread ignorance of the nature of sexual diseases and contagion.

Contemporary medical arguments resulting from investigations in anatomy and physiology were taken up by this erotica, and curiosity about the body showed itself in extended discussions on embryology and procreation. Attitudes to the body had become increasingly diverse and chaotic, and perceptions of the body became problematic. Theories queried ranged from whether or not the vagina produces its own juices, to the necessity of orgasm in sexual reproduction. More specifically, female orgasm had been seen to be necessary for pregnancy, but this idea was changing with William Harvey contending that the 'violent shaking and dissolution and spilling of humours' which occurs 'in women in the ecstasy of coitus' is not required for the real work of making babies.[43]

Fresh developments in science contradicted old ideas on generation. Galen's theory that both sexes contributed equally to conception and both had to experience pleasure, was countered by the ideas of Harvey who followed the epigenetic line and held that the egg was the product of conception, not the cause. Female orgasm was now seen by some medics as surplus to requirements in the matter of procreation, since it was no longer believed that her 'seeds' were essential in the creation of the new foetus. But the writers and readers of erotica were more interested in the idea of heightening women's sexual pleasure rather than abandoning its necessity, and hence satirized the medical views:

> It has long been warmly contested by the great *Botanists,* whether the *Vulvaria* is not a *succulent Plant.* Hippocrates and *Galen,* two eminent *Virtuosi* of former Ages, with abundance of their Followers, very obstinately contended that it was so; and that it has a balmy *Succus,* or *viscous Juice*, which distilled from it, upon being *lanced,* and at certain times, of the same Nature with that discharg'd at the *Pistillum* of the *Arbor Vitae,* which was absolutely necessary in order to its bearing. But the celebrated *Harvey,* with many other modern *Botanists,* famous for their useful Discoveries and Improvements, absolutely deny this, and affirm that it is impregnated solely by the *Succus* of the *Arbor Vitae,* without contributing any Juice thereto itself, in so much as this Opinion is now entirely exploded.[44]

Despite the fact that female orgasm was increasingly deemed unnecessary for procreation, the erotica recognized women's desire for sexual gratification. Indeed, the theme of uncontrollable female desire is expressed in the feigned concerns about nymphomania:

> Some *Vulvaria* are troubled with a very unaccountable Disorder, ... which they shew by the a continual *Opening* of the *Fissura,* or *Chink* above mention'd, and which is not to be remedied but by the Distillation therein of the balmy *Succus* of the *Arbor Vitae.* In this Case, one *Tree* seldom or never discharges a *quantum sufficit* to answer the Intent of Cure.

The depositing of an over-sexed woman in a brothel is seen as one way of curing nymphomania, or at least a way of containing female sexual desire, and constitutes an attack on the attempts at the regulation of sexuality currently in vogue: 'it has often been found necessary to remove the *Shrubs* to a *Hot-house* where there are several *Trees* provided, in order to compleat the Cure'.[45] It continues, 'Several of these *Hot-houses* are to be met with in and about the *hundred of Drury*', specifically mentioning those around St James and Westminster, St George's Fields, Vauxhall and Mother Needham's,[46] the latter bawd given the title 'Female Botanist'. Female insatiability is conveyed through lunar symbolism which reflects not only life-rhythms of change and renewal but also female sexual inconstancy. The menstrual cycle is referred to as a disorder 'which makes it believ'd that this *Shrub* is under the Dominion of the moon'.

Distinguishing between genuine medical practitioners and quacks (Figure 9.1) was increasingly difficult for the patient, and it was hard to divide eighteenth-century medical practitioners into professionals and opportunists, solely on the basis of performance.[47] In *Natural History of the Frutex Vulvaria*, reference is made to Sir Richard Manningham (1690–1759), a celebrated accoucheur of the period, who was involved in the unusual case of Mary Tofts, a woman who in 1726 alleged she had given birth to many rabbits: 'Accordingly, some Years ago, the Town was amus'd for a considerable Time with the Report of a *Vulvaria* that yielded Rabbits as fast as a tolerable Warren'. However, the secret is uncovered here in the surprising revelation that the woman put the rabbits in to her own vagina; 'it was discover'd that the Owner has found out the Secret to make it *open* as naturally for the introducing a Rabbit, as is generally does for the Inoculation of the *Arbor Vitae*'. Manningham narrowly escaped being duped by Tofts and such gullibility amongst those in the medical profession was eagerly seized upon.

Risk of pregnancy was ever present, and abortion fore-fronted as a means of contraception with female abortionists available to do the deed. Such 'tumours' could be removed and 'Female Botanists' were available who claimed to do this, but the author warns us, 'I would advise no Person, who have a Value for the Wellfare of their *Vulvaria*, to trust them in extraordinary Cases, but immediately to apply to the *Botanists* above mentioned'.[48]

FIGURE 9.1 *Thomas Rowlandson,* Death and the Apothecary, *a satire on quacks, c.1815. Wellcome Library, London.*

The fascination caused by botanical metaphors of the body is evident from the sheer volume of similar material; on the male model, *Wisdom Revealed; Or The Tree Of Life* (1725)[49] had been published earlier, in which the more virile of the male species, the 'manly men' are described as trees, but the weaker, less able men depict the man of sensibilities, the 'sensitive plant'. Other spoof pieces would follow and take up the theme: *The Manplants: Or, a Scheme for Increasing and Improving the British Breed* (1752)[50] and *Mimosa, Or A Sensitive Plant* (1779)[51] with a flourishing of double entendres; 'the *sensitive plant* is alive to the *touch*', and so on based around the name of a real plant *Mimosa* (L. *mimus*, mime) because it mimicked the sensitivity of animals. The 'sensitive plant' became a well-recognized metaphor; even Fanny Hill made reference to it: 'My fingers too had now got within reach of the true, the genuine sensitive plant, which, instead of shrinking from the touch, joys to meet it, and swells and vegetates under it.'[52] In a similar vein, parodies of the female model, connecting nature and sexual organs in the same metaphorical stance, can be seen as early as 1725 in *The Riddle Or A Paradoxical Character Of An Hairy Monster*, reprinted in 1741 along with *Little Merlin's Cave* (1741),[53] another metaphor for female genitalia.

By the end of the eighteenth century, scientist and social critic Erasmus Darwin melded the world of botany and erotica yet further as seen in his poetic depiction of the erotic garden in *The Botanic Garden* (Figure 9.2), comprising two poems, *The Loves of the Plants* (1789) and *The Economy of Vegetation* (1791). It was widely read and the poems well known, referred to in the letters of Horace Walpole, William Cowper, Walter Scott, S. T. Coleridge, William Wordsworth, Mrs Thrale, Percy Shelley and William Godwin. *The Loves of the Plants* was initially published anonymously and, according to Darwin, written solely for money and to make botany agreeable to 'ladies and other unemploy'd scholars'. The poem is significant in that it brings together Linnaeus's sexual classification of plants and the social position, behaviour and functions of women. According to Janet Browne, the garden metaphor played an important role in the courtship between Darwin and Elizabeth Pole; in a poem addressed to her in 1775, she notes that Darwin, 'thinly disguised as a wood nymph from his botanic garden, begs that she should not proceed to lop any more trees in the garden'.[54]

Erasmus Darwin's descriptions of 'mild' and 'retiring' plants expressed conservative attitudes in his use of metaphors which relegated the female to a secondary role.[55] Darwin was merely utilizing an already well-established structural organization of botany and nature which reflected the hierarchy of social relations between men and women in the external world. Plant sexuality was not incidental but lay at the core of the eighteenth-century revolution in the study of the plant kingdom and this was a place where Nature was firmly linked with femaleness. In Londa Schiebinger's words, the laws of nature were read through the lens of social and sexual relations between men and women. Gender was a main principle in attempting to

MEDICINE, THE BODY AND THE BOTANICAL SEXUAL METAPHOR

FIGURE 9.2 *Flora at play with cupid in Erasmus Darwin,* The Botanic Garden, *1791. Wellcome Library, London.*

organize revolutionary views on nature and gave rise to the emergence of sexual difference in plant terminology in the late seventeenth and eighteenth centuries.[56]

The gendering of plants and the sexual overtones of botanical terminology afforded too good an opportunity to miss for quick-witted satirists, and new theories on generation were thus incorporated within erotica. The 'discoveries' of the scientists were frequently questioned, as the theories were either too contradictory or sounded too far-fetched to be believed. Furthermore, well-known botanists and scientists were satirized in mock dedications, and cited in reference to gossip and scandal.

Most importantly, the use of botanical metaphors allowed concerns around the body to be raised in public without use of graphic detail. Although essentially this erotica is a celebration of sexuality which parodied the morals of the day, fears about male and female bodies are prevalent. Three concerns are prominent: first, men's anxieties about women's bodies are evident in their need to know more about the workings of the female's internal organs, and the fear of pregnancy and ensuing medical problems attached to the sexually active woman. Abortionists ('botanists') could deal with unwanted side-effects of sex, and such 'tumours' were to be avoided. Discussions on fertility and questions surrounding new scientific theories of the body are more concerned with relation to female sexual desire and enjoyment, rather than her actual fertility, although virility, potency and female sexuality are glorified. It was recognized that women enjoyed sex as an end in itself and not merely as a means to procreation.

Second, apprehension of women's sexual inconstancy was reflected in the constant expression of belief in female insatiability. Women appear to be an enigma, an unknown quantity and a mystery yet to be unveiled. Theorists of generation had merely clouded the issue with their conflicting conjectures about the necessity of female sexual pleasure in the act of procreation. Third, the fear of catching the pox was paramount: the sheer amount of space, not only in this erotica, but elsewhere, dedicated to discussion of causes of venereal disease and its potential cures and effects, highlight the dread which it instilled. Considering the lack of effective cures, it is unsurprising that male writers of erotica concentrate extensively on the possibilities of the spread of 'vermin' or the catching of crabs or the pox. Women seem to shoulder most of the blame for the spread of the pox, as depictions frequently attack the quality of the 'shrubs', its fruits and flowers, its wayward courses and allusions to the disease therein. Men, however, do not escape blame for this decline, as they are castigated for their lack of due care and attention and are also apportioned blame for degeneration of the body. Risks of pregnancy, the menstrual cycle, nymphomania and other 'female' disorders, along with impotence, are discussed in coached botanical terms in order to openly discuss the body.

The writers of botanical erotica, by indulging in metaphors, provided a method of discussing sex. Despite attacks by science on women's fertility and attempts to reconceptualize the biological roles, in this erotica we see a celebration of female sexuality and the maintenance of the traditional idea of female desire. Significantly, the tree or sensitive plant is important only in its relationship to the vulvaria or shrub.

CHAPTER TEN

The Eighteenth-century Erotic Garden

The erotic garden was established and became popular in two areas of eighteenth-century life – it evolved in reality, and in erotic literature. In the first, in the real world, this development can be seen with the emergence of the gentleman's classical estates with their huge grounds full of suggestive statues and imagery. In the second, in fantasy, the erotic classical garden was a setting for sex. Within this location, landscape gardening, science and botany came to exert a particular influence on both the stately gardens and erotic literature. In the former, it was used in the form of sexualized designs in landscapes, including erotic structures and statues; in the latter, it was used in the creation of a new form of stylized literature which used highly evolved metaphors of erotic trees and sexualized flowering shrubs to represent the genitalia.

This chapter will look at the reasons and influences which encouraged men to make their gardens and estates erotic; and why erotic literature took up such a strange subject – why did authors of erotica use gardens and flowers to write about sex? In order to understand the influences on this phenomena, I first want to look at the background and interests of the eighteenth-century gentleman and explore prominent events and stimuli which were affecting the thinking and fashion of the elite and middling sort. I will examine the growing interest in world exploration which affected collection and examination of plants, and connected it with sexuality.

Three main areas of development can be seen in the eighteenth century: increasing expeditions to faraway places; the influence of the neoclassical revival; and the changes taking place in botany through the influence of Carl Linnaeus. The first advance – that of travel – would influence the two other developments. Trips abroad encouraged the admiration of the classical world and spurred the neoclassical revival, fuelled by an increased curiosity about archaeological digs.[1] Pompeii and Herculaneum were rediscovered in

1738, stimulating further interest in archaeology and the classics, and the sites were incorporated into the Grand Tour. Every young man on his travels abroad would have stopped off to see the ancient locations to marvel at the cities captured in volcanic ash.[2]

German art historian and archaeologist Johann Joachim Winckelmann (1717–1768) was partly responsible for a Greek 'revival'. His *History of Ancient Art* (1764) was one of the first books written in German to become a classic of European literature. He also published various reports on antiquaries and was the first to point out the difference between Greek and Roman art which stimulated a growing interest in fertility rituals and ancient cultures. Earlier inspiration had come in the form of travelogues which instilled a revival of interest in classical Greece as seen in such books *The Villas of the Ancients* (1728) (based partly on Pliny) and James Stuart and Nicholas Revett's *Antiquities of Athens* (1762).

New ideas were brought back from gentlemen who had been on the Grand Tour and those who formed societies as a result of their interest in Greece and Rome. Sir Francis Dashwood, who owned an estate in Medmenham, West Wycombe, founded the Dilettanti Society in 1732/3, stemming from his fascination with Italy. He also subsidized expeditions to Greece. Members of his society took to travelling around ancient sites and publishing reports about their findings, thereby further stimulating excitement. Stuart and Revett published their *Antiquities of Athens* (1762) resplendent with impressive sketches of their findings, further encouraging archaeology. The Dilettanti elected Richard Chandler (1738–1810) as the leader of their first subsidized venture around Greece after his publication of *Marmora Oxoniensia* (1763) came to their attention, and Revett was picked to go with him. Robert Wood (1717–1771) took trips to Greece in 1742/3, on his way to Egypt and Syria. In 1750, when he returned, he took as his companions John Bouverie (c.1722–1750) and James Dawkins (1722–1757). As a keen member of the Dilettanti, Dawkins paid for all the expenses of the trip for all three travellers. Those remodelling their gardens were motivated by Greece and artists' depictions of them in paintings. Claude's picture *Coast View of Delos with Aeneas* seems to have been inspired Henry Hoare's building of the Pantheon temple in his gardens at Stourhead.[3] Expeditions to farther climes such as Captain James Cook's three-year voyage to the South Seas in 1767 also led to a spurt in interest in botany. Young naturalist Joseph Banks, who accompanied him on the *Endeavour*, brought back many different kinds of species of flora and fauna never previously seen by Europeans.

All these developments – interest in new archaeology digs, travel to ancient Greek sites and the South Seas, and the ensuing influence of travel writing and paintings – had an obvious influence on developments in both creation of the erotic garden in reality and in erotic literature. Thus armed, the English gentleman began to fill his garden with classical sculptures and follies.

The making of the gentleman's erotic garden

From the 1720s and 1730s, many gentlemen began to desire a more cultivated wilderness, the appearance of 'nature', on their estates. Classical temples and grottoes were an imperative part of the design. This was in contrast to earlier styles of gardens inherited from the Tudor, Dutch and French traditions which had contained clipped bushes, high walls and patterns of low box hedges, mainly of a geometric design. Anthony Ashley Cooper, 3rd Earl of Shaftesbury, in his *The Moralists* (1710) summed up his feelings for the new fashion:

> I shall no longer resist the passion in me for things of a *natural* kind; where neither *Art*, nor the *Conceit* or *Caprice* of Man has spoil'd their *genuine Order* by breaking up the *Primitive State*. Even the rude *Rocks*, the mossy *Caverns*, the irregular unwrought *Grotto's* and broken *Falls* of waters, with all the horrid graces of the *Wilderness* itself, as representing NATURE more, will be the more engaging, and appear with a magnificence beyond the mockery of princely gardens.[4]

Through the influence of landscape gardening, nature had to some extent been 'tamed', and it was now a nature created by man; despite landscape gardeners' intention to recreate nature, they were nonetheless cultivating a 'look'. The work of gardeners such as William Kent (1685–1784), 'Capability' Brown (1716–1783) and Humphry Repton (1752–1818), which brought nature under man's control, was emulated in the erotic garden, bringing sex under man's control.

Specially-created grottoes became popular, and grounds became dotted with statuettes. Classical style buildings, porticoes and grottoes were all important parts of the erotic garden, both in fictionalized accounts and in real gardens. These additions created another dimension to the garden, one which introduced a new place for social interaction and introduced a sexualized space in the garden. The intent was the creation of seclusion, a retreat into a more private sphere. This trend led to the making of the erotic landscape such as the Royal Gardens in Casserta. Friend of the King and Queen of Naples, William Hamilton, British Ambassador in Naples, engaged German botanist John Andreas Graefer to begin work on the 'English Garden' in the grounds of the Royal Palaces where the royal couple spent their summers. He filled the garden with grottoes, sexual symbols and a statue of Venus to delight visitors (Figure 10.1). Hamilton was a known roué, having married his mistress Emma Hart (later Lady Hamilton), but he was also a recognized scholar and botanist, and was also a respected member of the Royal Society (see Chapter 7).[5] In the creation of such a garden, Hamilton was simply following a line of elite men who had created erotic gardens in England. One of those was Sir Francis Dashwood who developed his estate from around 1739.

FIGURE 10.1 *William Hamilton's English garden, Caserta, near Naples. Wikimedia Commons.*

Sir Francis Dashwood's estate

Libertine Sir Francis Dashwood held various important eighteenth-century political offices – Treasurer of the Chamber, Chancellor of the Exchequer, Keeper of the Great Wardrobe and Joint Postmaster-General – and established one of the most notorious hell-fire clubs of the century at Medmenham. His sexual antics, along with those of his friends, became both the source and the subject of many an erotic tale and he was known for his libertinism; Horace Walpole MP commented, '[he has] the staying power of a stallion and the impetuosity of a bull'.[6] Dashwood formed the 'Knights of St Francis' or the 'Monks of Medmenham' in the 1750s basically as a sex club for himself and his friends, and created his own sexual playground on his West Wycombe estate and at Medmenham Abbey, a disused Gothic ruin which he rented and renovated for the use of his 'monks'. He invited his 'monks' (his male friends) and 'nuns' (prostitutes from London, mistresses of the monks, and women known from his circle) down to West Wycombe to 'chapter' meetings to indulge in sexual activities.

The grounds of his estate was full of sexual imagery, a place devoted to amorous pursuits and said to be a satire of Lord Cobham's garden of virtue at Stowe (Figure 10.2), and which represented the politics of elite male

FIGURE 10.2 *Temple of Ancient Virtue, Stowe. Imagno/Getty Images.*

culture.[7] John Wilkes, MP and member of Dashwood's hell-fire club, somewhat facetiously remarked that he was 'full of astonishment that any man should take so much pains and be at so great an expense, only to show a public contempt of all decency, order and virtue'.[8]

The gardens of the Dashwood estate were essentially designed as a utopia, a homage to classical love. At the entrance to the garden was a cave of Venus where, on the inside over a mossy couch was an inscription which sums up Dashwood's intention for the garden:

Ite, agite, o juvenices; partier fudate medullis
Omnibus inter vos; non murmura vestra columbae,
Brachia non hederae, non vincant oscula conchae.

[Go into action, you youngsters;
Put everything you've got into it together, both of you;
Let not doves outdo your cooings,
nor ivy your embraces, nor oysters your kisses.]

Many original porticoes and follies can still be found on the Dashwood estate, such as the Temple of Apollo, also known as Cockpit Arch as cockfights were supposed to have been held there. The Temple was built by Donowell probably in 1761, originally intended as a gateway but turned into a garden feature sometime after 1770; etched above the archway is the motto of the hellfire club, 'Liberatati Amicatiaeque Sac' (sacred to liberty and friendship). The late Sir Francis Dashwood (1925–2000) believed the lake to have been in the shape of a swan,[9] the legs were represented by two small streams which are crossed by bridges of rough knapped flints. It has been argued that the topography probably represented Leda and the Swan but the garden has since been redesigned and no longer retains its original form.[10] The Cascade has been attributed to Servandoni and Jolivet by the National Trust Guide. The Cascade originally consisted of a mass of stone boulders with a retiring statue of Father Neptune at the centre with grottoes on either side.

It is likely that, at some stage, Dashwood had the garden designed in the topographical shape of a woman's body, the form most suitably viewed from the top of the hill near Dashwood's family church. Daniel Mannix, author of *The Hell-Fire Club* who wrote about Dashwood, related the tale of a clergyman's visit, invited by Dashwood to view the garden from the church tower:

> The clergyman cheerfully agreed and followed Francis to the top of the tower. He had just time to realise that he was gazing down at a garden elaborately designed to represent the body of a naked woman when Sir Francis gave a signal. Instantly a stream of water gushed from the shrubbery triangle while two fountains concealed in the flowerbeds shot stream of milky water into the air.[11]

Fountains acting as female fluids were a novelty intended by Dashwood to thrill, or shock, his visitors. Such innovations were more than likely gleaned from popular erotic books such as those discussed below. When I queried this with the late Sir Francis Dashwood, he dismissed the idea as fantasy invented by Mannix, although there is plenty of evidence of the popularity of this topographical form indicated in erotica. Mannix also states that Dashwood hollowed out a tiny cave in a little hill which he called the Cave of Trophonius. The cave is possibly similar to the one as seen in the textual image of Merryland in *A New Description of Merryland*, a jovial piece of erotica which displays the world of sex in terms of the topography of a woman's body in terms of an extended allegory and in which the Landscaped Body acts as a mini-cosmos: 'Near the Fort is the Metropolis, called CLTRS [clitoris]; it is a pleasant Place, much delighted in by the Queens of MERRYLAND, and is their chief Palace, or rather *Pleasure Seat*; it was at first but small, but the Pleasure some of the Queens have found in it, has occasion'd their extending its Bounds considerably.'[12] Dashwood more than likely had access to this book, and is certain to have known about it as it was a commonly known joke in libertine circles, although I found no evidence of it in his library records. Dan Cruickshank has given credence to the idea that the West Wycombe estate was designed in the shape of a female body.[13]

Wilkes saw the grounds as a sexual playing field for Dashwood's friends. He described the shape and form of the estate in *The Public Advertiser* for 2 June 1763. In particular, he wrote of an astonishing temple where the entrance to it

> is the same Entrance by which we all come into the World, and the Door is what some idle Wits have called the Door of Life. It is reported that, on a late Visit to his Chancellor, Lord Bute particularly admired this Building and advised the noble Owner to lay out the £500 bequeathed to him by Lord Melcombe's Will, for an Erection, in a Paphian Column to stand at the Entrance, and it is said to be advised it to be made of Scottish pebbles .... and, at the Entrance to the Temple ... are two Urns sacred to the Ephesian Matron and to Potiphar's wife .... You ascend to the Top of the Building, which is crowned with a particular Column, designed (I suppose) to represent our former very upright State ...., and is skirted with very pretty Underwood.[14]

A painting by William Hannan (1725–1772) hangs in Dashwood's house which provided further evidence of the grounds being cultivated in the form of a female body; a pudenda was represented by a triangular clump of trees in the middle of a lake. A grotto called Venus's Parlour, entered by curving screen walls, gives the tale of the garden's female topography further veracity. Above it, on a small mound where the original house was, is the Temple of Venus (Figure 10.3) built in 1748.

Another connection between well-known gardeners and erotica can be seen through William Kent's work. A book on his work, *The Designs of Inigo Jones and Mr. William Kent*, carried Kent's design of 'Merlin's Cave' built in 1735 in the royal garden of Queen Caroline.[15] This instigated a response with a skittish poem called *Little Merlin's Cave* (1741) in homage to Kent's garden project. In fact, a whole badinage developed around Kent's design and its title applying erotic connotations. The frontispiece to the follow-up to *A New Description of Merryland* discussed above, *Merryland Displayed*, depicts the picture of Merryland as a woman's body under the title *Merlin's Cave* (a metaphor for the vagina); the image was again repeated in a publication of the notorious pornographer, Edmund Curll, *Poems on Several Occasions*.[16] These landscaped gardens became increasingly fashionable in bawdy and obscene writings.

The garden in erotic literature

These attempts to turn one's own estate into one's own private classical sexualized world were not isolated gardening projects, but reflected a well-developed theme in erotica; both the real gardens and the fictional erotic gardens were all part of the same cultural sphere. The authors of erotica

FIGURE 10.3 *Temple of Venus, Dashwood's estate, West Wycombe. Author's collection.*

emulated and assimilated utopian literature and travelogues into their narrative in an alternative portrayal of socio-sexual relations between men and women.

Geographical locations for sex in erotica were going through changes to reflect these fashions and changes taking place in the external environment. The allegorical utopian garden, popular in early eighteenth-century erotica, was very much connected with nature. But this was later to evolve, as erotica kept up with themes and ideas expressed by designers of landscaped estates, now incorporating the more cultivated garden – the garden as nature tamed – into its repertoire. This was a gradual development and the older classical garden would continue to be used alongside the new, more manicured, sexual garden.

If we first look at early eighteenth-century erotica we see that it displayed sex as taking place within the classical world as suggested by Ovid. An example of this classical sexualized world can be seen in a piece of erotica entitled *New Atalantis for the Year One Thousand Seven Hundred and Fifty-Eight* (1758) in one racy tale entitled 'An Introduction, Containing The Origin Of Love And Gallantry', which describes an Arcadia full of nymphs and shepherds, populated by the act of tossing rocks over their shoulders.[17] This depiction of Ovid's method of reproduction had already been satirized in a print which accompanied *Le Cabinet d'Amour* (c.1750), which depicts a picture of a couple scattering discorporate genitals in their wake producing babies, in a classical garden complete with temple in the background. The Arcadian setting had already been used as a backdrop in *La Nuit Merveilluese ou Le Nec Plus Ultra du Plaisir* (c.1800),[18] translated into English as *The Voluptuous Night, or, The Non Plus Ultra of Pleasure* (1830). The Idyllic Elysian Garden is described as a Garden of Eden, the lovers enjoying all its delights. With the effect of an ecstatic kiss, the protagonist is conveyed into a classical garden, declaring, 'I thought myself transported to the abode of the Gods, or that in the Garden of Imathontè. I was inhaling voluptuousness from the rosy mouth of the most enchanting of the Goddesses.'[19] Reflecting the gentlemen's estate, an evening's stroll leads the lovers to a captivating pavilion: 'We trembled as we entered. It was a sanctuary and that the sanctuary of love. The god took full possession of our knees – we lost every power and faculty but that of love.'[20] Once they have finished their love-making, they continue walking, their feelings heightened by the enchantment of the garden, a place which increases the passions. In the interior of the pavilion, they find secret compartments symbolic of the recesses of a woman's body. They follow a 'labyrinth of galleries and stairs passing through 'a dark narrow gallery.'[21] The descriptions convey an earthly paradise, a Grecian Garden of Eden, with birds singing and cool water flowing; the grotto or 'aerial grove' has a 'softened lustre', with 'suspended garlands of flowers' and 'green turf'.[22] The erotic garden had become a central backdrop for love-making.

Standing in opposition to the classical garden was the cultivated enclosed garden. This particular development in erotica was inherited from the French obsession with the setting of the monastery or nunnery, one which Britain inherited in its genre of anti-Catholic literature.[23] Within this location, the secretive walled garden came into its own, with its clipped confines conveying attempts at control of sexuality, yet its lushness and waters rebelling to encourage sexual freedom of the protagonists within the erotic tale. This theme was explored not only in fictional erotica, but in genuine accounts from excommunicated priests and dissatisfied nuns. The tales gave descriptions of life within the confines of religious houses thereby buttressing contemporary perceptions of convents as sexualized places: 'There are several narrow closets in the church, with a small iron grate: One side answers to the cloister, the other to the church; So the nun being on the inside, and father confessor on the outside, they hear one another.'[24] The nuns and priests invariably went on to have sex together in these accounts. Another account reported: 'The Cordeliers were not satisfied with seeing the nuns at the grate, they made *secret and nocturnal* entries into the Garden and Monastery by the help of *false keys*, or *ladders of cord, and in baskets*.'[25] Sensual monastic grounds adorned with veiled greenery and running waters were so erotic that they could raise sexual feelings in those who spent time there;

> those very Places of Retirement, with their large Gardens, adorned with Walks and Shades, and many times watered by pleasant Fountains, or

murmuring Streams, together with the idle Way of Living, seem to be accommodated to inspire them with amorous Sentiments, against which their Vows of Chastity, and the Rules of their Order, are so far from being Preservative, that they only act as Fuel to their Flames, and make them commit *Sin* with a higher *Relish*.[26]

These secret gardens screened behind cloister walls were part of the privatized erotic location, a repressed echo of the natural erotic gardens elsewhere. These ostensibly factual accounts raised issues about religious confinement and sexual repression which were to be reflected in purely fictional tales of the convent.

The more cultivated erotic garden can be seen in an erotica book entitled *Voyage to Lethe* (1741). The hero, the aptly named Captain Cock, had designed his garden in a typical example of corporeal analogy. (An accompanying picture of Captain Cock shows that he was none other than Captain James Cook, the name smudged to read 'Captain Sam Cock', an indication that the date of the image was later than the text. This was probably inserted after Cook's first expedition to make it more contemporary.) In the description of his manor at Allcock, the female body is displayed through erotic topiary:

> I must own most singularly curious Shape, and situate withall in a very pleasant and fertile Part of the Country, being a long Neck of Land, shaded by a Grove of Trees [pubic hair], and supported by a couple of Hills [the breasts],[27] impregnated according to the Virtuosi, with a white fort of Metal, which being liquify'd, is deem'd an Excellent Restorative [breast milk]. Its Figure towards the end is the Form of a large Nut [clitoris]; and there is an Aqueduct thro' it, that terminates in a *jette d'Eau,* [women were thought to ejaculate at orgasm] as often as it is properly suppl'd with Water [urine].[28]

By the second half of the eighteenth century, there was a shift in format to satisfy a more sophisticated audience. Although ribald allegories were still very much in circulation, the metalepsis became increasingly complex. In the mildly erotic *The Fruit-shop* (1765), a connection is made between topographical descriptions, botanical metaphors and the Garden of Eden. In the appendix, the author refers us to a 'fruit-shop' in St James's Street where satisfaction seems guaranteed, the term 'fruit-shop' indicating a brothel, the fruit being the whores. Horticulture plays a large part in chapter two, opening with a 'description of the garden [Eden] wherein the first fruit-tree stood', the fruit-tree being a synonym for the penis.[29]

The Fruit-Shop includes an attack on Dashwood and his friends, bringing together real-life libertines within a partly fantasized world, this critical fiction grounded in fact. The second edition contains a picture of a garden scene, a satire on Dashwood's estate which attacks Dashwood and his friends; and a phallic tree standing before a classical temple, a tribute to Dashwood's sexual prowess and an allusion to the sexual nature of his garden. A clergyman is holding an ass which is crushing the book, *Tristram Shandy*.[30] In front of the clergyman sits a monkey on the Holy Bible squirting a syringe. Both the picture and the accompanying text are an attack on Laurence Sterne,[31] possibly a visitor to Dashwood's estate. Donald McCormick, in his book *The Hell-Fire Club*, lists Sterne amongst the possible members of the order of St Francis.[32] Certainly his close friend John Hall Stevenson visited as he is recorded in the minutes of one of the meetings of the Knights.[33] References were made to Dashwood's garden as 'a fertile source of a thousand different and celebrated conjectures, even among those who were the best qualified to devote themselves to profound researches',[34] a 'fertile source' presumably in the double sense as a breeding ground for scandal, and a place of love-making. Sterne himself had possibly attended Dashwood's meetings at some point. There is also a similarity displayed to Dashwood's gardens in the frontispiece image of *The Fruit-Shop*, with its temple and phallic tree. The monkey aloft the Bible conveys an inner circle joke in which Dashwood allegedly gave unholy communion to Lady Wortley Montagu's monkey.[35]

So we have a very intimate and profound connection between the libertine man and his garden and the development of the garden in erotic literature. But it was not only changes in fashion and gardening that affected the development of the erotic garden in eighteenth-century perception. The same sort of connections were being made between botany and erotica.

Botanical developments and the fictional erotic garden

Newer developments and advances in science saw the introduction of the botanical garden. Botanists were making extensive voyages in search of botanical collections discovering new species of plants, trees, birds and animals. The main influence was due to Carl Linnaeus (1707–1778) who undertook expeditions into northern Sweden and established a complete new sexual hierarchical cataloguing system of the animal and plant kingdom. He became renowned for his reclassification of nature, famous for his taxonomy of the animal, vegetable and animal kingdoms, most notably his sexual classifications of plants in seven volumes.[36] He described the world of plants in sexual terms, based on the difference between the male and female parts of flowers. Linnaeus was not the first on this route and had been influenced by Nehemiah Grew who, in his *Anatomy of Plants* (1682), had already likened his plant specimens to male genitalia. He noted, 'The blade (or stamen) does not inaptly resemble a small penis, with the sheath on it.'[37] Two other botanist working at the end of the seventeenth century, John Ray and Joseph Tournefort, had also made significant inroads into classification of plants based entirely on the structure of their flower and fruit parts.

Unsurprisingly, as we have seen in the previous chapter, this system described by Linnaeus, which conveyed a sexual life for flowers, was not altogether immediately accepted by a sceptical public and certain wits were quick to take up an attack on the notion as ridiculous. As a result, writers of erotica began to play with metaphors. Edward Ward's *The Riddle Or A Paradoxical Character Of An Hairy Monster* (1725) used topographical allegories of the female body:

> When full 'tis round, when empty long,
> Sometimes a Hole, sometimes a Slit,
> Hairy when old, and bald when young,
> Too wide for some, for other fit.
>
> It justly may be stil'd a Well
> At each Spring-Tide it overflows;
> It's Depth no mortal Man can tell;
> That none but he that made it knows.

The famous English botanist Philip Miller who had adopted the Linnaeus system in his books entitled *Catalogus Plantarum Officinalium* (1730) and *The Gardener's Directory* (1731) (with all the ramifications of sexual classification of plants) became the butt of jokes. Grubb Street hacks such as Thomas Stretser used his name as a pseudonym in his works *Natural History of Arbor Vitae* (1732) and its counterpart *A Natural History of the Frutex Vulvaria* (1732), both discussed in depth in the previous chapter.

Flagellation and flowers in the erotic garden

By the 1770s a new wave of erotic material emerged shining a new light on the effects and meaning of flowers and the erotic garden. Within these stories, flowers were conveyed as an important aphrodisiac and nosegays became an open signifier of the female flagellant. The garden has now become the producer of erotic flowers.

A huge nosegay worn in the lapel acted as an advertisement of the female flagellant and became part of her essential dress code. The emergence of this new sub-genre of erotica can be seen with the publication of a plethora of pornographic novellas with titles such as *The Birchen Bouquet* (1770 or 1790); *Exhibition of Female Flagellants* (1777); *The Spirit of Flagellation; or The Memoirs of Mrs. Hinton, Who kept a School many years at Kensington* (c.1790);[38] *Manon La Fouëtteuse, or the Quintessence of Birch Discipline* (c.1805);[39] *Venus School-Mistress, or Birchen Sports* (c.1808–1810);[40] *Element of Tuition* ('1794'), printed around 1830; *The Bagnio Miscellany*[41] published in 1830.

In *The Birchen Bouquet*, some young libertines, 'after taking a few turns in the garden, and gathering a parcel of flowers, went into the parlour, and made a bouquet for each then went back to their carriage'. Later, the heroine, Harriet, on returning to school fired up with passion, flogged another young pupil, 'the fragrance of the bouquet, and above all, the latent effects of the well placed dildoe, Harriet soon lost her senses, and remained for some time absorbed in a rapturous stupor'.[42]

The accent on nosegays in *Female Flagellants, Part One* caused a similar stir, its sequel *Female Flagellants, Part Two* publishing letters from so-called satisfied customers, no doubt a fiction itself. One reader, apparently well acquainted with the connection between flogging and nosegays, allegedly wrote an account of one Miss N after visiting a friend who had just whipped her step-daughter:

> After she had done, she took Miss N. to the garden, and picked for her a beautiful nosegay, but so monstrously large that she was almost ashamed to wear it. However, as her friend wore one of equal size, she pinned it to her bosom. I see, my dear, said she, you are not acquainted with the secret influence of flowers; known, my dear, that their sweet perfume has an uncommon effect on men and women; but to have that effect on men they must adorn a lovely bosom like yours.[43]

We are not told what this influence is but it the aphrodisiac quality of the flowers is implicit.

Finally, it appears that flowers, or more specifically nosegays as symbols of flagellatory inclinations, were not confined to erotic books but were recognized by gentleman's magazines and in turn, the garden took on a new significance. The *Bon Ton* magazine for November 1791 published a letter from 'A. Rambler' who described the actions taken to entice an admired French governess: 'as she is extremely fond of flowers, I got my flower-garden enlarged and stocked with the most beautiful flowers that could be had'. A. Rambler follows her, secretly watching her make up a birch in the garden, which she later used for flagellation purposes: 'She, however, stopped in the shrubbery and seeing her cut some twigs from a birch tree, I retreated behind some trees unperceived; when she had got a large bundle of them, she bound them up in a rod with a ribbon, as she seemed to be in a great passion.' She went upstairs to the room where she sat with her pupils and commenced flogging the young girl who had scratched her brother all over in a fit of temper.[44]

The neoclassical revival, factual travelogues, together with the interest in archaeology and landscaping estates and gardens would all influence new erotic utopias. Developments in horticulture and botany were applied to create a new botanical garden, one which was to be infused with erotic content.

The interest in landscape gardening saw owners of large estates introducing major innovations to their properties, often in Arcadian fashion with nude statues, erotic grottoes, fluid cascades and sensual waterfalls. As a result of this, English erotic literature introduced similar features, with its own landscaped gardens and sexualized plants and flowers. The importance of the garden as a focus of sexual pleasure is striking in eighteenth-century erotica. The idea that 'nature knows best' was a notion culled from classical philosophy, one which celebrated sexual activity. The publishers and writers of erotica such as Edmund Curll and Erasmus Darwin were therefore reviving the equation between nature and sex in their neoclassical representations. The fictional landscape was Arcadian or pastoral, a sensual evocation of nature at its best; either free or wild, or both. The restraint of nature was condemned. Yet, in the real world, attempts were being made to recreate the Garden of Eden as an earthly paradise. The major pre-occupation of landscape gardeners such as William Kent, 'Capability' Brown and Humphry Repton was to reshape hills and lakes, moulding nature into patterns selected by man. These cultivated gardens would eventually become part of the new erotic utopias.

Finally, the erotic garden became the instigator of a new form of sexual release through its production of erotic flowers. The garden produced not only flowers with pungent aphrodisiac effects which whipped the protagonist into a form of flagellatory frenzy, but also provide the birches for the weapon of their pleasure. The erotic garden had found its new, peculiarly British form of excitement in nosegays and birches of the female flagellant.

NOTES

Introduction

1. Julie Peakman, *Mighty Lewd Books. The Development of Eighteenth-Centuy Pornography in England* (London, Palgrave, 2003), pp. 27–39; Tim Hitchcock, *English Sexualities, 1700–1800* (London, Macmillan, 1997), 11.
2. Robert Darnton, *The Forbidden Best-Sellers of Pre-Revolutionary France* (London: HarperCollins, 1996), 37. Darnton has identified female booksellers of erotic and pornographic material; one particular woman, Madame Charmet, obviously read material before ordering. In 1784, she wrote to her suppliers about Turgot's *Oeuvres Posthumes*, commentating on the power and energy of the book, displaying savvy of the trade.
3. A certain Mrs H. wrote racy poems and a sex manual, *Guide to Joy*. Mary Lyons (ed.), *The Memoirs of Mrs. Leeson* (Dublin, The Lilliput Press, 1995), p. 170.
4. M. Spufford, *Small Books and Pleasant Histories: Popular Fiction and its Readership in Seventeenth Century England* (Cambridge, Cambridge University Press, 1981). Spufford, in her study of early modern English chapbooks, claims that plebeian women read risqué stories and shared a raucous sense of humour with men.
5. A good place to start is Edward Stein (ed.), *Forms of Desire. Sexual Orientation and the Social Constructionist Controversy* (London, Routledge, 1990).
6. See the discussion by Professor Alun Munslow on 'What is History?' http://www.history.ac.uk/ihr/Focus/Whatishistory/munslow6.html

Chapter One   Continuities and Change in Sexual Behaviour and Attitudes from the Eighteenth Century

1. One of the great early pioneers was Vern Bullough; among other works, see his *Sexual Variance in Society and History* (New York, Wiley Interscience, 1976); Bullough, *Sex, Society and History* (New York, Science History, Neale Watson, 1976); and Reay Tannahill, *Sex in History* (London, H. Hamilton, 1980). Other earlier explorers include R. E. L. Masters, *Sex Crimes in History*

(New York, Julian Press, 1963); Gordon Rattray Taylor, *Sex in History* (London, Thames & Hudson, 1953); and George Ryley Scott, *Phallic Worship* (privately printed 1941).

2   For example on the body, see Thomas Laqueur, *Making Sex. Body and Gender from the Greeks to Freud* (Harvard, Harvard University Press, 1992); Helen Berry and Elizabeth Foster, *The Family in Early Modern England* (Cambridge, Cambridge University Press, 2007). On homosexuality and prostitution see sections below. On pornography see Julie Peakman, *Mighty Lewd Books. The Development of Pornography in Eighteenth-Century England* (Basingstoke, Palgrave, 2003); Lisa Sigal (ed.), *International Exposure. Perspectives on Modern European Pornography 1800–2000* (New Jersey, Rutgers University Press, 2005). On perversions, Jonathan Dollimore, *Sexual Dissidence. Augustine to Wilde, Freud to Foucault* (Oxford, Clarendon Press, 1991); James Penney, *The World of Perversion. Psychoanalysis and the Impossible Absolute of Desire* (Albany, State University of New York Press, 2006); Julie Peakman (ed.), *Sexual Perversions 1670–1890* (Basingstoke, Palgrave, 2009).

3   For an overview see John D. Delamater and Janet Shibley Hyde, 'Essentialism vs. Social Constructionism in the Study of Human Sexuality', *Journal of Sex Research*, Vol. 35, No. 1 (1998), pp. 10–18.

4   Michel Foucault (trans. Robert Hurley), *The History of Sexuality, Vol. I. An Introduction* (Harmondsworth, Penguin, 1990); Domna C. Stanton, *Discourses of Sexuality. From Aristotle to AIDS* (Michigan, University of Michigan, 1992).

5   See for example, Lois McNay, *Foucault, A Critical Introduction* (Cambridge, Polity Press, 1994); Lin Foxall, 'Pandora Unbound: A Feminist Critique of Foucault's History of Sexuality', in David H. Larmour, Paul Allen Miller and Charles Platter (eds), *Rethinking Sexuality* (Princeton, Princeton University Press, 1998), pp. 132–3; Ruth Mazo Karras, 'Prostitution and the Question of Sexual Identity in Medieval Europe', *Journal of Women's History*, Vol. 11, No. 2 (Summer 1999), pp. 159–77.

6   See for example Julie Peakman (general ed.), *A Cultural History of Sexuality* (Oxford, Berg, 2011); Phillip Ariès and George Duby, *A History of Private Life* (Cambridge, MA, Harvard University Press, 1990); Peter Gay, *Education of the Senses: The Bourgeois Experience, Victoria to Freud* (Oxford, Oxford University Press, 1984).

7   The term 'heterosexuality' was first used by Austro-Hungarian poet and translator Karl Maria Kertbeny in 1869. The current sociological argument is that heterosexuality is a learned behaviour, not a natural occurrence; Jonathan Katz, *The Invention of Heterosexuality* (Chicago, University of Chicago Press, 2007); Chrys Ingraham, *Thinking Straight. The Power, the Promise and the Paradox of Heterosexuality* (London, Routledge, 2005).

8   Ludmilla Jordanova, *Sexual Visions. Images of Gender in Science and Medicine between the Eighteenth and Twentieth Centuries* (London, Harvester Wheatsheaf, 1989); Londa Schiebinger, *Nature's Body. Sexual Politics and the Making of Modern Science* (London, Pandora, 1993); Roy Porter and Mikuláš Teich (eds), *Sexual Knowledge, Sexual Science. The History of Attitudes to Sexuality* (Cambridge, Cambridge University Press, 1994). Lyn Salkin Sbiroli,

'Generation and regeneration: reflections on the biological and ideological role in France (1786–96)', in Marie Mulvey Roberts and Roy Porter, *Literature and Medicine during the Eighteenth Century* (London, Routledge, 1993).

9   For examples covering the early modern period, see Margaret Somerville, *Sex and Subjection. Attitudes to Women in Early-Modern Society* (London, Arnold, 1995); and for the Victorian period, Susan Mendus and Jane Rendal (eds), *Sexuality & Subordination* (London, Routledge, 1989); Sarah Shaver Hughes and Brady Hughes, *Women in World History. Vol 2. Readings from 1500–the Present* (Armonk, New York, M.E. Sharpe, 1997); Vern Bullough, Brenda Shelton and Sarah Slavin, *The Subordinated Sex. A History of Attitudes towards Women* (Athens, GA, University of Georgia Press, 1998). On homosexuality, see section below.

10 G. R. Quaife, *Wanton Wenches and Wayward Wives: Peasants and Illicit Sex In Early Seventeenth Century England* (London, Croom Helm, 1979); Julie Peakman, *Lascivious Bodies. A Sexual History of the Eighteenth-Century* (London, Atlantic, 2004), pp. 32–5.

11 Henry Reed Stiles, *Bundling: Its Origin, Progress and Decline* (1871; reprint, Kessinger Publishing, 2005); Lawrence, *The Family, Sex and Marriage in England 1500–1800* (London, Penguin, 1997), pp. 349, 384–5; Benjamin B. Roberts and Leendert F. Groenendijk, '"Wearing out a Pair of Fool's Shoes": Sexual Advice for Youth in Holland's Golden Age', *Journal of the History of Sexuality*, Vol. 13, No. 2 (April 2004), pp. 139–56.

12 Allyson M. Poska, *Regulating the People. The Catholic Reformation in the Seventeenth-Century* (Leiden, Brill 1998), pp. 1–2, 101–10.

13 Bruno P. F. Wanrooij, 'Italy: Sexuality, Morality and Public Authority' in Franz x. Eder, Lesley Hall and Gert Hekma, *National Histories. Sexual Culture in Europe* (Manchester, Manchester University Press, 1999), pp. 114–37.

14 Lawrence Stone, *The Family, Sex and Marriage in England, 1500–1800* (London, 1977); Jean-Louis Flandrin (trans. Richard Southern), *Families in Former Times: Kinship, Household, and Sexuality* (Cambridge, 1979); Edward P. Thompson, 'Happy Families, Review of Lawrence Stone, The Family, Sex and Marriage in England, 1500–1800', *New Society*, Vol. XLI (1977), p. 500; Edward Shorter, *The Making of the Modern Family* (New York, Basic Books, 1975); see Berry and Forster, *The Family in Early Modern England*.

15 Peter N. Stearns, *Sexuality in World History* (London, Routledge, 2009), pp. 79–81.

16 Alexandre Avdeev, Alain Blum and Irina Troitskia, 'Peasant Marriage in Nineteenth-century Russia', *Population-E*, Vol. 59, No. 6 (2004), pp. 721–64.

17 For examples, see Ronald Hyam, *Empire and Sexuality. The British Experience* (Manchester, Manchester University Press, 1990); Albert L. Hurtado, *Sex Gender and Culture in Old California* (Albuquerque, University of New Mexico Press, 1999); C. Philippa Levine (ed.), *Gender and Empire* (Oxford, Oxford University Press, 2004); Carl J. Ekberg, *Sex and Empire in Netherlands, Spain: Stealing Indian Women, Native Slavery in the Illinois Country* (Urbana and Chicago, University of Illinois Press, 2007).

18 Richard C. Trexler, *Sex and Conquest. Gendered Violence, Political Order, and the European Conquest of the Americas* (Ithaca, NY, Cornell University Press, 1995); Ekberg, *Sex and Empire*.

19 John D'Emilio and Estelle Freedman, *Intimate Matters. A History of Sexuality in America* (Chicago, Chicago University Press, 1997), p. 7.

20 Stearns, *Sexuality in World History*, p. 67; Szreter, 'Falling Fertilities and Changing Sexualities', p. 168.

21 D'Emilio and Freedman, *Intimate Matters*, pp. xi–xii; Stone, *The Family*, p. 22.

22 Helen LefkowitzHorowitz, *Rereading Sex. Battles over Sexual Knowledge and Supression in Nineteenth-Century America* (New York, Alfred A. Knopf, 2002).

23 Stearns, *Sexuality in World History*, p. 69.

24 Hyam, *Empire and Sexuality*, p. 93.

25 See Peter W. Bardaglio, 'Rape and Law in the Old South: "Calculated to Excite indignation in Every Heart"', *Journal of Southern History*, Vol. 60 (November 1994), pp. 753–5; and Bardaglio, *Reconstructing the Household; Families, Sex and the Law in the Nineteenth-Century South* (Chapel Hill, University of North Carolina Press, 1995).

26 Sharon Block, *Rape and Sexual Power in Early America* (Chapel Hill, University of North Carolina Press, 2006), pp. 243–4; also see Bardaglio, 'Rape and Law in the Old South', pp. 753–5; and Bardaglio, *Reconstructing the Household*.

27 Sonia Nishat Amin, *World of Muslim Women in Colonial Bengal 1876–1939* (Leiden, New York and Koln, E. J. Brill, 1996).

28 See his chapter, 'From bibi to memsahib', Hyam, *Empire and Sexuality*, p. 115.

29 Anne de Courcy, *The Fishing-Fleet: Husband-hunting in the Raj* (London, Weidenfeld & Nicolson, 2012); Margaret MacMillan, *Women of the Raj* (London, Thames and Hudson, 1988), p. 16.

30 Ann Stoler, *Carnal Knowledge and Imperial Power: Race and the Intimate in Colonial Power* (University of California Press, 2002); Patricia Seed, *To Love, Honour and Obey in Colonial Mexico: Conflicts Over Marriage Choice, 1574–1821* (Palo Alto, CA, Stanford University Press, 1988), p. 238.

31 Stephen O. Murray and Will Roscoe, *Islamic Homosexualities. Culture, History and Literature* (New York, New York University Press, 1997), pp. 74, 262–6; Trexler, *Sex and Conquest*, p. 136; Gayatri Reddy, *With Respect to Sex: Negotiating Hijra Identity in South India* (Chicago, IL, Chicago University Press, 2005); Sue-Ellen Jacobs, Wesley Thomas and Sabine Lang (eds), *Two Spirit People: Native American Gender Identity, Sexuality, and Spirituality* (Chicago, University of Illinois, 1997).

32 On betrothal and marriage customs, see Henry Doré, *Chinese Customs* (Singapore, Graham Brash, 1987), pp. 47–59; Dabing Ye (trans. Mark Bender and Shi Kun), *The Bridal Boat. Marriage Customs of China's Fifty-Five Ethnic Minorities* (Beijing, New World Press, 1993).

33 Alison Sau-Chu Yeung, 'Fornication in the Late Qing Legal Reforms. Moral Teachings and Legal Principles', *Modern China*, Vol. 29, No. 3 (July 2003), pp. 297–328.

34　Vivien W. Ng, 'Ideology and Sexuality: Rape Laws in Qing China', *Journal of Asian Studies*, Vol. 46 (1987), pp. 57–60, 310–11.

35　Matthew H. Sommer, *Sex, Law and Society in Late Imperial China* (Stanford, CA, Stanford University Press, 2000), pp. 69, 318; Susan Mann, 'Widows in the Kinship, Class and Community Structures of Qing Dynasty China', *Journal of Asian Studies*, Vol. 46, No. 1 (1987), pp. 37–56.

36　Harry G. Gleber, *The Dragon and the Foreign Devils* (London, Bloomsbury, 2007), pp. 54–6.

37　Susan Mann, *Precious Records. Women in China in the Long Eighteenth-Century* (Stanford, CA, Stanford University Press, 1997), pp. 11, 35, 43.

38　Gail Lee Bernstein, *Recreating Japanese Women, 1600–1945* (Berkeley and Los Angeles, CA, University of California Press, 1991).

39　Judith R. Walkowitz and Daniel J. Walkowitz, '"We Are Not Beasts of the Field": Prostitution and the Poor in Plymouth and Southampton under the Contagious Diseases Acts', *Feminist Studies*, Vol. 1 (Winter-Spring 1973), pp. 73–106. Ruth Harris and Lyndal Roper (eds), *The Art of Survival. Gender and History in Europe, 1450–2000* (Oxford, Oxford University Press, 2006).

40　Randolph Trumbach, 'Prostitution' in Peakman (ed.), *A Cultural History of Sexuality in the Enlightenment*, pp. 183–202.

41　For a comprehensive bibliography of prostitution up to 1999, see Timothy J. Gilfoyle, 'Prostitutes in History: From Parables of Pornography to Metaphors of Modernity', *The American Historical Review*, Vol. 104, No. 1 (February 1999), pp. 117–41.

42　Tony Henderson, *Disorderly Women in Eighteenth-Century London. Prostitution and Control in the Metropolis, 1730–1830* (London, Longman, 1999), p. 2.

43　Julie Peakman, 'Introduction', in *Whore Biographies* (London, Pickering and Chatto, 2007–8); Sophie Carter, *Purchasing Power: Representing Prostitution in Eighteenth-century English Popular Print* (Aldershot, Ashgate, 2004); W. Speck, 'The Harlot in Eighteenth-Century England', *British Journal of Eighteenth-Century Studies*, Vol. III (1980), pp. 127–39; Susan Staves, 'British Seduced Maidens', *Eighteenth-Century Studies*, Vol. 14 (1980/1), pp. 109–34.

44　Sarah Lloyd, '"Pleasure's Golden Bait": Prostitution, Poverty and the Magdalen Hospital in Eighteenth-Century London', *History Workshop Journal* (1996), pp. 51–70; and Stanley Nash, 'Prostitution and Charity: The Magdalen Hospital, a Case Study', *Journal of Social History*, Vol. 17 (1984), pp. 617–28.

45　Sherrill Cohen, *Evolution of Women's Asylums Since 1500. From Refuges for Ex-Prostitutes to Shelters for Battered Women* (Oxford, Oxford University Press, 1992), pp. 165–76, 168.

46　Philippa Levine, *Prostitution, Race and Politics. Policing Venereal Disease in the British Empire* (London, Routledge, 2003); Raelene Frances, 'Prostitution: The Age of Empires', in Chiara Beccalossi and Ivan Crozier (eds), *A Cultural History of Sexuality in the Age of Empire* (Oxford, Berg, 2011), pp. 145–70.

47　Jeffrey Weeks, 'The "Homosexual Role". After 30 Years. An Appreciation of the Work of Mary McIntosh', *Sexualities*, Vol. 1, No. 2 (May 1998), pp. 131–52; Mary McIntosh, 'The Homosexual Role', *Social Problems*, No. 16 (1968), pp. 182–92.

48 For a good introduction to the various debates see D. Altman et al., *Which Homosexuality?* (London, GMP Publishers, 1989) and Edward Stein (ed.), *Forms of Desire. Sexual Orientation and the Social Constructionist Controversy* (London, Routledge, 1990). Also see Michel Foucault, *The History of Sexuality*, Vol. I (London, Penguin reprint 1990); Jeffrey Weeks, *Sex, Politics & Society in the Regulation of Sexuality Since 1800* (London, Longmans, 1989), pp. 96–21; Alan Bray, *Homosexuality in Renaissance England* (New York, Columbia University Press, 1995); Randolph Trumbach, *Sex and the Gedner Revolution Vol. 1: Heterosexuality and the Third Gender in Enlightenment* (London and Chicago, University of Chicago Press, 1998); Rictor Norton, *Mother Clap's Molly House: The Gay Subculture in England, 1700–1830* (London, GMP, 1992); George Haggarty, *Men in Love. Masculinity and Sexuality in the Eighteenth Century* (New York, Columbia University Press, 1999); Katherine O'Donnell and Michael O'Rouke, *Love, Sex, Intimacy and Friendship Between Men, 1550–1800* (London, Palgrave, 2003).

49 Norton, *Mother Clap's Molly House*; D. Higgs, 'Lisbon', in *Queer Sites. Gay Urban Histories Since 1600* (London, Routledge, 1999), pp. 112–37; M. Rey, 'Police and Sodomy in Eighteenth-Century Paris: From Sin to Disorder', in K. Gerard and G. Hekma, *The Pursuit of Sodomy. Male Homosexuality in Renaissance and Enlightenment* (New York, Harrington Park Press, 1989), pp. 129–46; R. D. Tobin, *Warm Brothers: Queer Theory and the Age of Goethe* (Philadelphia, University of Pennsylvania Press, 2000). Also Robert Aldrich (ed.), *Gay Life and Culture. A World History* (London, Thames & Hudson, 2006); David Halperin, *One Hundred Years of Homosexuality* (London, Routledge, 1990).

50 Judith Brown, *Immodest Acts: the Life of a Lesbian Nun in Renaissance Italy* (New York, Oxford University Press, 1986); Lillian Faderman, *Surpassing the Love of Men. Romantic Friendships and Love Between Women from the Renaissance to the Present* (London, Junction Books, 1981); Emma Donoghue, *Passions Between Women* (London, Scarlet Press, 1993); Valerie Traub, 'The Perversion of Lesbian Desire', *History Workshop*, No. 41 (1996), pp. 23–49; Alison Oram and Ann Marie Turnbull *A Lesbian Source History Book. Love & Sex Between Women 1780–1970* (London, Routledge, 2002), Judith M. Bennett, '"Lesbian-Like" and the Social History of Lesbianisms', *Journal of the History of Sexuality*, Vol. 9, No. 1–2 (January/April 2000).

51 Vivien W. Ng, 'Homosexuality and the State in Late Imperial China', in *Hidden from History, Reclaiming the Gay and Lesbian Past* (Nal Books, 1989), pp. 76–89.

52 Sommer, *Sex, Law and Society*, pp. 305, 310–11; Matthew H. Sommer, 'The Penetrated Male in Late Imperial China: Judicial Constructions and Social Stigma', *Modern China*, Vol. 23, No. 2 (April 1997), pp. 140–80.

53 Quoted in Khaled El-Rouayheb, *Before Homosexuality in the Arab-Islamic World, 1500–1800* (Chicago, University of Chicago Press, 2005), p. 1.

54 Murray and Roscoe, *Islamic Homosexualities*; Anne O'Brien, 'Missionary Masculinities: The Homosexual Gaze and the Politics of Race: Gilbert White in Northern Australia, 1885–1915', *Gender and History,* Vol. 20, No. 7 (2008), pp. 68–86.

55 Jonathan Ned Katz, *Love Stories. Sex Between Men Before Homosexuality* (Chicago, University of Chicago Press, 2001).

Chapter Two 'Perversion of the Course of Nature': Sexual Variations in the Eighteenth Century

1 *Old Bailey Proceedings Online* (www.oldbaileyonline.org, 26 December 2008), 11 July 1677 (t16770711-1).

2 Keith Thomas, *Man and the Natural World* (London, Allen Lane, 1983); also see www.oldbaileyonline.org for examples.

3 For arguments on this see Judith Butler, *Gender Trouble, Feminism and the Subversion of Identity* (London, Routledge, 1990); Eve Kosofsky Sedgwick, *Epistemology of the Closet* (Berkeley, University of California, 1990); Jonathan Dollimore, *Sexual Dissidence. Augustine to Wilde, Freud to Foucault* (Oxford, Clarendon Press, 1991); David Halperin, *One Hundred Years of Homosexuality* (London, Routledge, 1990).

4 See Julie Peakman, *The Pleasure's All Mine. A History of Perverse Acts* (London, Reaktion, 2013); Peakman, *Sexual Perversion, 1670–1890* (Basingstoke, Palgrave, 2010).

5 See Introduction to Peakman, *Sexual Perversions, 1670–1890,* Part I.

6 See chapters 2 and 3 in my edition of *Sexual Perversions*. Similar was to be found in French culture; see Natalie Zemon Davies, 'Women on Top', *Society and Culture in Early Modern France* (Stanford, CA, Stanford University Press, 1965), pp. 124–51, 136.

7 John Boswell has argued that negative views on homosexuality did not emerge until the thirteenth century which means that the influences of the Judeo-Christian ethic are not constant throughout the whole of the period. This may well be true of other behaviours thought of as deviant over the last two thousand years but, as yet, not enough work has been undertaken in this area. John Bosewell, *Christianity, Social Tolerance, and Homosexuality* (Chicago, Chicago University Press, 1980).

8 See Introduction, *Sexual Perversions,* Part I.

9 Foucault, *A History of Sexuality, Volume 1, An Introduction,* p. 36.

10 Although Jeffrey Weeks used the title for his book *Against Nature* (1991) to examine homosexuality it can, and was, frequently applied to other perceived sexual deviations.

11 Thomas Laqueur, 'Sexual Desire and the Market Economy', in Donma C. Stanton, *Discourses of Sexuality: From Aristotle to Aids* (Michigan, University of Michigan Press, 1992), p. 210.

12 On social control, see Herman Roodenburg and Pieter Spierenburg, *Social Control in Europe*, Part 1, 1500–1800, Clive Emsley, Eric Johnson and Pieter Spierenburg (eds) Part 2, 1800–2000 (Columbia, Ohio University Press, 2004); on sexual slander, see Laura Gowing, 'Language, Power and the Law: Women's Slander Litigation in Early Modern England', in Jenny Kermode and Garthine Walker (eds), *Women, Crime and Courts in Early Modern England* (Chapel Hill, University of North Carolina Press, 1995), pp. 26–47; on rough music and 'skimmington rides', see E. P. Thompson, *Customs in Common* (London, Penguin, 1991), pp. 467–533.

13 See Julie Peakman on science and nature in her *Mighty Lewd Books* (Basingstoke, Palgrave, 2003), pp. 67–92; James Penney, *World of Perversion: Psychoanalysis and the Impossible Absolute of Desire* (Albany, State University of New York Press, 2006).

14 Pierre Hurteau, 'Catholic Moral Discourse on Male Sodomy and Masturbation in the Seventeenth and Eighteenth Centuries', *Journal of the History of Sexuality*, Vol. 4, No. 1 (July 1993), pp. 1–26, p. 4.

15 Quoted in Hurteau, p. 10.

16 As Sean Brady points out, there was a cascade of new legislation introduced in the nineteenth century but the Buggery Act remained the basis for legislation in prohibited sex between men right up until its repeal in 1967. Despite the introduction of new laws in 1823, 1861 and 1885, the laws remained highly ambivalent; Sean Brady, *Masculinity and Male Homosexuality in Britain, 1861–1913* (Basingstoke, Palgrave, 2005), p. 51.

17 Cynthia B. Herrup, *A House in Gross Disorder, Sex, Law and the 2nd Earl of Castlehaven* (Oxford, Oxford University Press, 1999); Mervin Touchet, *The Arraignment and Conviction of Mervin Lord Audley, Earl of Castlehaven ... at Westminster on Monday April 25, 1631* (London, 1642).

18 *Old Bailey Proceedings Online* (www.oldbaileyonline.org, accessed 26 December 2008), December 1776, Thomas Burrows (t17970215-46).

19 *Old Bailey Proceedings Online* (www.oldbaileyonline.org, accessed 26 December 2008), February 1797, William Winklin (t17761204-2).

20 Hurteau, 'Catholic Moral Discourse', p. 11.

21 See Julie Peakman, *Lascivious Bodies. A Sexual History of the Eighteenth Century* (London, Atlantic, 2004), pp. 174–200; Judith C. Brown, 'Lesbian Sexuality in Renaissance Italy: The Case of Sister Benedetta Carlini', *Signs*, Vol. 9, No. 4 (Summer 1984), pp. 751–8; G. P. S. Bianchi, *An Historical and Physical Dissertation on the Case of Catherine Vizzani, containing the adventures of a young woman who for eight years poised in the habit of a man ... with some curious and anatomical remarks on the nature and existence of the hymen. ... On which are added certain needful remarks by the English editor* (London, 1751); *The True History and Adventures of Catherine Vizzani* (London, W. Reeve, and C. Sympson, 1755); Brigette Eriksson, 'A Lesbian

Execution in Germany, 1721. The Trial Records', *Journal of Homosexuality*, Vol. 6, No. 1–2 (1980/81), pp. 27–40.
22. On toleration of lesbianism see A. D. Harvey, *Sex in Georgian England. Attitudes and Prejudices from the 1720s to the 1820s* (London, Duckworth, 1994), pp. 111–15.
23. *The Annual Register*, 5 July 1777, pp. 191–2.
24. Henry Fielding, *The Female Husband: or the Surprising History of Mrs. Mary, alias George Hamilton* (London, M. Cooper at the Globe in Paternoster Row, 1746).
25. See Peakman, *Lascivious Bodies*, pp. 174–218.
26. The Llangollen Ladies, Sarah Ponsonby and Eleanor Butler, were frequently visited by writers, artists and visitors from London and accepted as a couple. They were therefore upset when the newspaper *General Evening Post* ran an article on them in 1790 insinuating lesbianism, but their friend Edmund Burke advised them against suing for libel. Elizabeth Mavor, *The Ladies of Llangollen* (London, Penguin, 1973); also see the case of Anne Lister, Helena Whitbread (ed.), *'I Know My Heart' The Diaries of Anne Lister 1791–1840* (New York, New York University Press, 1992).
27. *Old Bailey Proceedings Online* (www.oldbaileyonline.org, 26 December 2008), March 1776, Christopher Saunders (t17760417-28).
28. See Jonas Liliequist, 'Peasants Against Nature: Crossing the Boundaries between Man and Animal in Seventeenth and Eighteenth Century Sweden', in John C. Fout (ed.), *Forbidden History. The State, Society and the Regulation of Sexuality in Modern Europe* (Chicago, University of Chicago Press, 1990), pp. 57–88; for the British case described in Peakman, *Lascivious Bodies*, p. 258; and French cases in William Naphy, *Sex Crimes From Renaissance to Enlightenment* (Stroud, Tempus, 2002), pp. 43, 81, 95, 157.
29. G. Hickes, *Rabillac Redivivus* (London, Henry Hills, 1678). Also see Ashbee, Vol. II, pp. 51–61.
30. Jens Rydström, '"Sodomitical Sins Are Threefold": Typologies of Bestiality, Masturbation, and Homosexuality in Sweden, 1880–1950', *Journal of the History of Sexuality*, Vol. 9, No. 3 (July 2000), pp. 240–76; Jens Rydström *Sinners and Citizens: Bestiality and Homosexuality in Sweden, 1880–1950* (Chicago, University of Chicago Press, 2003).
31. Penney, *World of Perversion*, p. 55.
32. *William Perkins, 1558–1602: English Puritanist: his pioneer works on casuistry: 'A discourse of conscience' and 'The whole treatise of cases of conscience'*, edited with an introduction by Thomas F. Merrill (1966), quoted by Dollimore, p. 288.
33. Nadezhda Durova, *The Cavalry Maiden. Journals of a Female Russian Officer in the Napoleonic Wars* (London, Angel Books, 1988); Julie Wheelwright, *Amazons and Military Maids* (London, Pandora Press, 1989); Suzanne J. Stark, *Female Tars. Women Aboard Ship in the Age of Sail* (Maryland, Naval Institute Press, 1996), pp. 102–7.
34. For example see Anon, *Lives and Adventures of a German Princess, Mary Read, Anne Bonny, Joan Philips . . . etc* (London, M. Cooper, 1755).

35 Although Faderman has argued that female transvestism was perceived as threatening, others have found the opposite in cases of mere cross-dressing, where no sex was involved. Peakman, Donaghue and Friedli have found friendly support for the women in such tales of cross-dressing. Lillian Faderman, *Surpassing the Love of Men* (London, Junction Books, 1982); Peakman, *Lascivious Bodies*, pp. 214–35; Emma Donoghue, *Passions Between Women* (London, Scarlet Press, 1993), pp. 87–108; and Lynne Friedli, 'Passing Women, a Study of Gender Boundaries in the Eighteenth Century', in G. S. Rousseau and Roy Porter (eds), *Sexual Underworld of the Enlightenment* (Manchester, Manchester University Press, 1987).

36 This has now been well-documented, first addressed by Rictor Norton, *Mother Clap's Molly House: The Gay Subculture in England, 1700–1830* (London, GMP, 1992).

37 P. J. Carter, '"Mollies", "Fops", and "Men of Feeling": Aspects of Male "effeminacy" and masculinity in Britain, c.1700–80' (PhD, 1995); Philip Carter, 'Men about Town: Representations of Foppery and Masculinity in Early Eighteenth-Century Urban Society', in Hannah Barker and Elaine Chalus (eds), *Gender in Eighteenth-Century England* (Longman, 1997); and more recently his *Men and the Emergence of Polite Society, Britain 1660–1800* (London, Longman, 2001). Also on masculinities in the early modern period see Elizabeth Foyster, *Manhood in Early Modern England* (London, Longman, 1999); Tim Hitchcock and Michèle Cohen (eds), *English Masculinities 1666–1800* (London, Longman, 1999); Michèle Cohen, *Fashioning Masculinity: National Identity and Language in the Eighteenth Century* (London, Routledge, 1996).

38 R. Blanchard, I. G. Racansky and Betty W. Steiner, 'Phallometric Detection of Fetishistic Arousal in Heterosexual Male Cross-Dressers', *Journal of Sex Research*, Vol. 22, No. 4 (November 1986), pp. 452–62.

39 On D'Eon, see Peakman, *Lascivious Bodies*, pp. 211–18.

40 Chevalier D'Eon, *Mémoires pour servir á l'histoire générale des finances* (London, 1758); and *Letters, mémoires and négociations particulières* (London, 1764); Gary Kates, *Monsieur D'Eon is a Woman. A Tale of Political Intrigue and Sexual Masquerade* (London, HarperCollins, 1995).

41 Lisa Forman Cody, 'Sex, Civility, and the Self: Du Coudray, d'Eon, and Eighteenth-Century Conceptions of Gendered, National, and Psychological Identity', *French Historical Studies*, Vol. 24, No. 3 (Summer 2001), pp. 379–407; Vern L Bullough, *Cross Dressing, Sex and Gender* (Philadelphia, University of Pennsylvania Press, 1993); also see Marjorie Garber, *Vested Interests. Cross-dressing and Cultural Anxiety* (London, Routledge, 1992).

42 Dollimore, *Sexual Dissidence: Augustine to Wilde, Freud to Foucault* (Oxford, Clarendon Press, 1991), pp. 284–5, 290.

43 David Kunzle's definition in his book *Fashion and Fetishism. A Social History of the Corset, Tight-Lacing and Other Forms of Body-Sculpture in the West* (New Jersey, Rowan and Littlefield, 1982), p. 1

44 William Rossi, *The Sex Life of the Foot and the Shoe* (London, Routledge & Kegan Paul, 1977), p. 171. The term 'fetish' was adopted in medical and sex literature by Alfred Binet in 1888.

45 Rossi, *The Sex Life of the Foot and the Shoe*, p. 1.
46 Kunzle, *Fashion and Fetishism*, quoting Rossi, p. 15.
47 Rossi, *The Sex Life of the Foot and the Shoe*, pp. 158–70.
48 See Sandra Adams, 'Chinese sexuality and the Bound Foot', in Peakman (ed.), *Sexual Perversions*, pp. 246–75.
49 *Memoirs of Harriette Wilson*, reprinted in Lesley Blanche (ed.), *The Game of Hearts. Harriette Wilson and Her Memoirs* (London, Gryphon Books, 1957), pp. 135, 158.
50 Mary Lyons (ed.), *The Memoirs of Mrs. Leeson, Madam 1727–1797* (Dublin, Lilliput Press, 1995), pp. 176–7.
51 *Oxford English Dictionary*.
52 For example see George Etherege's play *Man of the Mode, or, Sir Fopling Flutter*.
53 Both Chevalliers De Choissy and D'Eon had left their memoirs. See R. H. F. Scott (ed.), *The Transvestite Memoirs of The Abbé De Choisy* (London, Peter Owen, 1973); and note above on D'Eon.
54 Julie Peakman, *Mighty Lewd Books*, pp. 182–5.
55 Patricia Ann Meyer Spacks, *Privacy: Concealing the Eighteenth-Century Self* (Chicago, University of Chicago Press, 2003), p. 141.
56 Peakman, *Mighty Lewd Books*, pp. 12–15.
57 H. Montgomery Hyde, *A History of Pornography* (London, Heinemann, 1964), p. 122. For biographies on de Sade see Neil Schaeffer, *The Marquis de Sade. A Life* (New York, Knopf, 1998); Maurice Lever, *Marquis de Sade. A Biography* (London, HarperCollins, 1993); Francine du Plessix Gary, *At Home with Marquis de Sade* (London, Chatto & Windus, 1999).
58 'Pisanus Fraxis' [Henry Spencer Ashbee], *Index Librorum Prohibitorum*, *Centuria Librorum Absconditorum* and *Catena Librorum Tacendorum* (London, privately printed, 1877), reprinted as *Bibliography of Forbidden Books* (New York, Jack Brussel, 1962), Vol. I, p. 37; Vol. II, pp. xliii, 133, 247.
59 Peter Mendes, *Clandestine Erotic Fiction in English 1800–1930. A Bibliographical Study* (Aldershot, Scholar Press, 1998), pp. 187–8.
60 For a discussion of French influences on English pornography, see Peakman, *Mighty Lewd Books*, pp. 17–22.
61 Jonathan G. W. Conlin, 'High Art and Low Politics: A New Perspective on John Wilkes,' *The Huntington Library Quarterly*, Vol. 64, No. 3/4 (2001), pp. 357–81.
62 Angelica Gooden, *Diderot and the Body* (Oxford, Legenda, 2001), pp. 4, 12.
63 Julie Peakman, 'Bodily Anxieties in Enlightenment Sex Literature', *Studies on Voltaire & the Eighteenth-Century*, No. 1 (2005); Gail Kern Paster, *The Body Embarrassed, Drama and the Disciplines of Shame in Early Modern England* (Ithaca, Cornell University Press, 1993).
64 Phillippe Ariès, *Centuries of Childhood* (New York, Vintage Books, 1962).
65 James R. Kincaid, *Child-Loving. The Erotic Child and Victorian Culture* (London, Routledge, 1992); Louise Jackson, *Child Sexual Abuse in Victorian England* (London, Routledge, 2000).

66 Jad Adams, 'William and Edna Clark Hall: Private and Public Childhood "Your Child Forever"', *English Literature in Transition, 1880–1920*, Vol. 49, No. 4 (2006), pp. 398–417.

67 George Rousseau (ed.), *Child Sexuality. From the Greeks to the Great War* (Basingstoke, Palgrave, 2007).

68 Although a book entitled *The Quintessence of Birch Discipline* is mentioned in the Public Records Office in a prosecution case for the eighteenth century, I have been unable to trace an eighteenth-century edition. The nineteenth-century edition is probably an extended and more advanced and explicit version of the earlier one.

69 Lisa Z. Sigel, 'Name Your Pleasure: The Transformation of Sexual Language in Nineteenth-Century British Pornography', *Journal of the History of Sexuality*, Vol. 9, No. 4 (October 2000), pp. 395–419.

70 See Peakman, *Mighty Lewd Books*, pp. 126–60.

71 See Peakman (ed.), *Sexual Perversions*.

72 Joanna Bourke, *Rape* (London, Virago, 2007), p. 11.

73 Sylvana Tomaselli and Roy Porter (eds), *Rape. An Historical and Cultural Enquiry* (Oxford, Basil Blackwell, 1986).

74 Barbara J. Baines, *Representing Rape in the English Early Modern Period* (New York, Edward Mellen Press, 2003), pp. 2, 261.

75 *Oxford English Dictionary*.

76 On medieval understanding of rape see Ruth Mazo Karras, *Sexuality in Medieval Europe. Doing unto Others* (Oxford, Routledge, 2005), pp. 112–16.

77 Julie Peakman, 'Memoirs of Women of Pleasure: The Whore Biography', *Women's Writing*, Vol. 11, No. 2 (2004).

78 Anna Clark, *Women's Silence, Men's Violence: Sexual Assault in Britain, 1770–1845* (London, Pandora, 1987).

79 Roy Porter, 'Rape – Does it have a historical meaning?' in Sylvana Tomaselli and Roy Porter (eds), *Rape: An Historical and Cultural Enquiry* (Oxford, Basil Blackwell, 1986), p. 218, summing up Susan Brownmiller, *Against Our Will. Men, Women and Rape* (London, Secker and Warburg, 1975).

80 Laura Hinton, *The Perverse Gaze of Sympathy: Sadomasochistic Sentiments from Clarissa to Rescue* 911 (Albany, NY, State University of New York Press, 1999), pp. 36, 74.

81 See John Aitkins, *Sex in Literature: Vol. IV. High Noon: The Seventeenth and Eighteenth Centuries* (London, John Calder, 1982), p. 91.

82 Porter, 'Rape – Does it have a historical meaning?', p. 222.

83 Antony E. Simpson, 'Popular Perceptions of Rape as a Capital Crime in Eighteenth-Century England: The Press and the Trial of Francis Charteris in the Old Bailey, February 1730', *Law and History Review*, Vol. 22, No. 1 (Spring 2004), pp. 27–70.

84 A. D. Harvey, *Rape and Seduction in Early Nineteenth-Century England London* (London, John Nold Books, 1991) quoting from T. E. Tomlins,

The Law Dictionary: Explaining the Rise, Progress and Present State of the English Law (1810), p. 1.

85   See Jennie Mills, 'Rape in Early Eighteenth-Century London: A Perversion "so very perplex'd"', in Peakman, *Sexual Perversions 1670–1890*, pp. 140–66.

86   Harvey, *Rape and Seduction*, quoting from Tomlins, *The Law Dictionary*, p. 1.

87   *Old Bailey Proceedings Online* (www.oldbaileyonline.org, 26 December 2008), April 1707, Alice Grey (t17070423-26).

88   Elizabeth Bronfen, *Over Her Dead Body. Death, Femininity and the Aesthetic* (Manchester, Manchester University Press, 1992); Camille Naish, *Death Comes to the Maiden. Sex and Execution 1431–1933* (London, Routledge, 1991); Janet Todd, *Gender, Art and Death* (New York, Continuum Publishing Company, 1993).

89   Beverley Clack, *Sex and Death. A Reappraisal of Human Mortality* (Cambridge, Polity, 2002), p. 81.

90   Jolene Zigarovich (ed.), *Sex and Death in Eighteenth-Century Literature* (London and New York, Routledge, 2013).

91   Lisa Downing, *Desiring the Dead: Necrophilia and Nineteenth-Century French Literature* (Oxford, Legenda, 2003), p. 11.

92   Jonathan P. Rosman and Phillip J. Resnick, 'Sexual Attraction to Corpses: A Psychiatric Review of Necrophilia', *Bulletin of the American Academy of Psychiatry and the Law*, Vol. 17 (1989), pp. 153–63.

93   On necrophilia, see Julie Peakman, *The Pleasure's All Mine: A History of Sexual Perversion* (London, Reaktion, 2014), pp. 239–69.

94   Joseph Loach, 'History, Memoir and Necrophilia' in Peggy Phelan (ed.), *The End of Performance* (New York University Press, 1998), pp. 23–30.

95   See Ashbee, *Bibliography of Forbidden Books*, Vol. II, p. 6; Vol. III, p. 15.

96   Scott Dudley, 'Conferring with the Dead, Necrophilia and Nostalgia in the Eighteenth Century', *ELH*, Vol. 66, No. 2 (Summer 1999), pp. 277–94.

97   For cultural influences and dissection see Jonathan Sawday, *The Body Emblazoned. Dissections and the Human Body in Renaissance Culture* (London, Routledge, 1995); Tom Marshall, *Grave-Robbing, Frankenstein and the Anatomy Literature* (Manchester, Manchester University Press, 1995); Ruth Richardson, *Death, Dissection and the Destitute* (London and New York, Routledge, 1997); Richardson, *The Human Corpse and Popular Culture* (Brighton, University of Sussex, 1985).

98   A copy of the *The Lascivious Hypocrite* (1790) is in the Dawes Bequest at the British Library; Ashbee cites the book entitled *La Tartufe [sic] Libertin ou Le Triomphe du Vice (Par Le Marquis DE SADE) En Holland Chez Les Libraires Associés 1789* (Fraxis, *Centuria*, Vol. II, pp. 267–8).

99   Translations announcing themselves as 'true and accurate' were frequently freely altered, if not completely spurious.

100 For his categorizations of sexual anomalies see Kraft-Ebbing, *Psychopathia Sexualis* (1886, English trans. 1892).

101 Hyman believes the erosion of respect of other races of the British Empire took place between the 1790s and 1840s, and the growth of prejudice against them took place between the mid-1850s and the late 1860s, although I have found lack of respect and prejudice from much earlier explorations. Ronald Hyman, *Empire and Sexuality. The British Experience* (Manchester, Manchester University Press, 1900); Julie Peakman, *Civilising Sex. Two Thousand Years of History* (London, forthcoming).

102 Philippa Levine, *Prostitution, Race and Politics. Policing Venereal Disease in the British Empire* (London, Routledge, 2003). Also see her chapter in Levine (ed.), *Gender and Empire* (Oxford, Oxford University Press, 2004), pp. 134–55.

103 George L. Mosse, 'Nationalism and Respectability: Normal and Abnormal Sexuality in the Nineteenth Century', *Journal of Contemporary History*, Vol. 17, No. 2 (April 1982), pp. 221–46.

104 Ibid.

105 The concept of normality as 'constituting, conforming to, not deviating or differing from the common type of standard' and the term 'abnormal as 'deriving from the ordinary rule or type, contrary to the rule or system', appears only to have become common from the 1830s or 1840s onwards; as did its opposite abnormal 'deviating from the ordinary rule or type; contrary to the rule or system; irregular unusual aberrant'.

Chapter Three Blaming and Shaming in Eighteenth- and Early Nineteenth-century Print Culture

1 Norbert Elias, *The Civilizing Process* (Oxford, Blackwell, 2000); Michel Foucault, *Madness and Civilization. A History of the Age of Reason* (London, Tavistock, 1965); Foucault, *Discipline and Punishment* (Harmondsworth, Penguin, 1991). For a discussion, see Judith Rowbotham, Marianna Muravyeva and David Nash, *Shaming, Blaming and Culpabilities. Crime and Violence in the Modern State* (London, Routledge, 2013), p. 3.

2 Margaret R. Hunt, *The Middling Sort: Commerce, Gender, and the Family in England, 1680–1780* (California, University of California Press, 1996).

3 See Paul Langford, *A Polite and Commercial People, England 1727–1783* (Oxford, Clarendon Press, 1996).

4 As well as Foucault's books above, see his 'Two Hectares', in Colin Gordon (ed.), *Power and Knowledge* (New York, Pantheon, 1980).

5 David Nash, 'Agenda for the Wider Study of Shame', in Rowbotham et al., *Shaming, Blaming and Culpabilities*, pp. 43–50, p. 47; Jürgen Habermas, *The Structural Transformation of the Public Sphere: Inquiry into a Category of Bourgeois Society* (Cambridge, Polity Press, 1992).

6 Muravyeva, 'Litigating for Shame and Dishonour in Early Modern Europe', in Rowbotham et al., *Shame, Blame and Culpability*, pp. 17–31.

NOTES

7   There was a cascade of new legislation introduced in the nineteenth century but the Buggery Act remained the basis for legislation in prohibited sex between men right up until its appeal in 1967.

8   Cynthia B. Herrup, *A House in Gross Disorder, Sex, Law and the 2nd Earl of Castlehaven* (Oxford, Oxford University Press, 1999).

9   The sheer number of editions and reprints point to the pamphlet's popularity, for example: *The Arraignment and Conviction of Mervin Lord Audley, Earl of Castlehaven . . . at Westminster on Monday April 25, 1631. As also the beheading of the said Earle shortly after on Tower Hill, Mervin Touchet, Earl of Castlehaven* (London, T. Thomas, 1642); *The Trial of the Lord Audley, Earl of Castlehaven, for inhumanely causing his own wife to be ravished, and for buggery, Mervin Touchet, Earl of Castlehaven* (London, 1679); *The Memoirs of James Lord Audley, Earl of Castlehaven, his engagement and carriage in the wars of Ireland from the year 1642 to the year 1651. [Written by himself.] James TOUCHET, Earl of Castlehaven* (London, C. Brome, 1684); *The Tryal and Condemnation of Mervin, Lord Audley Earl of Castle-Haven, at Westminster, April the 5th 1631. For abetting a rape upon his Countess, committing sodomy with his servants, etc. Mervin Touchet, Earl of Castlehaven* (London, 1699); *The Case of sodomy in the tryal of Mervin Lord Audley, Earl of Castlehaven . . . Printed from an original manuscript. Mervin Touchet, Earl of Castlehaven* (London, 1708); *The Case of Sodomy in the Tryal of Mervin Lord Audley, Earl of Castlehaven* (London 1710).

10 For more information on Curll, see Paul Baines and Pat Rogers, *Edmund Curll, Bookseller* (Oxford, Oxford University Press, 2007).

11 *The Case of Impotency as debated in England in that remarkable tryal An. 1613, between Robert, Earl of Essex, and the Lady Frances Howard, etc. (Vol. II. Containing The Tryal of Mervin, Lord Audley, Earl of Castlehaven, for sodomy, and a rape, Anno 1631. The Proceedings upon the Bill of Divorce between His Grace Henry, Duke of Norfolk, and the Lady Mary Mordant . . . Anno 1699)* (London, E. Curll, 1715).

12 See my chapter on 'The Erotic Book Trade', in Julie Peakman, *Mighty Lewd Books. The Development of Pornography in Eighteenth-Century England* (Basingstoke, Palgrave, 2003), pp. 12–44.

13 Also see *The Tyburn Chronicle, or, Villainy Display'd in All its Branches, Containing an authenic account of the lives, adventures, tryals, executions, and last dying speeches of the most notorious malefactors . . . who have suffered . . . in England, Scotland, and Ireland, from the year 1700, to the present time* (London, J. Cooke, 1768), Vol. IV, pp. 137–42. This carried the news about another sodomitical rape in *A Narrative of the Behaviour of Thomas Andrews, who was convicted of committing the detestable Crime of Sodomy, on the Body of John Finnimore* (1768). For a comprehensive look at the trials, see http://rictornorton.co.uk/eighteen, accessed 2 August 2015.

14 *The Trial of Richard Branson for an attempt to commit sodomy on the body of James Fassett* (London, T. Drake, 1760).

15 *Some Particulars Relating to the Life of William Dillon Sheppard, Who was executed at St Michael's Hill Gallows, for Sodomy on Monday the 1st June, 1761* (Bristol, E. Ward, 1761), p. 21; 'sold opposite the post-office'.

16 *Some Particulars . . . Sheppard*, p. 23.
17 *The State of the Case of Captain Jones* (London, T. Peat 1772), which could be purchased in a shop opposite St Dunstan's church in Fleet Street.
18 Rictor Norton had discussed the case in detail on his website where the full text has been transposed: http://rictornorton.co.uk/eighteen/jones1.htm. Norton also provides newspaper reports about the case.
19 *The State of the Case of Captain Jones*, p. 18
20 Ibid., pp. 21–2.
21 See my chapter on 'Anti-Catholic Erotica' in *Mighty Lewd Books*, pp. 126–60.
22 Nicholas Bernard, *The Penitent Death of a Woefull Sinner. Or, the penitent death of John Atherton executed at Dublin the 5. of December. 1640 . . . As also the sermon . . . preached at his burial* (Dublin, Printed by the Society of Stationers, 1641); *The Life and Death of John Atherton, Lord Bishop of Waterford and Lysmore, who for incest . . . and many other enormous crimes was hanged on the Gallows Greene at Dublin* [in verse] (London, 1641); *The Case of John Atherton Bishop of Ireland* (London, J. Morphew, 1710). For the 1641 text, see http://rictornorton.co.uk/eighteen/atherton.htm and his entry on Atherton in *Who's Who in Gay & Lesbian History*, ed. Robert Aldrich and Garry Wotherspoon (London and New York, Routledge, 2001), Vol. I, pp. 31–2.
23 Anon, *A Correct Account of the Horrible Occurrence which took place at the pubic house in St James's market in which it was discovered that The Right Rev Father in God the Bishop of Clogher Lately transferred from the Bishopric of Ferns was a principal actor with A Common Soldier!* (London, J. Marks 1822), p. 8. Also see *The Bishop!! Particulars of the Charge against the Hon. Percy Jocelyn, Bishop of Clogher* (London, 1822); and William Benbow, *Crimes of the Clergy* (1823), pp. 41–4.
24 *A Correct Account of the Horrible Occurrence*, p. 23.
25 See Lawrence Stone, *Roads to Divorce 1530–1987* (Oxford, Oxford University Press, 1990), pp. 1, 347.
26 M. Harris, 'Trial and Criminal Biographies. A case study in Distribution', in R. Myers and M. Harris (eds), *Sale and Distribution of Books from 1700* (Oxford, Oxford Polytechnic Press, 1982), pp. 1–36.
27 Richard Lydell, *Account of the Tryal of R. L. . . . for criminal conversation with Lady Abergavenny* (London, 1730); *The Tryal of Mr Harvey for having Criminal Conversation with the wife of Mr Gouldney in Pall-Mall Miscellany* (1732); *The Tryal for the cause for the Criminal Conversation between Theophilus Cibber, Gent and Willim Sloper* (London, T. Trott, 1734); J. G. Biker, *The Tryal between J. G. Biker, Plaintiff; and M. Morley, Doctor of Physic, Defendant; for criminal conversation with the plaintiff's wife* (London, J. Huggonson, 1741); *The Tryal between Sir W----m M--rr--s, baronet, plaintiff, and Lord A---gst---s F---tz-R--y, defendant, for criminal conversation with the plaintiff's wife, at the Kings-Bench Bar, Westminster. William Morice, Sir* (c.1707–1750); *Tryal before the Lord chief [sic] Justice R-y---d at [sic] Guild Hall between Mr. J--c – a mercer at Aldgate, and Mr. J. E—for criminal conversation with his wife . . .* (London, printed for J. Huggonson, in

Sword-and-Buckler Court, over-against the Crown Tavern, on Ludgate-Hill, 1742); Gawler, afterwards Ker, John Bellenden, *The genuine trial of J. B. Gawler for criminal conversation with . . . Lady Valentia* (London, 1799); Charles Sturt, M.P. for Bridport, *Report of the cause between C. S., plaintiff, and . . . the Marquis of Blandford [afterwards Duke of Marlborough], defendant, for criminal conversation with . . . Lady M. A. Sturt* (London, J. Ridgway, 1801); Charles Massy, *A Report of the Trial on an action for damages, brought by the Reverend C. Massy against . . . the Marquis of Headfort, for criminal conversation with Plaintiff's Wife, etc.* (London, H. D. Symmonds, 1804).

28 *His Grace, the Duke of Norfolk's Charge Against the Dutchess [sic] before the House of Lords, and the Dutchesses [sic] Answer* (London, 1692), p. 1.

29 Ibid., p. 2.

30 For example, see Laura Gowing, *Domestic Dangers: Women, Words and Sex in early Modern London* (Oxford, Oxford University Press, 1996); Elizabeth A. Foyster, *Manhood in Early Modern England, Honour, Sex and Marriage* (London, Longman, 1999).

31 David Turner, '"Nothing is so secret but shall be revealed"; the scandalous life of Robert Foulkes', in Tim Hitchcock and Michèle Cohen, *English Masculinities 1660–1800* (London, Longman, 1999), pp. 169–92.

32 *The Tryals of the Two Causes between Theophilus Cibber Gent and Plaintiff William (1710)* (London, 1710), p. 2

33 E. P. Thompson, *Customs in Common* (Harmondsworth, Penguin, 1978), p. 443

34 John Stevenson, *Popular Disturbances in England 1700–1832* (London, Longman, 1992).

35 *The Whole Tryal of Richard Lydell Esq. At his Majesty's Court of Common-Pleas Before the Right Honourable Lord Chief Justice Eyre for Carrying on a Criminal Conversation with the late Lady Abergavenny on Monday the 16th of February, 1729/30* (London, A. Moore near St Paul's and sold by the booksellers of London and Westminster, 1730), p. A2.

36 Ibid., p. 4.

37 Ibid., p. 4.

38 Ibid., pp. 9–10.

39 Ibid., pp. 10–11.

40 For a discussion on the author and other anti-clerical material, see Peakman, *Mighty Lewd Book. The Development of Eighteenth-Century Pornography in Eighteenth-Century England* (London, Palgrave, 2003), pp. 126–60.

41 Gabriel D'Emiliane, *A Short History of Monastical Orders* (London, Robert Clarvell, 1693), pp. 133–4.

42 Anon, *The Case of Seduction Being an Account of the late Proceedings at Paris, as well Ecclesiastical; as Civil Against the Reverent Abbé Claudius Nicholas des Rues for committing rapes on 133 Virgins* (London, E. Curll, 1726).

43 *Tryal of Father John-Baptist Girard on an Accusation for Quietism, Sorcery, Incest, Abortion and Subornation Before the Great Chamber of Parlement at Aix. At the Instance of Miss Mary-Catherine Cadiere* (London, Printed for J. Isted, at the Golden Ball in Fleet-Street; T. Astley in St. Paul's Churchyard;

E. Nutt at the Royal-Exchange; A. Dod, without Temple-Bar; and J. Jollifre, in St. James's Street, 1732).

44 John Hill, *The Story of Elizabeth Canning, considered. With remarks on what has been called, A clear state of her case, by Mr Fielding, etc.* (London, 1753) which refers to Henry Fielding, *A clear state of the case of Elizabeth Canning, who hath sworn that she was robbed and almost starved to death by a gang of gipsies and other villains in January last, for which one Mary Squires now lies under sentence of death* (Dublin, George Faulkner, 1753). For other examples see Daniel Cox, M.D., *An Appeal to the Public, in behalf of Elizabeth Canning, in which the material facts in her story are fairly stated, and shewn to be true, etc.* (London, W. Meadows, 1753); 'Philologus' [John Hill], The Inspector inspected: or, Dr Hill's story of *Elizabeth Canning, examined: in which all his subterfuges are detected and confuted* (London, 1752); A Complete Answer to the Clergyman's Letter to the Right Honourable the Earl of ------ concerning the affair of *Elizabeth Canning, . . . By a Wild Indian, suddenly landed in England from California* (London, Printed for the Author, 1753); *A Collection of Several Papers relating to Elizabeth Canning* (London, E. Innocent, 1754); Mary Squires, *A full and authentic account of the . . . affair between Mary Squires . . . and Elizabeth Canning,; . . . with all the particulars of the trial of E. Canning* (London, 1754).

45 John Hill, *The Story of Elizabeth Canning, considered. With remarks on what has been called, A clear state of her case, by Mr Fielding, etc.* pp. 14–15.

46 Ibid., p. 15.

47 Ibid., pp. 19–20.

48 Ibid., p. 24.

49 *Rape And Murder!!The Trial Of Abraham Thornton, For The Wilful Murder Of Mary Ashford; With Copius Elucidations* (London, John Fairburn, 1817), p. 5; as well as a flurry of pamphlets on this case, many others would follow, for example *The life, trial and execution of George & Henry Knowles, two brothers, who underwent the awful sentence of the law, for a rape, robbery, & murder of Ann Vale, between Abington and Sutton, in the county of Berks, on Thursday last, March 3rd, 1825*; *The Trial and Lamentation of Patrick Duffy for a Rape, sentenced to be hung at Oakham Gallows* (1826); and *The Trial and Execution of the Burkers for Murdering a Poor Italian Boy* (1831).

50 For example, *Tryal of Jane Wenham, witch* (1712).

Chapter Four   Whore Biographies in the Eighteenth Century

1 See Julie Peakman, *Lascivious Bodies. A Sexual History of the Eighteenth-Century* (London, Atlantic, 2004); Peakman, *Mighty Lewd Books. The Development of Pornography in Eighteenth-Century England* (London, Palgrave, 2003); Tony Anderson, *Disorderly Women in Eighteenth-Century London, 1730–1830* (London, Longman, 1999); Randolph Trumbach, *Sex and the Gender Revolution. Heterosexuality and the Third Gender in*

Enlightenment London (Chicago and London, University of Chicago Press, 1998).
2 Sophie Carter, *Representing Prostitution in Eighteenth Century English Popular Print Culture* (Aldershot, Ashgate, 2004).
3 Patricia Meyers Spacks asserts 'the material of biography obviously resembles that of gossip': Patricia Meyer Spacks, *Gossip* (New York, Alfred A. Knopf, 1985), p. 118.
4 'One would make no mistake in calling you a pornographer . . .', Athenaeus' *Deipnosophistae*, Vol. 13, Section 567b.
5 For a history of foreign influences on erotic literature and the development of modern pornography see Peakman, *Mighty Lewd Books*; 'Initiation, Defloration and Flagellation: Sexual Propensities in *Memoirs of a Woman of Pleasure*', in Patsy Fowler and Alan Jackson (eds), *This Launch into the Wide World: Essays on Fanny Hill*, (New York, AMS Press, 2003); Melissa M. Mowry, *The Bawdy Politic In Stuart England, 1660–1714: Political Pornography and Prostitution* (Aldershot, Ashgate Publishing, 2004); James Grantham Turner, *Schooling Sex: Libertine Literature and Erotic Education in Italy, France, and England 1534–1685* (Oxford, Oxford University Press, 2003); Ian Frederick Moulton, *Before Pornography. Erotic Writings in Early in Modern England* (Oxford, Oxford University Press, 2000); Bradford K. Mudge, *The Whore's Story. Women, Pornography and the British Novel, 1684–1830* (Oxford, Oxford University Press, 2000); Robert Darnton, *The Forbidden Best-Sellers of Pre-Revolutionary France* (London, HarperCollins, 1997); Jean Marie Goulemot, *Forbidden Texts. Erotic Literature and its Readers in Eighteenth-Century France* (Cambridge, Polity Press, 1994); Lynn Hunt (ed.), *The Invention of Pornography: Obscenity and the Origins of Modernity, 1500–1800* (New York, Zone Books, 1993); Peter Wagner, *Eros Revived. Erotica of the Enlightenment in England and America* (London, Secker & Warburg, 1988); Patrick Kearney, *The History of Erotica* (London, Macmillan, 1982); Maurice Charney, *Sexual Fiction* (Iowa, Kendall Hunt Publishing Company, 1981); David Foxon, *Libertine Literature in England 1660–1745* (New York, University Books, 1965).
6 For examples, 'Charles Johnson' [Daniel Defoe], *A History of the Lives of all the Notorious Pirates* (Dublin, 1727); Henry Fielding, *The Life of Mr Jonathan Wild the Great* (London, 1743); as well as female adventurers as found in *The Lives and Adventures of a German Princess, Mary Read, Anne Bonny, Joan Philips . . . etc* (London, 1755).
7 For fuller details, see Julie Peakman, *Whore's Biographies 1700–1825* (London, Pickering & Chatto, 2006–7), 8 Vols, accompanied by reprints of original texts.
8 For further discussions on whores' narratives see Julie Peakman, 'Memoirs of Women of Pleasure: the Whore Biography', *Women's Writing*, Vol. 11, No. 2 (2004), pp. 163–83; Alison Conway, 'Defoe's Protestant Whore', *Eighteenth-Century Studies*, Vol. 35, No. 2 (2002); Vivien Jones, 'Scandalous Femininity: Prostitution and Eighteenth-Century Narrative', in Dario Castilione and Lesley Sharpe, *Shifting the Boundaries* (Exeter, Exeter University Press, 1995), pp. 54–70; James Grantham Turner, '*The Whore's Rhetorick*: Narrative,

Pornography and the Origins of the Novel', *Studies in Eighteenth-Century Culture*, Vol. 24 (1995), pp. 297–306.

9   *The Genuine History of Mrs. Sarah Prydden, usually called Sally Salisbury and her Gallants* is reprinted in *Eighteenth-Century British Erotic II* (London, Pickering and Chatto, 2001).

10 'Annodyne Tanner MD', *The Life of the Late Celebrated Mrs Elizabeth Wisebourn, vulgarly call'd Mother Wybourn* ('Published for A. Moore, near St. Pauls', 1721). This is the earliest extant English whores' biography of its type in the British Library catalogue but more might emerge from other archives.

11 BL shelfmarks, 808g36; 635f11 (12);1419k.21.

12 See Burford, *Wits*, pp. 42–52.

13 *Pharmacopaeia Venerea or a Compleat Venereal Dispensory. By Anodyne Necklace Tanner* (London, H. Parker, 1724), p. 18.

14 *Weekly Journal, or The British Gazetteer*, 7 February 1719.

15 *An Account of the Tryal of Salley Salisbury* (London, 1723); *The Effigies, Parentage, Education, Life, Merry-Pranks and Conversation of the Celebrated Mrs Sally Salisbury* (Cornhill, London, John Wilkes, 1722–3); *Sally Salisbury's Letter to Frank Rigg* (Dublin, J. Carson, 1723).

16 Captain Charles Walker, *Authentick Memoirs of the Life, Intrigues and Adventures of the Celebrated Sally Salisbury* (London, 1723), p. 8; Anon, *The Genuine History of Mrs. Sarah Prydden, Usually Called Sally Salisbury and Her Gallants* (London, Andrew Moore, 1723), pp. 39–41.

17 For further details about her life, see Peakman, *Whores Biography*.

18 Old Bailey Proceedings online, 24 April 1723. Reference Number: 17230424–2.

19 There is another copy of *An Account of the Tryal of Salley Salisbury* in the back of the second edition of Captain Charles Walker's *Authentick Memoirs of the Life, Intrigues and Adventures of the Celebrated Sally Salisbury*, held at the British Library.

20 *Memoirs of the Celebrated Miss Fanny M____* [Murray] (London, J. Scott in Pater-noster-Row; and M. Thrush at the Kings Arms, second edition, 1759). This edition sold for three shillings. The first edition came out in 1758, a copy of which is extant in the University of Chicago, Los Angeles.

21 Hinde and Walters believe she came from London; T. Hinde, *Taken from the Pump Room; 900 years of Bath, the place, its people and its gossip* (1988), p. 40; John Walters, *Splendours and Scandal. The Reign Of Beau Nash* (London, Jarrolds, 1968), p. 73.

22 Her current biographer (correctly, I believe) runs with the *Memoirs* asserting Murray was born in Bath in 1729; Barbara White, *Queen of the Courtesans* (Stroud, The History Press, 2014), p. 13.

23 Walters, p. 31, quoting an unreferenced contemporary source.

24 See for example, *Kitty's Stream, Or the Noblemen Turned Fisher-Men. A comic Satire* (Printed for A. Moore, near St. Pauls, 1759); *Horse and Away to St. James's Park Or, a Trip for the Noontide Air Who Rides Fastest, Miss Kitty Fisher or her Gay Gallant* (Printed at Strawberry Hill, 1760); *A Sketch of the*

Present Times and the Time to come: In an Address to Kitty Fisher (London, T. Waller, 1762); price one shilling, a poem dedicated to Kitty Fisher.

25 Casonova stated it was Ensign Anthony George Martin, but *Town and Country Magazine* believed it to be Captain Augustus Keppel; Jacques Casanova de Seingalt, *Memoirs of Casanova*, Vol. II (privately printed for the Navarre society), p. 222; *Town and Country Magazine,* September 1771.

26 *Genuine Memoirs of the Celebrated Miss Nancy Dawson* (London, Printed for R. Stevens, at Pope's Head in Paster-Noster-Row, 1760) was followed by the second edition entitled *Authentic Memoirs of the Celebrated Miss Nancy Dawson* (London, Tom Dawson, 1762).

27 *Of All the Girls in our Town. Nancy Dawson, a New Song* (London, 1760).

28 *Oxford Dictionary of National Biography.*

29 *Genuine Memoirs of the Late Celebrated Jane D******s* [Douglas] (London, Printed for J. Simpson at Shakepear's Head in Paul's Alley, St Paul's Churchyard, 1761). Price two shillings.

30 *The Whole Life and Adventures of Miss Davies Commonly called The Beauty in Disguise. With a full, true, and particular Account of her robbing Mr. W. of Gosfield, in Essex, of Eleven Hundred Pounds in Cash and Bank notes, for which she now lays to take her trial at Chelmsford* (1785), pp. 3–4. [BL shelfmark: 1077g36(2).]

31 National Archives: Ref Assi 31/14 and Assi 94 1270.

32 See Peakman, 'Women in Breeches', *Lascivious Bodies*, pp. 219–25.

33 *See Secret Memoirs of Miss Sally Dawson; Otherwise Mrs. Sally McClane; Otherwise Mrs Sarah Mayne, _____Widow* (London, Holmes & Charles, 1805), note to p. 8, l. 25.

34 Both Peg Plunkett and Harriette Wilson mention encounters with the Prince of Wales.

35 W. Speck, 'The Harlot in Eighteenth-Century England', *British Journal of Eighteenth-Century Studies*, Vol. III (1980), pp. 127–39. For images in literature, see Susan Staves, 'British Seduced Maidens', *Eighteenth-Century Studies*, Vol. 14 (1980/1), pp. 109–34; and Patricia Meyer Spacks, '"Ever'y Woman is at Heart a Rake"', *Eighteenth-Century Studies*, Vol. 8, No. 1 (1974), pp. 27–46. For an analysis of visual images see Sophie Carter, *Purchasing Power: Representing Prostitution in Eighteenth-century English Popular Print* (Aldershot, Ashgate, 2004).

36 In both of William Hogarths's series of prints, the *Harlot's* and *Rake's Progress,* both images of Seduced Maiden and Brazen Whore run concurrently in a gritty portrayal of seduction by a procuress and the poor 'fallen' millineress who then becomes the brazen whore, an inevitable result.

37 Jonas Hanaway, *Thought On The Plan For A Magdalen House* (1758); Sarah Lloyd, '"Pleasure's Golden Bait": Prostitution, Poverty and the Magdelen Hospital in Eighteenth-Century London', *History Workshop Journal* (1996), pp. 51–70; and Stanley Nash, 'Prostitution and Charity: The Magdalen Hospital, a Case Study', *Journal of Social History,* Vol. 17 (1984), pp. 617–28.

38 M. Ludovicus, *A Particular but Melancholy Account of the Great Hardships, Difficulties, and Miseries that . . . the Common Women of the Town are Plung'd into at this Juncture, etc.* (London, 1752); John Fielding, *A Plan or the Preventing of Robberies within Twenty Mile of London. With an account of the rise and establishment of the real Thieftakers* (London, 1955) and *A Plan for a Preservatory and Reformator, for the benefit of deserted girls and penitent prostitutes* (London, 1758).

39 Cambridge University Library, shelf mark Hh1138(2); BL shelf mark C124g15.

40 Edward J. Bristow, *Vice and Vigilance. Purity Movements in Britain since 1700* (London, Macmillan, 1977).

41 Saunders Welch, *A Proposal To Render Effectual A Plan To Remove The Nuisance Of Common Prostitutes From The Street Of This Metropolis* (London, 1758); Baron von Uffenbach (trans. W. Quarrell and Margaret Moore), *London in 1710* (London, Faber, 1934).

42 Roy Porter and Lesley Hall, *Facts of Life: The Creation of Sexual Knowledge in Britain, 1650–1950* (Yale University Press, 1995), p. 15.

43 Boswell's London Journal, 14 December 1762.

44 Tony Henderson, *Disorderly Women in Eighteenth-Century London. Prostitution and Control in the Metropolis, 1730–1830* (London, Longman, 1999).

45 Thomas, Keith, 'The Double Standard', *Journal of History of Ideas*, Vol. 20 (1959), pp. 195–216; Vivien Jones (ed.), *Women in the Eighteenth Century. Constructions of Femininity* (London, Routledge, 1990); Margaret Sommerville, *Sex and Subjugation. Attitudes in Early-Modern Society* (London, Arnold, 1995).

46 For the history of sexuality in the eighteenth century see Julie Peakman, *Lascivious Bodies. A Sexual History of the Eighteenth Century* (London, Atlantic, 2004); Tim Hitchcock, *English Sexualities, 1700–1800* (Basingstoke, Macmillan, 1997); Roy Porter and Lesley Hall, *Facts of Life: The Creation of Sexual Knowledge in Britain, 1650–1950* (New Haven, CT, Yale University Press, 1995); Roy Porter and Mikuláš Teich (eds), *Sexual Knowledge and Sexual Science. The History of Attitudes to Sexuality* (Cambridge, Cambridge University Press, 1994); Robert Purks Maccubbin (ed.), *'Tis Nature's Fault. Unauthorised Sexuality during the Enlightenment* (Cambridge, Cambridge University Press, 1987); G. S. Rousseau and Roy Porter (eds), *Sexual Underworlds of the Enlightenment* (Manchester, Manchester University Press, 1987); Paul-Gabriel Boucé (ed.), *Sexuality in Eighteenth-Century Britain* (Manchester, Manchester University Press, 1982).

47 Anne-Marie Kilday and Katherine Watson, 'Child Murder in Georgian England', *History Today*, Vol. 55, No. 1 (2005), pp. 40–46; Josephine McDonagh, *Child Murders and British Culture, 1720–1900* (Cambridge, Cambridge University Press, 2003); Mark Jackson (ed.), *Infanticide: Historical Perspective on Child Murder and Concealment, 1500–2000* (Aldershot, Ashgate, 2002); Marilyn Francis, 'Monstrous Mothers, Monstrous Societies: Infanticide and the Rule of Law in Eighteenth-Century England', *Eighteenth-Century Life* (1997), pp 133–56; Mark Jackson, *New-Born Child Murder:*

Women, Illegitimacy and the Courts in Eighteenth-Century England (Manchester, Manchester University Press, 1996).

48 Hogarth's *Before* and *After* (1736) shows the seduction of a young woman; in *Before* the girl has anticipated her lover's advances and removed her shackling underwear beforehand. The source of her 'fall' is to be found in the reading material on her bedside cabinet, the poems of Rochester and a novel, 'The Practice of Piety', lies adjacent, in vain also resting beside a love letter. *After* shows the girl in clinging defeat. A book lies on the floor entitled 'Omne Animal Post Coitum Triste/Aristotle' (Every animal is sad after intercourse).

49 For further discussions on venereal disease in the eighteenth century, see Kevin P. Siena, *Venereal Disease, Hospitals and the Urban Poor* (Rochester, NY, Woodbridge, University of Rochester Press, 2004); Linda Merians, *The Secret Malady. Venereal Disease in Eighteenth-Century Britain and France* (Lexington, University of Kentucky, 1996); David Innes, *The London Lock Hospital 1746–1952* (London, Royal Society of Medicine, 1995); W.F. Bynum, *Treating the Wages of Sin. Venereal Disease and Specialism in Eighteenth-century Britain* (London, Wellcome, 1987).

50 *Gentleman's Magazine,* Vol. 1 (1731), p. 15.

51 For further information on the erotic book trade, see Peakman, *Mighty Lewd Books*, pp. 12–44. Spufford suggests a shared appreciation of rude humour between plebeian men and women in their reading of cheap popular ribald material, declaring that 'even the most cultivated early seventeenth-century ladies enjoyed dirty jokes'; Margaret Spufford, *Small Books and Pleasant Histories. Popular Fiction and its Readership in Seventeenth-Century England* (Cambridge, Cambridge University Press, 1981), p. 62.

Chapter Five   Memoirs of Women of Pleasure: Autobiographies

1 Ann Lewis and Markman Ellis (eds), *Prostitution and Eighteenth-Century Culture: Sex, Commerce and Morality* (London, Pickering & Chatto, 2011), p. 1.

2 Eric Trudgill, *Madonnas and Magdalenes* (London, Heinemann, 1976). For an overview of images of women in the eighteenth century, see Paul Fritz and Richard Morton (eds), *Women in the Eighteenth Century and Other Essays* (Toronto and Sarasota, 1976); Katherine Rogers, *Feminism in the Eighteenth Century* (London, Harvester, 1982); Alice Brown, *The Eighteenth Century Feminist Mind* (London, Harvester Press, 1987). For useful anthologies see Bridget Hill, *Eighteenth-Century Women: An Anthology* (London, Allen & Unwin, 1984) and Vivien Jones, *Women in the Eighteenth Century* (London, Routledge, 1990).

3 See Thompson, *The Scandalous Memoirists,* pp.19–79 and 81–122.

4 John Carroll (ed.), 'Samuel Richardson, letters to Sarah Chapone, 6 December 1750 and 11 January 1751', in *Selected Letters of Samuel Richardson* (Oxford, Clarendon Press, 1964), p. 173.

5   Norma Clarke, *Queen of Wits. A Life of Laetitia Pilkington* (London, Faber and Faber, 2008), p. xv.
6   Lynda M. Thompson, *The 'Scandalous Memoirists'. Constantia Phillips, Laetitia Pilkington and the Shame of 'Publick Fame'* (Manchester, Manchester University Press, 2000), p. 14.
7   Harriet Blogden, *The English Women's Diary: An Anthology* (London, Fourth Estate, 1992), pp. 1–2.
8   Elizabeth W. Bruss, *Autobiographical Acts. The Changing Situation of a Literary Genre* (Baltimore and London, Johns Hopkins University Press, 1976), p. 7; Laura Marcus, *Autobiographical Discourses. Theory, Criticism, Practice* (Manchester, Manchester University Press, 1994), p. 12.
9   Felicity A. Nussbaum, *The Autobiographical Subject. Gender and Ideology in Eighteenth Century England* (London and Baltimore, Johns Hopkins University Press, 1989), p. 1.
10 Marcus, *Autobiographical Discourses*, p. 7.
11 Claire Brant, 'Speaking of Women: Scandal and Law in the Mid-Eighteenth-Century', in C. Brant and D. Purkis (eds), *Women, Texts and Histories 1575–1760* (London and New York, Routledge, 1992), pp. 242–70.
12 Isaac D'Israeli, *Miscellanies; or Literary Recreations* (London, T. Catell, 1796), p. 95 quoted in Treadwell, *Autobiographical Writing and British Literature, 1783–1834* (Oxford, Oxford University Press, 2002), p. 13.
13 I use the term 'whore biographies'; Nussbaum uses the term 'scandalous memoirs', as does Lynda M. Thompson; Vivien Jones uses 'prostitutes' narratives' or 'prostitutes' memoirs'; James Treadwell uses 'courtesans' memoirs'; Linda Peterson uses both 'chroniques scandaleuse' and 'scandalous memoirs'. Essentially we are all writing about the same material. See Julie Peakman, 'Memoirs of Women of Pleasure: the Whore Biography', *Women's Writing*, Vol. 11, No. 2 (2004), pp. 163–83; Nussbaum, *The Autobiographical Subject*, chapter 8 on 'Scandalous Memoirs', pp. 178–200; Thompson, *The 'Scandalous Memoirists'*; Vivien Jones, 'Scandalous Femininity: Prostitution and Eighteenth-Century Narrative', in Dario Castiglione and Lesley Sharpe, *Shifting the Boundaries* (Exeter, Exeter University Press, 1995), pp. 54–70; Treadwell, *Autobiographical Writing*, pp. 21, 164; Linda H. Peterson, *Traditions of Victorian Women's Autobiography* (Charlottesville, University Press of Virginia, 1999).
14 Katheryn Norberg states, 'The libertine whore is utterly fictional, an image which had more to do with male fantasy than with social reality'; 'The Libertine Whore: Prostitution in French Pornography', in Lynn Hunt (ed.), *The Invention of Pornography: Obscenity and the Origins of Modernity, 1500–1800* (New York, Zone Books, 1993), pp. 225–52.
15 I have examined all volumes and editions of the *Memoirs of Mrs Margaret Leeson* held in the National Library of Ireland and in the British Library and Harriette Wilson and Julia Johnson's memoirs, both held in the British Library; Harriette Wilson, *The Interesting Memoirs and Amorous Adventures of Harriette Wilson* (London, Published by W. Chubb, 7 Fetter Lane; T. Blacketer, 19 Vere Street, Clare Market; and T. Reed, 90, Drury Lane, 1825);

Julie Johnstone, *Confessions of Julia Johnstone* (London, Benbow, 1825). For easy access to references for readers, here I have used the reprints of Harriette Wilson's memoirs in Lesley Blanch (ed.), *The Game of Hearts. Harriette Wilson and Her Memoirs* (London, Gryphon Books, 1957) and Mary Lyons (ed.), *The Memoirs of Mrs. Leeson 1727–1797* (Dublin, Lilliput Press, 1995), using LB and ML respectively, and JJ for Julia Johnstone, *Confessions of Julie Johnstone* (London, Benbow, 1825).

16 Joanna Richardson, *The Courtesans: The Demi-monde in 19th Century France* (Weidenfeld and Nicolson, 1967).

17 M. D'Archenholz, *A Picture of England; Containing a Description of the Laws, Customs and Manners of England* (Dublin, P. Byre, 1790), p. 189.

18 Margaret's birth date was stated as 1727 by the editor of her memoirs, Mary Lyons, but I have amended this to fit with the dates I think more likely. For a full biography, see my *Peg Plunkett, Memoirs of a Whore* (London, Quercus, 2014).

19 JJ, p. 6.

20 W. Speck, 'The Harlot's Progress in Eighteenth-century England', *British Journal of Eighteenth-Century Studies*, Vol. 3 (1980); Susan Staves, 'British Seduced Maidens', *Eighteenth Century Studies*, Vol. 14 (1980/1).

21 See Julie Peakman, *Mighty Lewd Books. The Development of Pornography in Eighteenth-Century England* (London, Palgrave Macmillan, 2003).

22 ML, p. 10. Spotted fever – a febrile disease typically characterized by a skin eruption.

23 ML, p. 10.

24 ML, p. 13.

25 ML, p. 15.

26 LB, p. 63.

27 LB, p. 63.

28 JJ, p. 8.

29 LB, p. 117.

30 LB, p. 87.

31 JJ, p. 115.

32 ML, p. 5.

33 LB, p. 78.

34 JJ, p. 96.

35 JJ, p. 9.

36 Peakman, *Mighty Lewd Books*.

37 JJ, p. 29.

38 JJ, pp. 42–3.

39 LB, p. 148.

40 LB, p. 129.

41 ML, p. 9.
42 LB, p. 86.
43 LB, p. 87.
44 LB, p. 89.
45 JJ, p. 50.
46 LB, p. 177.
47 LB, p. 178.
48 ML, pp. 4–5.
49 ML, p. 19.
50 LB, p. 63.
51 JJ, p. 52.
52 JJ, p. 53.
53 ML, p. 61.
54 LB, p. 69.
55 LB, p. 200.
56 LB, p. 73.
57 JJ, p. 45.
58 ML, p. 41.
59 JJ, p. 244.
60 JJ, p. 173.
61 ML, p. 52.
62 ML, p. 53.
63 ML, p. 55.
64 ML, p. 58.
65 ML, p. 107.
66 LB, p. 99.
67 JJ, p. 39.
68 LB, p. 128.
69 LB, p. 176.
70 JJ, p. 68.
71 JJ, p. 238.
72 JJ, pp. 55–6.
73 JJ, p. 57.
74 ML, p. 49.
75 LB, p. 85.
76 LB, p. 156.
77 LB, pp. 301–2.
78 ML, p. 97.
79 ML, p. 72.

80 *A Commentary in the Licentious Liberty of the Press In which the recent Publication, entitled 'Memoirs of Harriette Wilson' is severely censured* (London, 1825), pp. 10, 21.
81 JJ, p. 247.

Chapter Six   Initiation, Defloration and Flagellation: Sexual Propensities in *Memoirs of a Woman of Pleasure*

1   John Cleland, *Memoirs of a Woman of Pleasure*, Vol. II (London, G. Fenton, 1749), p. 109.
2   See Chapter 8.
3   Peter Gay uses the terms 'pornography', 'erotica' and 'smut' indiscriminately to describe this material as a separate entity, suggesting that pornography belongs in a world of its own, and should be seen as separate from the dominant culture; Peter Gay, *The Education of the Senses*, Vol. 1, *The Bourgeois Experience: Victoria to Freud* (New York, Open University Press, 1984), pp. 358–79, 495–7.
4   Randolph Trumbach, 'Modern Prostitution and Gender in Fanny Hill: Libertine and Domesticated Fantasy', in G. S. Rousseau and Roy Porter (eds), *Sexual Underworlds of the Enlightenment* (Manchester, Manchester University Press, 1987), pp. 69–85.
5   Ruth Bernard Yeazell, *Fictions of Modesty: Women and Courtship in the English Novel* (Chicago, Chicago University Press, 1990).
6   See Chapter 9.
7   This earlier British erotica shows influence from the Greek and Roman classicists.
8   Cleland's expurgating of *MWP* in attempts to sanitize it in the later *Fanny Hill* saw impoverishment of his earlier stylistic accomplishments. See Peter Sabor, 'The Censor Censured: Expurgating *Memoirs of a Woman of Pleasure*', in Robert Purks Maccubin (ed.), *'Tis Nature's Fault. Unauthorized Sexuality during the Enlightenment* (Cambridge, Cambridge University Press, 1987), pp. 192–201.
9   Trumbach, 'Modern Prostitution and Gender in Fanny Hill', pp. 69–85.
10 Peakman, *Lascivious Bodies,* pp. 174–200.
11 *MWP*, Vol. I, pp. 30–31.
12 See my *Mighty Lewd Books* for further information on these texts.
13 Anon, *A Dialogue between a Married Lady and a Maid* (London, n.p., 1740).
14 David Foxon, *Libertine Literature in England 1660–1745* (New York, University Books, 1965), points to later copies being recorded but which cannot be found: *Delights of the Nuptial Bed, or a Lady's Academy in Dialogues* ('Printed in the island of Paphos', 'Philadelphia, May 1806'); *Delights of the*

Nuptial Bed Laid Open in Luscious Dialogues, translated from an original manuscript (Printed in the island of Paphos, Cannon, c.1830); *The Bedfellows; or Young Misses Manual* (London, Dickinson, c.1820).

15 See Robert Darnton, *The Forbidden Best–Sellers of Pre-Revolutionary France* (London, HarperCollins, 1996).

16 *Venus in the Cloister*, p. 11.

17 'Roger Pheuquewell' (Thomas Stretser?), *A New Description of Merryland* (London, J. Leake and E. Curll, 1741). Price 1/6d.

18 *MWP*, Vol. I, p. 109.

19 *MWP*, Vol. I, p. 109

20 *MWP*, Vol. I, p. 113.

21 *MWP*, Vol. I, p. 197.

22 *MWP*, Vol. II, p. 35.

23 Bloch was among the first to describe the Victorian 'defloration mania' in the 1920s; David Loth also refers to the Victorian defloration mania, although he recognizes that this interest in virgins was evident earlier. Simpson and Trumbach provide ample evidence of the reality of defloration of young girls in the eighteenth century. Iwan Bloch, *Sexual Life in England. Past and Present* (reprint: London, Arco, 1958); Loth, *The Erotic in Literature*, p. 182; Anthony E. Simpson, 'Vulnerability and the Age of Female Consent', in Rousseau and Porter (eds), *Sexual Underworlds*, pp, 181–205; Trumbach, *Sex and the Gender Revolution*, pp. 212–18.

24 Roy Porter and Lesley Hall, *The Facts of Life. The Creation of Sexual Knowledge in Britain* (London and New Haven, Yale University Press, 1995), pp. 36, 298.

25 Anon, *Rare Verities, The Cabinet of Venus Unlocked and her Secrets Laid Open* (London, P. Brigg, 1657), p. 58.

26 Nicolas Venette's *Tableau de L'Amour Conjugal* first appeared in 1686 and went through over thirty editions, enjoying success in England on its translation. Porter and Hall, *Facts of Life*, p. 36.

27 John Cleland, *Memoirs of a Woman of Pleasure* (London, George Fenton, 1749), Vol. II, pp. 119–20.

28 Written by Nicolas Chorier, the earliest edition was published in Latin, *Satyra Sotadica* in 1659 or 1660. The French edition, *L'Académie des Dames*, appeared in 1680, translated as *The School of Women* in 1682 and as *A Dialogue Between a Married Lady and a Maid* in 1688 and 1740. For a history of the book see Kearney, *History of Erotica*, pp. 34–46 and Foxon, *Libertine Literature*, pp. 38–51.

29 Anon, *Dialogue Between a Married Lady and a Maid* (London, n.p., 1740), p. 18.

30 Ibid., pp. 21–7.

31 Tassie Williams, 'Female Fraud: Counterfeit Maidenheads in the Eighteenth Century', *Journal of the History of Sexuality*, Vol. 6, No. 41 (1996), pp. 518–48.

32 'By A Monk Of The Order Of St. Francis', *Nocturnal Revels, Or, The History Of King's-Palace and Other Modern Nunneries Containing Their Mysteries,*

Devotions And Sacrifices. Comprising Also, The Ancient And Present State Of Promiscuous Gallantry: With The Portraits Of The Most Celebrated Demireps And Coutezans [sic] *Of This Period: As Well As Sketches Of Their Professional And Occasional Admirers*. In Two Volumes (London, M. Goadby, 1779), pp. 141–2. The book was translated into French as *Les Sérails de Londres* (1801), 'Pisanus Fraxi' [Henry Spencer Ashbee], *Index Librorum Prohibitorum*, Vol. I (London, privately printed, 1877: reprint Jack Brussel, *Bibliography of Forbidden Books*, London, 1962), p. 321.

33 I have found no evidence of Hayes's account book apart from its mention in the scurrilous *Nocturnal Revels*, an exaggerated spurious attack on Dashwood and his friends. Mannix appears to take it as genuine. Daniel P. Mannix, *The Hell-Fire Club* (London, The New English Library, 1961), p. 33.

34 *Nocturnal Revels*, pp. 49–51.

35 Anon, *Kitty's Attalantis for the Year 1766* (London, J. Harrison, 1766), pp. 20–21.

36 *Bon Ton*, Vol. 3 (March 1793).

37 *MWP*, Vol. II, p. 155.

38 John Henry Meibomius, *A Treatise Of the Use of Flogging In Venereal Affairs: Also of the Office of the Loins and Reins* (London, E. Curll, 1718), p. 34.

39 Lawrence Stone, 'Libertine Sexuality in Post-Restoration England: Group Sex and Flagellation among the Middling Sort in Norwich in 1706–07', *Journal of the History of Sexuality*, Vol. 2, No. 4 (1992), pp. 551–5.

40 *Venus in the Cloister*, pp. 20–21.

41 Anon, *Tryal of Father John-Baptist Girard On an Accusation for Quietism, Sorcery, Incest, Abortion and Subornation Before the Great Chamber of Parlement at Aix. At the Instance of Miss Mary-Catherine Cadiere* (London, Printed for J. Isted, at the Golden Ball in Fleet-Street; T. Astley in St. Paul's Churchyard; E. Nutt at the Royal-Exchange; A. Dod, without Temple-Bar; and J. Jollifre, in St. James's street, 1732).

42 *Tryal of Father John-Baptist Girard*, p. 9.

43 This interest in exposed bloodied internal parts has to some extent already been recognized by Jonathan Sawday in which he investigates the culture of dissection in the English Renaissance exploring the dark, morbid eroticism of the anatomy theatre. Jonathan Sawday, *The Body Emblazoned. Dissection and the Human Body in the Renaissance* (London, Routledge, 1995).

44 *Bon Ton*, March 1792.

45 Anon, *Exhibition of Female Flagellants* (London, 'Printed at the Expense of Theresa Berkeley for the Benefit of Mary Wilson', n.d.). The edition used here is William Dugdale's edition c.1860. J. C. Hotten reprinted it in 1872, along with a second part. This has led some historians to believe neither are eighteenth-century works. However, this earlier edition of *Exhibition of Female Flagellants* is extant in the British Library. The preface states, 'this work was originally published about fifty years since and is [sic] now become so very scarce as seldom to be obtained'. According to Ashbee, Cannon's 1830 version also carried this preface, thereby dating the original as far back as at least c.1780.

46 *Exhibition of Female Flagellants*, p. 14.

47 *Exhibition of Female Flagellants*, p. 53.
48 Jean-Jacques Rousseau, *Confessions* (reprint; London, Everyman, 1931), pp. 10–11.
49 Mark Bence-Jones, *The Catholic Families* (London, Constable, 1992), p. 84.
50 'Theresa Berkeley', *Venus School-Mistress: or Birchen Sports* (London, 'Mary Wilson', '1788'). The imprints are false but Ashbee believed this book to be taken from the genuine memoirs of notorious prostitute Theresa Berkeley and dated it to c.1808 or 1810. *Index Librorum Prohibitorum*, pp. xliii, and 397–401. It is likely that the preface is a later addition c.1830. The copy seen by Ashbee can no longer be traced, and a reprint from 1917 has been used here.
51 Erasmus Perkins, who was editing, translating and publishing books on 'the philosophy of the birch discipline', had taken the pseudonym 'Mary Wilson' from a famous prostitute of the day. Iain McCalman, *Radical Underworlds. Prophets, Revolutionaries and Pornographers in London 1795–1840* (Oxford, Clarendon Press, 1988), p. 204.
52 *Venus Schoolmistress*, p. x.

Chapter Seven   'The Best Freind in the World': The Relationship Between Emma Hamilton and Queen Maria Carolina of Naples

1 The British Library Manuscripts Collection contains most of the letters of Emma Hamilton, the Queen of Naples, Greville Hamilton, Horatio Nelson, William Hamilton, and various other key characters. Many of the letters have been printed in the Alfred Morrison Collection, as *The Collection of Autograph Letters and Historical Documents Formed by Alfred Morrison: The Hamilton and Nelson Papers*, 2 vols (London, Printed for Private Circulation, 1893–94) (BL Shelf Mark LR 4 e 1). For ease of reference in the notes, I have cited this printed collection wherever possible, using the short form 'Morrison MS', although I have examined the original manuscripts.
2 Brian Fothergill, *Sir William Hamilton: Envoy Extraordinary* (London, Faber & Faber, 1969), 219.
3 Lois G. Schwoerer, 'Women's public political voice in England: 1640–1740', in Hilda L. Smith (ed.), *Women Writers and the Early Modern British Political Tradition* (Cambridge, Cambridge University Press, 1998), pp. 57–8.
4 James Daybell observes that the basis upon which women laid claim to this language was 'founded for a large part on material power, social status and influence', and points to the fact that this mainly applied to aristocratic women, usually within the family but sometimes on the wider political stage. This rhetoric was often deployed in patronage letters. James Daybell, 'Women's Letters of Recommendation and the Rhetoric of Friendship in

Sixteenth-century England', in Jennifer Richards and Alison Thorne (eds), *Rhetoric, Women and Politics in Early Modern England* (London, Routledge, 2007), p. 179. On the eighteenth century, see Amanda Vickery (ed.), *Women, Privilege and Power: British Politics, 1750 to the Present* (Stanford, CA, Stanford University Press, 2001).

5   On writers, see Norma Clarke, *Ambitious Heights. Writing, Friendship, Love: The Jewsbury Sisters, Felicia Hemans and Jane Welsh Carlyle* (London, Routledge, 1990); and Pauline Nestor, *Female Friendships and Communities: Charlotte Bronte, George Eliot, Elizabeth Gaskell* (Oxford, Clarendon, 1985). On lesbians, see Elizabeth Susan Wahl, *Invisible Relations: Representations of Female Intimacy in the Age of Enlightenment* (Stanford, CA, Stanford University Press, 1999) and Lillian Faderman, *Surpassing the Love of Men: Romantic Friendship and Love between Women from the Renaissance to the Present* (New York, William Morrow, 1981).

6   One of the few parallels which might be drawn with the relationship between Emma and Maria Carolina might be that which subsisted between Sarah, Duchess of Marlborough and Queen Anne; but Sarah was a noblewoman serving as handmaid to her queen, employed in a position in court as Groom of The Stole, Mistress of the Robes and Keeper of the Privy Purse. See Ophelia Field, *The Favourite: Sarah, Duchess of Marlborough* (London, Hodder & Stoughton, 2002). Also see Kate Davies, *Catherine Macaulay and Mercy Otis Warren: The Revolutionary Atlantic and the Politics of Gender* (Oxford, Oxford University Press, 2005), but this is mainly in relation to American politics.

7   One of the best biographies is still Walter Sichel, *Emma Lady Hamilton* (London, Archibald Constable, 1905). For further references see my biography *Emma Hamilton* (London, Haus Publishing Ltd., 2005).

8   Although Emma always gave 1765 as her birth date, it is possible she was born earlier: she may have wished to conceal her illegitimacy, as her parents did not marry until 1764. See Peakman, *Emma Hamilton*, p. 4.

9   Sir Nathaniel Wraxall, *The Historical and the Posthumous Memoirs of Sir Nathaniel William Wraxall, 1772–1784*, ed. Henry B. Wheatley, 5 vols (London, Bickers & Son, 1884), Vol. 1, pp. 163–4.

10 Morrison MS 142, 2 December 1785.

11 Add. MS 34048 ff. 61–2, 6 April 1790.

12 Morrison MS 199, 20 December 1791.

13 Morrison MS 208, 17 April 1792.

14 T. J. Pettigrew, *Memoirs of the Life of Vice-Admiral Lord Viscount Nelson*, 2 vols (London, Boone, 1849), Vol. 1, p. 40.

15 Morrison MS 221, 2 June 1793.

16 Ibid.

17 Morrison MS 250, 18 December 1794.

18 Egerton MS 1615 f. 18, 17 April 1795.

19 Morrison MS 263, 19 April 1795.

20 Add MS 34710 f 23, 17 November 1795.
21 Egerton MS 1615 ff 20–22, 17 April 1795.
22 Morrison MS 263, 19 April 1795.
23 Morrison MS 274, [n.d.] February 1796.
24 Morrison MS 282, 7 June 1796.
25 Morrison MS 287, 21 September 1796.
26 Egerton MS 1615 ff 8, 69, 4 June 1795, 3 December 1796.
27 Morrison MS 290, 1 December 1796.
28 Horatio Nelson, *The Letters of Lord Nelson to Lady Hamilton. With a Supplement of Interesting Letters by Distinguished Characters*, 2 vols (London, T. Lovewell & Co., 1814), Vl. 1, p. 181.
29 Pettigrew, Vol. 1, p. 119.
30 Add. MS 34989 f 3, 8 September 1798.
31 Geoffrey Rawston (ed.), *Nelson's Letters* (London, J. M. Dent, 1960), 182, 17 June 1798.
32 Morrison MS 320, 18 June 1798.
33 Add. MS 34989 f 15, 20 October 1798.
34 Ibid.
35 Add. MS 34989 f 20, 27 October 1798.
36 Egerton MS 1616 f 38.
37 Egerton MS 1615 ff 8, 129.
38 Anon., *Memoirs of Lady Hamilton* (London, Henry Colburn, 1815), 195–6.
39 Morrison MS 370, 7 January 1799.
40 Ibid.
41 Ibid.
42 Ibid.
43 Morrison MS 369, 6 January 1799.
44 Pettigrew, *Memoirs*, Vol. 1, p. 187, 17 January 1799.
45 Morrison MS 381, 8 April 1799.
46 Sichel, *Emma Lady Hamilton*, p. 284.
47 Fothergill, *Sir William Hamilton*, p. 359.
48 Morrison MS 411, 19 July 1799.
49 Ibid.
50 Morrison MS 444, 25 January 1800.
51 *The Letters of Lord Nelson to Lady Hamilton*, Vol. 1, p. 272.
52 Morrison MS 1046, [n.d.] March 1813.
53 O. A. Sherrard, *A Life of Emma Hamilton* (London, Sidgwick & Jackson, 1927), 186.

Chapter Eight Bodily Anxieties in Enlightenment Sex Literature

1. Ian McCalman, *Radical Underworld. Prophets, Revolutionaries and Pornographers in London, 1795–1840* (Oxford, Clarendon Press, 1988); Peter Wagner, *Eros Revived* (London, Secker & Warburg, 1988); Lynn Hunt (ed.), *The Invention of Pornography: Obscenity and the Origins of Modernity, 1500–1800* (New York, Zone Books, 1993).

2. I have described this lack of classification of printed matter in more depth in chapter 2 of my book, Julie Peakman, *Mighty Lewd Books. Pornography in the Eighteenth Century* (London, Palgrave MacMillan, 2003). Also see P. J. Kearnery, *A History of Erotic Literature* (London, Macmillan, 1982); Patrick Spedding (ed.), *Eighteenth-Century British Erotica* (London, Pickering and Chatto, 2002).

3. This description is used purely as a means to give the modern-day reader an idea of the type of material being described. As Darnton has quite rightly pointed out, Frenchmen (and this applies to English men and women too) did not distinguish a genre of 'pure pornography' from erotic fiction, anti-clerical tracts, and other varieties of 'philosophical books'; Wagner defines pornography as that which is prohibited, 'the written or visual representation in a realistic form of any general or sexual behaviour with a deliberate violation of existing and widely accepted moral and social taboos'; Hunt takes pornography to be 'the explicit depiction of sexual organs and sexual practices with the aim of arousing sexual feeling'. Robert Darnton, *The Forbidden Best-Sellers of Pre-Revolutionary France* (London, HarperCollins, 1996), p. 87; Wagner, *Eros Revived*, p. 7; Hunt (ed.), *The Invention of Pornography*, p. 10.

4. See Helen King's chapter on 'green sickness' in her *Hippocrates' Women. Reading the Female Body in Ancient Greece* (London, Routledge, 1998), pp. 188–204.

5. Thomas Laqueur, *Making Sex. Body and Gender from the Greeks to Freud* (Cambridge, MA, Harvard University Press, 1992); Caroline Bynum, 'The Body of Christ in the Later Middle Ages', *Renaissance Quarterly*, Vol. 39, No. 3 (1986), pp. 399–439.

6. See Judith Butler, 'Subversive Bodily Acts', in *Gender Trouble. Feminism and the Subversion of Identity* (London, Routledge, 1990), pp. 79–141; Peter Stallybrass, 'Patriarchal Territories', in Margaret W. Ferguson, Maureen Quilligan and Nancy J. Vickers (eds), *Rewriting the Renaissance* (Chicago, Chicago University Press, 1986), pp. 123–42.

7. Norbert Elias, *The Civilising Process. Sociogenetic and Psychogenetic Investigations* (Oxford, Basil Blackwell, 1982).

8. Roy Porter and Lesley Hall, *Facts of Life, The Creation of Sexual Knowledge in Britain, 1650–1950* (London and New Haven, Yale University Press, 1995), pp. 36, 298.

9. Wagner, *Eros Revived*, p. 11.

10 Roy Porter has already thoroughly examined the impact of *Aristotle's Masterpiece* and Venette's *The Mysteries of Conjugal Love Reveal'd* in Porter and Hall, *Facts of Life*, pp. 33–90.

11 Roy Porter and Lesley Hall, *Facts of Life*, p. 7; Kathryn Shevelow, *Women and Print Culture* (London, Routledge, 1989): Shevelow perceives a shared knowledge between the writer and readers of their material, and readers would necessarily understand the set of codes being transmitted in order to render it comprehensible.

12 For example, *Rare Verities* expressed disingenuous concern in the preface relating fears that the book might slip into the wrong hands – maid-servants were thought to be reading it, with improper consequences.

13 See Chapter 6.

14 *Rare Verities*, p. 24.

15 Anon, *Arisotle's Masterpiece, Or the Secrets of Generation* (London, J. How, 1690), p. 71.

16 Ibid., p. 88.

17 See Chapter 6.

18 Ibid., p. 33.

19 Ludmilla Jordanova, 'The Popularisation of Medicine: Tissot and Onanism' in her *Nature Displayed. Gender, Science and Medicine 1700–1820* (London, Longman, 1999), pp. 103–17; also see the chapter on 'Masturbation in the Enlightenment', Porter and Hall, *Facts of Life*, pp. 91–105.

20 The first French edition came out in 1760, the English translation reaching British audiences in 1766. I have found at least four English-language copies listed in the British Library catalogue, one from 1766, two from 1772 and one from 1781, the latter being a fifth edition. Unfortunately, only two from 1772 survive, the two other editions having been destroyed, and possibly others not carried in the catalogue. Within the text, Tissot refers to, and agrees with, Hippocrates. S. A. A. D. Tissot MD, *Onanism; or a Treatise upon the Disorders produced by Masturbation, or the Dangerous Effects of Secret Excessive Venery* (London, B. Thomas, 1766), p. 57.

21 Tissot, *Onanism*, p. 24.

22 According to L. Vern and Bonnie Bullough, Tissot's views were widely accepted. L. Vern and Bonnie Bullough, *Sexual Attitudes* (London, Prometheus Books, 1995), p. 71.

23 Tissot, *Onanism*, pp. 41–2.

24 Paul-Gabriel Boucé, 'Imagination, Pregnant Women and Monsters, in Eighteenth-Century England and France', in G. S. Rousseau and Roy Porter (eds), *Sexual Underworlds of the Enlightenment* (Manchester, Manchester University Press, 1987), pp. 86–100.

25 Little is known about Bienville except that he may have lived in Holland for most of his life and that he wrote several other scientific works including two treatises defending smallpox inoculation – no biographical materials have been found. Rousseau cites various French editions, two in 1771; one in 1772, 1778 and 1784; a French edition appeared as 'Published in London', 1789; and two

English translations for 1775 and c.1840; G. S. Rousseau, 'Nymphomania, Bienville and the Rise of Erotic Sensibility', in Paul-Gabriel Boucé (ed.), *Sexuality in Eighteenth-Century Britain* (Manchester, Manchester University Press, 1982), pp. 95–119. I have found eight French-language copies and three English copies in the British Library catalogue, one for 1775 and two for 1840, the former which I have used. Another English-language copy for 1766 has been destroyed. There is also one Italian and one German edition for 1760.

26 M. D. T. Bienville, *Nymphomania, or a Dissertation Concerning the Furor Uterinus* (London, J. Bew, 1775), p. 36.
27 Ibid., p. 74.
28 Ibid., p. 50.
29 Anon., *A Dialogue between a Married Lady and Maid* (London, n.p., 1740), p. 13.
30 Attributed to Jacques Charles Gervaise de Latouche, *Histoire de Dom B* (London, n.p., 1743) saw various translations into English which, according to Kearney, date as far back as the French original; Kearney, *The Private Case*, p. 193. Reprinted and reworkings of this book appeared under various titles including *Dom Bougre* (i.e. Master Bugger), *Portier des Chartreux*, *Mémoires de Saturnin Histoire de Gouberdon*, and later translations such as *The Life and Adventures of Uncle Silas* (London, private edition, 1907 – although the British Library catalogue states that the imprint is false and it was printed in Paris) and *The Lascivious Monk* (Marlborough, Venus Classic, 1993).
31 *The Life and Adventures of Uncle Silas*, based on the original, 1742, pp. 30–31.
32 Hunt mentions the latter and Rosario describes both books. Hunt (ed.), *The Invention of Pornography*, p. 324; Rosario, *The Erotic Imagination*, p. 31.
33 *A Dialogue* . . . ., p. 16.

Chapter Nine   Medicine, the Body and the Botanical Sexual Metaphor in Erotica

1 Anon, *Arbor Vitae Or, The Natural History of the Tree of Life* (London, W. James, 1732). *Arbor Vitae* was originally published as a poem and frequently emulated. It was reprinted along with prose, and the *Natural History of the Frutex Vulvaria*. Both sets of material were probably written by Thomas Stretser, or Stretzer, one of Edmund Curll's hacks. 'Roger Pheuqewell' is given as the pseudonym in the 1741 edition, the same author of *A New Description of Merryland* (see below).
2 'Philogynes Clitorides', *Natural History of the Frutex Vulvaria* (London, W. James, 1732).
3 For a history of generation theories see Angus McLaren, *Reproductive Rituals: The Perception in Fertility in England from the Sixteenth to the Nineteenth Century* (London and New York, Methuen, 1984); Nancy Tuana, *The Less Noble Sex* (Bloomington and Indianapolis, Indiana University Press, 1983);

Elizabeth B. Gasking, *Investigations into Generation, 1651–1828* (London, Hutchinson, 1967); Joseph Needham, *History of Embryology* (Cambridge, Cambridge University Press, 1934; 2nd edn., 1959); and on William Harvey, *The Works of William Harvey*, trans. R. Willis (London, Sydenham Society, 1847).

4   Roy Porter, *Health for Sale: Quackery in England 1650–1850* (Manchester, Manchester University Press, 1989), chapter six. Also see Edward Shorter, *A History of Women's Bodies* (Harmondsworth, Penguin, 1983).

5   For discussions on the nature of female sexuality, see Vivien Jones (ed.), *Women in the Eighteenth Century. Constructions of Femininity* (London and New York, Routledge, 1990); Bridget Hill (ed.), *Eighteenth-Century Women: An Anthology* (London, Allen & Unwin, 1984).

6   Roy Porter, 'Mixed Feelings: the Enlightenment and Sexuality in Eighteenth Century Britain', in Paul-Gabriel Boucé (ed.), *Sexuality in Eighteenth-Century Britain* (Manchester, Manchester University Press, 1982), pp. 1–27.

7   For studies discussing aspects of 'medical' erotica see Peter Wagner, 'The Discourse on Sex – or Sex as Discourse: Eighteenth-century Medical and Paramedical Erotica', in G. S. Rousseau and Roy Porter (eds), *Sexual Underworlds of the Enlightenment* (Manchester, Manchester University Press, 1987), pp. 46–69; Peter Wagner, *Eros Revived: Erotica of The Enlightenment in England and America* (London, Secker and Warburg, 1987), pp. 8–46; Roy Porter, 'Spreading Carnal Knowledge or Selling Dirt Cheap? Nicolas Venette's *Tableau de l'Amour Conjugal* in Eighteenth Century England', *Journal of European Studies*, Vol. xiv (1984), pp. 233–55.

8   N. Venette, *Tableau de l'Amour Conjugal* (New York, Garland, 1984); English trans., *The Mysteries of Conjugal Love Reveal'd* (London, S.N., 1712).

9   *The Works of Aristotle* (printed for Archibald Whistleton, Chiswell Street, n.d. but c.1810) quoted in Roy Porter and Lesley Hall, *The Facts of Life: The Creation of Sexual Knowledge in Britain, 1650–1950* (New Haven and London, Yale University Press, 1995), p. 44.

10 See Angus McLaren, *Reproductive Rituals: The Perception of Fertility in England from the Sixteenth Century to the Nineteenth Century* (London and New York, Methuen, 1984), p. 18.

11 Dr James quoted in Paul-Gabriel Boucé, 'The Secret Sex Nexus: Sex and Literature in Eighteenth Century Britain', in Alan Bold (ed.), *The Sexual Dimension in Literature* (London, Vision Press Ltd, 1983), p. 79.

12 According to L. Vern and Bonnie Bullough, Tissot's views were widely accepted. L. Vern and Bonnie Bullough, *Sexual Attitudes* (London, Prometheus Books, 1995), p. 71.

13 John Marten, *Gonosologium Novum; or A New System of all the Secret Infirmities and Diseases, Natural, Accidental, and Venereal in Men and Women* (6th ed.; London, Crouch, 1709), p. 10.

14 Robert Erickson, '"The Books of Generation": Some Observations on the Style of the British Midwife Books, 1671–1764', in Boucé (ed.), *Sexuality in Eighteenth-century Britain*, pp. 74–94.

15 Jane Sharp, *The Midwives Book* (London: Simon Miller, 1671), pp. 10–19.

16 Indeed, whole landscapes were depicted as women's bodies in such erotica as John Cotton's *Erotopolis, The Present State of Bettyland* (1684), reprinted in *Potent Ally* (London, E. Curll, 1741).

17 Peter Wagner, *Eros Revived. Erotica of the Enlightenment in England and America* (London, Secker and Warburg, 1987), pp. 191–2.

18 See M. C. Howatson (ed.), *The Oxford Companion to Classical Literature* (Oxford, Oxford University Press, 1989), p. 462; and Felix Guirand (ed.), *New Larousse Encyclopaedia of Mythology* (London, Hamlyn Publishing, 1959). The tree as phallic symbol of fertility can be seen in the worship of Priapus and is also the source of life, the tree of knowledge from the Garden of Eden and the focal point in the Fall from Paradise.

19 Simon Schaffer, 'The Earth's Fertility as Social Fact in Early Modern Britain', in Mikulás Teich, Roy Porter and Bo Gustafsson (eds), *Nature and Society in Historical Context* (Cambridge, Cambridge University Press, 1997), pp. 124–47.

20 As quoted in Robert Olby, *Fontana History of Biology* (London, Fontana, 2000), chapter 8.

21 Earlier botanists had suggested the idea of the sexuality of plants, including Nehemiah Grew, *Anatomy of Plants* (1672), but Linnaeus was the one to develop and popularize it. At least one edition of *Arbor Vitae* was dedicated to the London botanist Phillip Miller and would have been recognized as a skit of his serious study of plants, *Catalogus Plantarum Officinalium* (1730). Miller was to adopt the system of Linnaeus.

22 Londa Schiebinger, *Nature's Body: Sexual Politics and the Making of the Modern Science* (London, Pandora, 1993), pp. 4, 37.

23 Londa Schiebinger, 'The Private Life of Plants: Sexual Politics in Carl Linnaeus and Erasmus Darwin', in Marina Benjamin (ed.) *Science and Sensibility: Gender and Scientific Enquiry 1780–1945* (Oxford, Basil Blackwell, 1991), p. 126. Also see Londa Schiebinger, *The Mind Has No Sex. Women in the Origins of Modern Science* (Cambridge, MA, Harvard University Press, 1989).

24 According to Schiebinger, 'Linnaeus saw plants as having sex, in the fullest sense of the term, sometimes illicit, and sometimes the sanctified expression of love between husband and wife'; Schiebinger, *Nature's Body,*. p. 23.

25 See Carl Linnaeus (trans. M. S. J. Engel-Ledeboer and H. Engel), *Systema Naturae* (1735) (Nieuwkoop, B. de Graaf, 1964).

26 This was a reference to William Kent (1686–1748), a landscape gardener who freed the English Garden from formality using winding paths and wooded glades, contrasting the wilderness of nature with small classical temples.

27 *Arbor Vitae* (London, E. Hill, 1741), p. 3. The picture of Merryland comes from this edition which is used forthwith.

28 *Arbor Vitae,* pp. 2–4.

29 Julie Peakman, 'Flagellation in Eighteenth-Century Erotica' (MA Dissertation, London University, 1992).

30 Curll defended himself against accusations of pornography on the grounds that 'the Fault is not in the Subject Matter, but in the Inclination of the Reader,

that makes these Pieces offensive'; see Roger Thompson, *Unfit for Modest Ears* (London, Macmillan, 1979), pp. 164–6.
31 See Trial at the Old Bailey, 23 April 1718; *Dictionary of National Biography*.
32 Green sickness (otherwise known as chlorosis) tended to particularly affect young or pubescent girls and was seen as a 'wasting disease'. Physical symptoms included pallid skin, loss of appetite, amenorrhoea and was often accompanied by behavioural changes such as lethargy or desire for solitude. See Roy and Dorothy Porter, *In Sickness and in Health* (London, Fourth Estate, 1988), pp. 51, 83.
33 *Arbor Vitae*, p. 9.
34 *Arbor Vitae*, pp. 6, 7.
35 Dr Misaubin, along with Dr Rock, can be found in Hogarth's *The Harlot's Progress*, shown as money-grabbing quacks haggling while Moll dies of VD in front of them. On the floor lies an advert for an 'anodyne' (pain-killing) necklace bought to cure syphilis and on the coal shuttle lies the remnants of Moll's teeth, fallen out as a result of taking mercury on his advice; see Fiona Haslam, *From Hogarth to Rowlandson in Eighteenth Century Britain* (Liverpool, Liverpool University Press, 1997). The doctor's office in *Marriage à la Mode*, Plate III, is said to be that of Misaubin at 96 St Martin's Lane, Westminster: Sean Shesgreen (ed.), *Engravings by Hogarth* (New York, Dover Publications Inc., 1975), p. xx.
36 Lynn Hunt (ed.), *Eroticism and the Body Politic* (Baltimore and London, Johns Hopkins University Press, 1991).
37 *The Potent Ally: or Succours from Merryland. With three essays (in verse) in praise of the cloathing of that country: and the Story of Pandora's Box ... To which is added Erotopolis, the Present State of Merryland*. Second edition (London, Curll, 1741).
38 *Frutex Vulvaria*, p. 7.
39 *Frutex Vulvaria*, p. 11.
40 Richard Davenport-Hines, *Sex, Death and Punishment. Attitudes to Sex and Sexuality in Britain since the Renaissance* (London: Collins, 1990), p. 47.
41 Roy Porter, *Health for Sale: Quackery in England 1650–1850* (Manchester, Manchester University Press, 1989); see chapter 6, 'Quacks and Sex: Pioneering or Anxiety Making?'.
42 *Frutex Vulvaria*, p. 12.
43 William Harvey (trans. Gweneth Whitteridge), *Disputations Touching the Generation of Animals* (1653), (Oxford, Blackwell Scientific Publications, 1981), p. 65.
44 *Frutex Vulvaria*, pp. 7/8.
45 *Frutex Vulvaria*, p. 14.
46 Elizabeth Needham (1680–1731) kept an opulent brothel in Park Place, St James. In 1721, she went before the courts for entrapment of young girls and she can be seen corrupting a fresh-faced country girl into prostitution in Hogarth's *The Harlot's Progress*, Plate I; see J. Burford, *Wits, Wenches and*

Wantons. London's Low Life: Covent Garden in the Eighteenth Century (London, Robert Hale, 1986), pp. 32, 69–71.

47 Margaret Pelling, 'Medical Practitioners in Early Modern England: Trade or Profession?' in Wilfred Prest (ed.), *The Professions in Early Modern England* (London, Croom Helm, 1987), p. 104.

48 *Frutex Vulvaria*, p. 13.

49 Anon, *Wisdom Revealed; Or the tree of life, discover'd and describ'd. By a Studious enquirer into the mysteries of Nature. To which is added The Crab-Tree: or; Sylvia Discover'd* (London, W. Shaw, 1725). The frontispiece states that it was sold at all the 'Pamphlet-shops in London and Westminster, price Six-Pence'.

50 Vincent Miller, *The Manplants: Or, a Scheme for Increasing and Improving the British Breed* (London, M. Cooper, at the Globe in Pater-noster-Row, 1752). Price one shilling.

51 The Sensitive Plant had been given the generic name *Mimosa* (L. *mimus* mime) as far back as 1619 because the plants 'mimick' the sensitivity of animals; see Olby, *History of Biology*, chapter 8. *Mimosa or the Sensitive Plant* has been attributed to James Perry (London, 1779); see *Eros Revisited*, p. 194. The poem was prefaced with a dedication to Joseph Banks and links him with an aristocratic intrigue. The veracity of the story is questionable but he does appear to have had an illegitimate child in 1773. It also slanders the Duke of Queensbury and Kitty Fisher, his mistress, a celebrated courtesan of the day mentioned in the dedication.

52 John Cleland, *Memoirs of a Woman of Pleasure* (Herts, Wordsworth Classics, 1993), p. 192.

53 Caves and grottoes have a history of association with female genitalia; see Mary Russo, *The Female Grotesque; Risk, Excess and Modernity* (London, Routledge, 1994).

54 Janet Browne, 'Botany for Gentlemen. Erasmus Darwin and *the Love of the Plants*', *Isis*, No. 80 (1989), pp. 593–612.

55 Londa Schiebinger cites John Fraley, *Gamete and Spires: Ideas about Sexual Reproduction, 1750–1914* (Baltimore, Johns Hopkins University Press, 1982); Londa Schiebinger, 'The Private Life of Plants: Sexual Politics in Carl Linnaeus and Erasmus Darwin', in Marina Benjamin (ed.), *Science and Sensibility: Gender and Scientific Enquiry 1780–1945* (Oxford, Basil Blackwell, 1991), p. 126. Also see Londa Schiebinger, *The Mind Has No Sex. Women in the Origins of Modern Science* (Cambridge, MA, Harvard University Press, 1989).

56 Schiebinger, *Nature's Body*, pp. 4, 37.

Chapter Ten   The Eighteenth-century Erotic Garden

1 G. Tolias, *British Travellers in Greece, 1759–1820* (London, Foundations of Hellenic Culture, 1995).

2   Jeremy Black, *The Grand Tour* (London, Croom Helm, 1985); Jeremy Black, *The British and The Grand Tour* (Stroud, Alan Sutton, 1992).

3   Tolias, *British Travellers*, p. 32.

4   Anthony Ashley Cooper, *The Moralists* (London, 1709).

5   Julie Peakman, *Emma Hamilton* (London, Haus, 2004).

6   Sir Francis Dashwood, *The Dashwoods of West Wycombe* (London, Aurum Press, 1987), p. 18. For other main biographies of Sir Francis Dashwood, see Ronald Fuller, *Hell-Fire Francis* (London, Chatto and Windus, 1939); Donald McCormack, *The Hellfire Club* (Norwich, Jarrolds, 1958); Daniel P. Mannix, *The Hell-Fire Club* (London, New English Library Ltd., 1962); Betty Kemp, *Sir Francis Dashwood* (London, Macmillan, 1967); Eric Towers, *Dashwood. The Man and The Myth* (London, Crucible, 1986); Gerald Suster, *The Hell-fire Friars. Sex, Politics and Religion* (London, Robson, 2000). These biographies are of varying quality, some based on fact, some apparently complete fabrication. Written documents, including letters, cellar books and inventories, about the meetings do exist in the private papers of the twentieth-century Sir Francis Dashwood who was kind enough to let me research them. I use both Dashwood's original private papers and the more spurious contemporary revelations to provide an overview of both the factual events and the gossip surrounding the Medmenham set.

7   Patrick Eyres's Editorial in 'Gardens of Desire', *The New Arcadian Journal*, No. 49/50 (2000), pp. 5–24.

8   Stowe MSS (BM) quoted in Fuller, *Hell-Fire Francis*, p. 92

9   Dashwood, *The Dashwoods of West Wycombe*, p. 223.

10 Richard Wheeler, '"Pro Magna Charta" or "Fay ce que Voudras": Political and Moral Precedents for the Garden of Sir Francis Dashwood at West Wycombe', in 'Gardens of Desire', *The New Arcadian Journal*, No. 49/50 (2000), pp. 26–61; see p. 58

11 Mannix, *The Hell-Fire Club*, p. 5; *The Times*, 17 April 2000, p. 8.

12 Anon, *A New Description of Merryland* (London, E. Curll, 1741), p. 15. This, and *Merryland Displayed*, was probably written by one of Curll's hacks, Thomas Stretser, the author of the prose version of *Arbor Vitae*.

13 *The Times*, 17 April 2000, p. 8.

14 *The Public Advertiser*, 2 June 1763, p. 2, col. a/b; reprinted in John Wilkes, *The New Foundling Hospital for Wit* (London, 1786), Vol. III, p. 75.

15 *The Designs of Inigo Jones and Mr. William Kent* (London, J. Vardy, 1744).

16 Ibid.

17 Anon, *A New Atalantis for the Year One Thousand Seven hundred and Fifty-Eight* (2nd ed.; London, M. Thrush, 1758).

18 *La Nuit Merveilluese ou Le Nec Plus Ultra du Plaisir* (no details).

19 Ibid., p. 23.

20 Ibid., p. 33.

21 Ibid., pp. 46, 49.

22 Ibid., pp. 49–50.
23 Julie Peakman, *Mighty Lewd Books, The Development of Pornography in Eighteenth-century England* (Basingstoke, Palgrave Press, 2003), pp. 126–60.
24 Antonio Gavin, *Master-Key to Popery* (Dublin, J. Walthoe, 1724), p. 43.
25 Nuns were given presents such as ribbons, watches, looking glasses and seals, and the priests sent them amorous letters declaring their passion. The Fathers were declared unfit to govern the nuns as charged in the court of France by the nuns of St Katherin [*sic*], near Provins, in France, against the Father Cordeliers their confessors. *The Nunns Complaints Against The Fryars* (London, E. H. and Robert Pawlett, 1676. Reprint by Alfred Harper Free Press Office, 1865), p. 34. This was reprinted several times in France, and 'faithfully done into English'.
26 Anon, *The Priest Gelded: Or, Popery At The Last Gasp Shewing* (London, A. McCulh, 1747), pp. 10–11.
27 A couple of hills as breasts had already been used in the frontispiece for *A New Description of Merryland*.
28 'Captain Samuel Cock', *A Voyage to Lethe* (London, J. Conybeare, 1741), p. 8.
29 *The Fruit-shop, A Tale Vol. I.* (London, C. Moran, 1765), p. 19. A second edition was printed in 1766 for J. Harrison, near Covent Garden.
30 *Tristram Shandy* had been brought out in a version containing pornographic prints.
31 'Pisanus Fraxi' [Henry Spencer Ashbee], *Catena Librorum Tacendorum*, 1877; reprinted as *Bibliography of Forbidden Books* (London, Jack Brussell, 1962), Volume III, p. 108. The author rails, 'You are displayed in our frontispiece, by way of a satirical gibbet'. The ass in the picture is referred to as 'the four-footed philosopher you cultivated an intimacy with at Lyons', a reference to Crébillon whom Sterne met in Paris in 1762 where they agreed to exchange specimens of their own pornography; Jean-Jacques Mayoux, 'Laurence Sterne', in John Traugott (ed.), *Laurence Sterne. A Collection of Critical Essays* (New Jersey, Spectrum, 1968), p. 108. Crébillon is most famous for *Le Sopha* (1742).
32 McCormick, *The Hell-Fire Club*, pp. 195–8.
33 Julie Peakman, *Lascivious Bodies. A Sexual History of the Eighteenth Century* (London, Atlantic, 2004), p. 112.
34 Ibid., p. 22.
35 Mannix, *The Hell-Fire Club*, p. 56.
36 Carl Linnaeus, *System of Nature; a general system of nature through the three grand kingdoms of Animal, Vegetable and Minerals* (1802 edition); original *System Naturae* (1735).
37 Quoted in Londa Schiebinger, *Nature's Body*, p. 19.
38 Anon, *The Spirit of Flagellation* (London, Mary Wilson, n.d.). Ashbee points to three different editions, one by Cannon in 1827; one by E. Dyer in 1852; and one c.1870. Ashbee, *Bibliography of Forbidden Books*, Vol. III, pp. 238–9.
39 *Manon La Fouëtteuse, or the Quintessence of Birch Discipline*, 'Translated from the French by Rebecca Birch, late teacher at Mrs. Busby's Young Ladies

Boarding School' (London, Society of Vice, n.d.). This is Dugdale's reprint of 1860. Rose mentions an edition by Canon, c.1830 in his *Registrum Librorum Eroticorum*, and dates the first edition c.1805. Mendes lists editions of *The Quintessence of Birch Discipline* as from 1883 (with a false imprint of 1870). Yet later, he points to an edition of *Manon la Fouëtteuse*, c.1805, remarking, 'Though probably written in French, it seems to have been published solely in this English translation', citing *Margot, the Birching Beauty* (1905) as the title of the English translation. There appears to be no connection made between the earlier *The Quintessence of Birch Discipline* and *Manon La Fouëtteuse*; Mendes, *Clandestine Erotic Fiction in England 1800–1930* (Hants, Scolar Press, 1993), pp. 158, 368. Ashbee dates it between 1805 and 1810.

40 Peakman, *Mighty Lewd Books*; Mendes, *Clandestine Erotic Fiction*, p. 426.
41 *The Bagnio Miscellany* (London, John Jones, '1792'). This edition is 1870, the imprint being false. See Ashbee, *Bibliography of Forbidden Books*, Vol. 1, p. 113.
42 Anon, *The Birchen Bouquet* (London, c.1770 or 1790), pp. 14–15.
43 Anon, *Exhibition of Female Flagellants, Part Two*, p. 9.
44 *Bon Ton*, June 1792, pp. 323–56.

INDEX

Abergavenny, Lady 52–4
abortifacients 75, 109
abortion 75, 109, 149, 155, 158
Acton, Sir John 118
actresses 77, 80, *see also* theatres
Adam and Eve Club 107
adultery
    adultery trial reports 48–51, 52–4
    categorization as a 'whore' 74
    East Asia 10, 11
advertisements 63, 74, 81, 153
advice manuals 106, 133, 135–8, 147–9
Africa 8, 10, 15
agricultural metaphors 148
alcohol 97
anodyne necklace 63–4
aphrodisiacs 29, 171–2
Arbor Vitae (1732) 145–6, 150–2, 170
Aretino, Pietro 61–2, 104
Ariés, Philippe 32
aristocracy, *see* upper classes
Aristotle's Masterpiece (1684) 106, 136–7, 139
arranged marriages 6, 10
asexuality 26
Ashbee, Henry Spencer 29
Ashford, Mary 56
Astell, Mary 146
asylum commitals 13, 29
Atherton, Bishop John 45–6
Audley, Lord Mervin, *see* Castlehaven, Earl of
Australia 8
autobiographies 79–99

Baddely, Sophia 80
Baines, Barbara 34
Banks, Sir Joseph 160
Bath 66–7, 76
bawdy houses 111
Bellamy, Anne 80
berdaches 10
Berkeley, Theresa 111

Berkeley horse 111
bestiality
    as 'abnormal' behaviour 4, 17, 21
    beyond control of the individual 32
    in the Bible 23
    as 'unnatural' behaviour 23–4
Bible
    bestiality 23
    botanical sexual metaphors 148
    cross-dressing 24
    homosexuality 20, 22
    onanism 140
    rape 34
Bienville, M. D. T. 141
Billington, Mrs 80
biography
    autobiographies 79–99
    whore biographies 61–78
Birchen Bouquet, The (1770/1790) 170–1
birchen twigs 150–1, 171
blaming and shaming 41–57
Bloch, Iwan 200 n.23
blood
    in erotica 105–8, 109, 112, 138–9, 143
    in medical texts 138–9
    menstruation 135, 138
    as proof of virginity 106, 139
boarding schools in erotica 109–11
bodily fluids, *see also* sexual fluids
    humoral system 135–8
    in pornography 133–4
Bogden, Harriet 81
Bonacina, Martin 21
Bond, Anne 55
Bon Ton 27, 107, 109–10, 171
Boswell 74
botanical erotic gardens 159–72
botanical sexual metaphors 145–58
Bourke, Joanna 34
Bouverie, John 160
Bowen, Humphrey 151

Brady, Sean 180 n.16
Branson, Richard 44
Brant, Claire 81
Bronfen, Elizabeth 36
brothels
    brothel keepers 63, 69–70, 82
    as cure for nymphomania 154
    legalisation of 74
    in London 76
    and theatres 77
Brown, 'Capability' 161, 172
Browne, Janet 156
Brownmiller, Susan 34
Bruss, Elizabeth 81
Buddhism 10
buggery, *see* sodomy
Bullough, Vern and Bonnie 26
bundling 6
Burrows, Thomas 21
Butler, Eleanor 23

Camerarius, R. J. 149
Campbell, John 72–3
Canada 13
Canning, Elizabeth 55–6
capital punishments 35–6, 44, 75
Carlini, Bernedetta 22
Carlo Alberto, Prince 125
Carolina, Queen 113, 117–29
Carty, Mary 56
Casanova 69, 71
Castlehaven, Earl of 21, 43
castration 151
Cately, Anne 80, 98
Catholicism
    anti-Catholic pamphlets 54–5, 56–7
    clergy 45–7, 54–5
    in erotica 104, 108–9, 167
    and flagellation 33
    and 'perversion' 19
    sex and marriage in 5–7
    and sodomy trials 45–6
Caxton, William 19
celibacy 54, 75
Chamberlain, Dr Paul 63
Chandler, Richard 160
Charke, Charlotte 80
chastity, female
    Chaste Ideal 90–2
    checking of virginal status 107, 139
    cult of chastity in East Asia 10
    double moral standards towards 75, 90–2
    in Europe 5–6

Chatres, Colonel 55
Childe, John 45–6
children
    flagellation of 109–11
    rape of 35–6
    sexual desire for 32–3
China
    bound feet 27
    homosexuality 14–15
    sex and marriage in 10–12
Christian missionaries 7
Cibber, Mrs 51, 55
civilizing processes 42, 51, 134, 135
Clack, Beverley 36
clap (gonorrhoea) 76
Clarissa 34–5
Clark, Anna 34
Clarke, Norma 80
class, *see also* upper classes
    and cross-dressing 26
    and honour 50
    Napoleonic Wars 123–4
    rise of the middle class 42
    whore biographies 61, 63
Cleland, John 22, 33, 62, 101, 111
clerics 45–7, 54–5
clitoris 141, 142–3
Cody, Lisa 26
colonies and empires 7–10, 15, 37–8
communal social control 20–1
companionate marriage 6
concubines 10, 12
Confucianism 10, 12
Conjugal Love Reveal'd, Mysteries of (Venette, 1712) 106, 136, 139, 147
Conlin, Jonathan G. W. 32
contraception 155
Cooke, George 97
Cooper, Anthony Ashley 161
coquette 92–4
Cornelys, Madame 71
Cotton, Colonel 86–7, 90
courtesans, *see* prostitution
court reports 43–57, 64
courtship fiction 102
Craven, Earl of 83, 86, 91
Cresswell, Mother 78
criminal acts 17, 20
criminal conversations 47–9, 51, 52
Crivelli, Bartolomea 22
cross-dressing 15, 20, 24–8, 71
Cruickshank, Dan 164
cuckolding 49, 50, 52

Curll, Edmund 43, 44, 55, 151, 166, 172

Daoism 10
Darnton, Robert 205 n.3
Darwin, Erasmus 156, 172
Dashwood, Sir Francis 67–8, 107, 160, 162–6, 168–9
Davies, Fanny 70–1
Dawkins, James 160
Dawson, Nancy 65, 66, 69, 77
Dawson, Sally 71–2, 76
Daybell, James 202 n.4
death and sex, links between 36–7
death penalties, *see* capital punishments
defloration 74, 75–6, 102, 105–8, 139
Defoe, Daniel 62, 72, 73
D'Emiliane, Gabriel 54
D'Emilio, John 8
demi-reps 82
D'Eon, Chevalier 26
de Rais, Gilles 24
Derham, William 18–19
De Sade, Marquis 28–33
devil 23–4, 32
Dialogue Between a Married Lady and a Maid, A (1688 and 1740) 62, 104, 107, 142, 143
diarists 81
Diderot, Denis 31–2
dildos 21, 22
Dilettanti Society 160
disgust thresholds 135
D'Israeli, Isaac 81
Divan Club 67–8
divorce laws 47–8, 50–1, 56
dogs 21, 23
Dollimore, John 26
dominatrices 27, *see also* flagellation
Douglas, Jane 65, 69–70
Downing, Lisa 36
Dublin 76, 82
Dunton, John 73–4

East Asia 10–12
Ecclesiastical courts 45
educated hostess 87–9
effeminacy 20, 25
ejaculation
    and definitions of sodomy 21, 43
    in erotica 143
    female ejaculation 142–3
Elias, Norbert 42, 51, 135
elite classes, *see* upper classes

Ellis, Markman 79
elopements 34
Enlightenment 38, 133–44, 147
erotica, *see also* pornography
    biography 61–78, 79–99
    botanical sexual metaphors 145–58
    definitions of 134
    development of erotic book trade 43
    development of erotic genre 102, 147–9
    and the erotic garden 159, 166–72
    fetishisms 27
    French erotica 62, 63, 102, 104, 108–9, 111, 143, 167
    history of the word pornography 61–2
    memoirs as 81–2
    novels 62, 80, 102, 110
    as perversion 28–33
    types of reader 78
erotic gardens 159–72
essentialism 3, 13–14
Europe 5–7
evil 18–19, 23, 92
Exhibition of Female Flagellants (1777) 27, 29, 110–11
experimentation, sexual 28
extramarital sex, *see* adultery

false modesty 92
family structures 6
Female Husband, The (Fielding, 1746) 22
feminism 51
Ferdinand IV, King 114, 117
fertility imagery 148–9
Fetherstonhaugh, Sir Harry 115
fetishism
    and cross-dressing 26
    definition of 26–8
    dress fetishism 26
    feet/shoes 26–7
Fielding, Henry 22, 55–6, 103
Fielding, John 73
Finch, Hon. John 64, 65
Fisher, Kitty 65, 69, 70, 77
'fishing fleet' 9
flagellation
    botanical sexual metaphors 150–1
    and the erotic garden 170–2
    Marquis de Sade 29
    in pornography 32–3
    as self-mortification 33
    as a stimulant 27, 33, 108

as theme in erotica 102, 108–12
women as flagellators 32–3, 108, 110, 170
'flash' houses 82
Florentine inquisitional records 22
fluids, sexual
   body beyond control 32
   and conception 147
   in erotica 31, 142–4
   in medical texts 140–2
   portrayed in erotic gardens 164
   semen 135, 142, 143, 147–8, 151
   vaginal fluids 141, 142–3, 147, 153, 164
foot fetishism 27
fornication 5, 45
Foucault, Michel 4, 13, 20, 28, 42
foundling hospitals 72–3
Foyster, Elizabeth 50
France
   courtesans 82
   French erotica 62, 63, 102, 104, 108–9, 111, 143, 167
   French sex advice manuals 133
   homosexuality 13, 14, 15
   Napoleonic Wars 118–29
fraud 14, 22
Freud, Sigmund 23, 39

gardens, erotic 159–72
Gavin, Antonio 54
Gay, Peter 199 n.3
gender
   asexuality 26
   botanical sexual metaphors 149
   and cross-dressing 26
   and honour 50
   and the laws of nature 156–7
   and politics 113, 115
   'proper' gender roles 25
   and sexual identity 12
   third gender 10
   women seen as inferior to men 4, 19, 22, 144, 152
Geneanthropeiae (Sinibaldus, 1642) 106, 136
Gentleman's Magazine 76, 109–10
Germain, Sir John 49
Germany 14
Girard, Father 37
gonorrhoea (clap) 76
Gothic literature 37
Gowing, Laura 50
Graefer, John Andreas 161

Gray, Alice 35–6
green sickness 139, 151
Greville, Charles Francis 115–16, 120–1, 125, 126, 127
Grew, Nehemiah 169–70, 209 n.21
guilt 23, 41–2, 44

Habermas, Jürgen 42, 51
Hale, Mathew 35
Hamilton, Emma 113–29, 161
Hamilton, Mary 22
Hamilton, William 113, 114, 116–17, 118, 120–9, 161
hangings, public 46
Hannan, William 165–6
Harlot's Progress, The (Hogarth, 1732) 7, 72, 73
Harvey, William 153
Hayes, Charlotte 107
Hayes, Sally 94
hell-fire clubs 160–2, 164, 169
Herrup, Cynthia 43
heterosexuality
   and cross-dressing 25
   learned behaviour 174 n.7
   as 'normal' behaviour 4, 14, 75
hijras 10
Hill, Fanny, *see Memoirs of a Woman of Pleasure*
Hill, John 55–6
Hinduism 8
Hinton, Laura 34–5
Hogarth, William 36, 72, 73
homosexuality, *see also* lesbianism; sodomy; tribadism
   as 'abnormal' behaviour 14
   association with cross-dressing 25
   in the Bible 20, 22
   changes in perceptions of 18
   eighteenth-century attitudes to 13–15
   female homosexuality ignored 14, 105
   and prostitution 12
   sodomy between women 22
Hone, Nathaniel 69
honour 42–3, 50, 90, 93, *see also* shame
Hopping, Elizabeth 52
Horowitz, Helen 8
humoral system 135–8, 143
Hurteau, Pierre 21
Hyam, Richard 8–9
hymen, breaking of 106, 139
hysteria 140–2

Ideal Woman (versus the whore) 75, 79–80
identity, sexual
　historical development of 3–4
　homosexuality 14
illegitimate children 75
impotence
　botanical sexual metaphors 150
　flagellation as cure for 108, 111
　and the heating of sexual fluids 140
incest
　as 'abnormal' behaviour 4
　Diderot on 32
　and witchcraft 24
India 8–9, 10
industrialization 6–7, 42
infanticide 75
inheritance, threats to 43
initiations
　Catholic priests 55
　defloration 102, 105–8, 139
　in early French erotica 30–1
　and flagellation 110
　in *Memoirs of a Woman of Pleasure* 102–5
　as theme in erotica 102
　violent 101
　women by men 105–8
　women by women 102–5
inter-racial relationships 8–9, 10
Irish women 71–2, 76
Islam 8, 15
Italy 6, 13, 102

James, Dr Robert 147
Japan 12
jealous lovers 96–7
Jersey, Lord 27
Jocelyn, Bishop Percy 46–7
Johnstone, Julia 82, 84, 86–99
Jones, Captain 44–5
Judeo-Christian ethic 20
Justine (de Sade, 1899) 29

Kent, William 161, 166, 172
Kertbeny, Karl-Maria 14
kiltgang 6
Knights of St Francis 160, 162, 169
Krafft-Ebing, Richard von 36, 37, 39
Kunzle, David 26–7

L'Académie des Dames (1680) 62, 104, 107, 139
Lamb, Lord 87

Laqueur, Thomas 20
Lawless, Mr 95, 96
Leeson, Margaret ('Peg Plunkett') 72, 82, 83, 85–99
legislation
　capital crimes 35–6, 44
　prostitution 12–13, 74
　to protect children 32
　to protect women 4
　public indecency laws 15
　and race 10, 11
　rape 35
　rape as a property crime 34
　religious basis 20
　sodomy 14–15, 21, 43
lesbianism
　in early French erotica 30–1
　and fraud 14
　initiations of women by women 102–5
　and the law 22
　natural part of woman's sexual initiation 31, 105
　tribadism 102–5, 143
Levine, Philippa 37–8
Lewis, Ann 79
Lewis, Matthew 37
Life of the Late Celebrated Mrs Elizabeth Wisebourn, The (Annodyne Tanner, 1721) 63
life-writing 80–1
Liliequist, Jonas 23
Linck, Catherina Margaretha 22
Linnaeus, Carl 149–50, 156, 159, 169–70
literacy, increasing 43
Llangollen Ladies 23
London 13, 74, 76–7
Loth, David 200 n.23
Ludovicus, M. 72–3
Lydell, Richard 52–4, 55

Madan, Martin 72, 73
Magdalene houses 13, 72
Mandeville, Bernard 74
Manningham, Sir Richard 155
Mannix, Daniel 164
Marcus, Laura 81
Maria Carolina, Queen 113, 117–29
Marie Antoinette 114, 117, 124
marriage
　arranged marriages 6, 10
　colonies and empires 7–10
　companionate marriage, history of 6

divorce laws 47–8, 50–1, 56
and premium of virginity 4
and rape 34
and religion 5–6
sex and marriage in Europe, history of 5–7
women pretending to be men 14, 22, 25
Marshall, Timothy 36–7
Marten, John 148, 153
masturbation
   in erotica 104–5, 106, 143
   in medical texts 140–2
   mutual masturbation 103, 143
Maubray, John 147
McCormick, Donald 169
M'Clean, Sally 72
medical texts
   blood 138–9
   botanical sexual metaphors 150–8
   and the humoral system 135–8
   necrophilia 36
   quasi-medical erotica 147, 151
   sexual fluids 138–9
medicine
   abortifacients 75, 109
   and flagellation 108
   humoral system 135–8
   sex as cure for ailments 147–8, 151
   sperm as 147–8
   venereal disease 63–4, 75, 76, 153
Medmenham 160, 162
Meibomius, John Henry 150–1
melancholia 135, 141–2
memoirs 80, 81–2, *see also* autobiographies
Memoirs of a Woman of Pleasure (Cleland, 1748/49) 33, 62, 101–12, 156
men
   cross-dressing 25
   male-orientated view presented in whore biographies 72
   male prostitutes 12, 14, 15
   pretending to be women 22
   recipients of flagellation 108
menstruation 135, 138
Merryland books 105, 148, 164, 166
Miller, Philip 170
Misaubin, Dr 151–2
misogyny 34–5
mistresses
   colonies and empires 8–9
   versus courtesans 82

Emma Hamilton 115–17
whore biographies 69
mollies 25
monks 33, 54, 104, 167–8
Montagu, Sir John (Lord Sandwich) 67, 68, 69, 107
morality
   blaming and shaming 41–57
   colonies and empires 7–8, 10
   courtesans' 90
   double standards 75, 90–2
   East Asia 11, 12
   and the Magdalene houses 13
   moral movements 73–4
   moral shaming 45
   and religion 18, 20
   social morality 20
Mosse, George L. 38
Mother Clap's Molly House 25
Motteux, Peter Anthony 151
Muravyeva, Marianna 42
Murray, Fanny 65, 66–9, 76, 77
mutual masturbation 103, 143
Mysteries of Conjugal Love Reveal'd (Venette, 1712) 106, 136, 139, 147

Nash, Beau Richard 67, 68
Nash, David 42
nationalism 37–8
Native Americans 7, 10
Natural History of Arbor Vitae (1732) 145–6, 150–2, 170
Natural History of the Frutex Vulvaria (1732) 145–6, 152–8, 170
nature
   botanical sexual metaphors 145–58
   erotic gardens 159–72
   natural versus unnatural sex 18–21
   perversion of 18–19
necrophilia 33, 34–7
Needham, Elizabeth 78
Nelson, Horatio 113, 114, 118, 122, 124–5, 126–9
neoclassical revival 159–60, 168–9, 171
newspapers
   investigative journalism 56
   letters to 45
   offering access to erotica 78
   and sodomy trials 45, 47
   trial by journalism 52
New Zealand 8
Ng, Vivien 10
Norfolk, Duke and Duchess of 49
North America 8, 10, 13

nose-gays 27–8, 170–1
Nourse, Captain Sir Joseph 95, 98
novels 62, 80, 102, 110, *see also* whore biographies
nuns 33, 54, 104, 108–9, 143, 167–8
Nussbaum, Felicity 81
nymphomania 32, 141, 154

onanism 140
orange girls 77
orgasm 140, 143, 147, 153
Other 37–8

paedophilia 32–3
pain and pleasure, links between 105
Pallavicino, Ferrante 62
Paris 13, 14
Parsons, Nancy 77
Pascal, Blaise 23
patriarchy 34, 80
pederasty 35–6
penetration
    and blood 105
    and definitions of sodomy 21, 25, 43
    as 'normal' behaviour 75
    in pornography 33
penis 108, 145, 148, 150, 168, 169
Penney, James 24
penny dreadfuls 36
Pensées ('Thoughts', Pascal, 1660) 23
Pepys, Samuel 36
Perkins, Erasmus 202 n.51
Perkins, William 24
perversions 17–39
    definition of 18–19
Phillips, Constantia 80
Pilkington, Laetitia 80
pillories 22, 23, 45, 51
plants, sexuality of 149–50, 156–7, 169–70
pleasure gardens 76–7
Plunkett, Peg (Margaret Leeson) 72, 82, 83, 85–99
politics
    and gender 113, 115
    political satire 152
    sodomy 21, 43
polygamy 8, 12, 73
Ponsonby, Lord 90, 95
Ponsonby, Sarah 23
pornography, *see also* erotica
    advertisements 63
    the body in 133–44
    conservative nature of 133–4
    definitions of 134
    Edmund Curll 43, 44, 55, 151, 166, 172
    history of the word 61–2
    memoirs as 81–2
    and necrophilia 37
    novels 62
    and perversion 28–33
    quasi-pornographic pamphlets 55
    and taboo 133
Porter, Roy 34, 35
pox (syphilis) 76, 151, 152–3, 158
pregnancy 75, 148–9, 155, 158, *see also* procreation
pre-marital sex 5–7
printing developments 28, 43
privacy, increasing 28
procreation
    as baseline 'normal' sex 21, 75
    and the definitions of 'perversion' 37
    emission of seed from both sexes 147, 153–4
    and orgasm 140, 147, 153–4
    separation from sex 3
    wasted seminal fluid 140
prostitution, *see also* brothels
    autobiographies 79–99
    characterizations of 84
    East Asia 10
    'fallen' women 13, 84, 85, 91
    history of 12–13
    male prostitutes 12, 14, 15
    memoirs 81–2
    prostitutes as victims 84, 87
    the redeemable prostitute 13, 72
    solutions to 72–4
    and venereal disease 13, 76, 152–3
    and virginity 107
    whore biographies 61–78
Protestantism
    anti-Catholic pamphlets 54
    and 'perversion' 19
    and the regulation of sex 20
    religious perversion and sexual corruption 33
    sex and marriage in 5–7, 8
    and sodomy trials 45
Prussian Secret Archives 22
public indecency laws 15
public punishments 21, 45–6, 51–2
purple gloves 27–8

queer theory 14

rabbits, giving birth to 155
race 8–10, 37–8
'rags to riches' tales 63, 113–14, 115
rape
  East Asia 10
  history of 34
  homosexual rape 14
  as perversion 34–7
  as property crime 34
  rape and murder in pamphlets 55, 56–7
  and slavery 8
Rare Verities, The Cabinet of Venus Unlocked and her Secrets Laid Open (1657) 106, 136, 138
Ray, John 169
regulation of sex
  Church to medicine shift 4
  colonies and empires 8
  of homosexuality 14–15
  prostitution 12–13
  religion 4, 10, 20, 21
religion, *see also* Bible; *specific religions*
  clerics 45–7, 54–5
  and cross-dressing 24–5
  in erotica 104, 167
  and homosexuality 15
  monks and nuns 33, 54, 104, 108–9, 143, 167–8
  and 'perversion' 19, 24
  and the regulation of sex 4, 10, 20, 21
  sinfulness of sex 5–6, 18–19, 20, 23
  and sodomy trials 44, 45–7
  and 'unnatural' acts 18
Repton, Humphrey 161, 172
reputation, upholding of 50–1, 75, 79–80, 92, 98
Resnick, Phillip 36
revenge 80–1, 97–9
Revett, Nicholas 160
Reynolds, Joshua 69
Richardson, Joanna 82
Richardson, Ruth 36–7
Richardson, Samuel 80
Robinson, Mary 80
Romano, Giulio 61
Rosman, Jonathan 36
Ross, David 69
Rossi, William 26

rough music 20, 51
Rousseau, George S. 32
Russia 6–7

sadism 33, *see also* flagellation
Salisbury, Sally 64–5, 76, 77
satires 69, 72, 73, 146, 155, 157
Saunders, Christopher 23
Sawday, Jonathan 36–7, 201 n.43
Schiebinger, Londa 156–7
Schurig, Martin 36
science 145–50, 159, 169–70
Scottish kirk courts 45
sedation 37
seduction
  courtesans' first sexual encounters 89–90
  with force 34
  ploys of seduction 75
  with promises of marriage 74
self-pollution, *see* masturbation
Selwyn, George 36
semen 135, 142, 143, 147–8, 151
sensationalism 56
sexology 39, *see also* Freud, Sigmund; Krafft-Ebing, Richard von
sexual fluids
  body beyond control 32
  and conception 147
  in erotica 31, 142–4
  in medical texts 140–2
  portrayed in erotic gardens 164
  semen 135, 142, 143, 147–8, 151
  vaginal fluids 141, 142–3, 147, 153, 164
sexual instruction/advice manuals 106, 133, 135–8, 147–9
sexually transmitted diseases (STDs), *see* venereal disease
Shaftesbury, Earl of 161
shame 20, 41–57
Sharia law 15
Sharp, Jane 148
Sheppard, Dillon 44
Sheridan, Tom 93
shoe fetishism 27
Shorter, Edward 6
Sigel, Lisa 33
Simonis, Johan George 36
sinfulness of sex 5–6, 18–19, 20, 23
Sinibaldus 106, 136
skimmington rides 21, 51
slavery 8
Sloper, Theophilus 51

Smith, Thomas 35–6
social constructionism 3–4, 13–14
social morality 20
social movement 11
Societies for the Reformation of
 Manners 73–4
sodomy
 as 'abnormal' behaviour 4
 association with cross-dressing 25
 beyond control of the individual
  32
 blame and shame pamphlets 43–5,
  56–7
 definitions of 21, 25, 43
 in erotica 105
 in *Memoirs of a Woman of
  Pleasure* 105
 as perversion 'against nature' 21
 regulation of sex 15
 between two women 22
 types of 21
Sommer, Matthew 10
South America 10
South Asia 8–10
Spacks, Patricia Meyer 28
Spain 6
Spencer, Jack 67
sperm, as medicine 147–8, *see also*
 semen
Spit-Fires 94–6
Spufford, Margaret 196 n.51
Stanhope, Sir William 67
Stearns, Peter 8
Sterne, Laurence 169
Stevenson, John Hall 169
Stone, Lawrence 6
Stowe gardens 162–3
Stretser, Thomas 170
Stuart, James 160
Sweden 23–4
syphilis (pox) 76, 151, 152–3, 158

taboo 133, 135
theatres 20, 77
Thompson, E.P. 51
Thomspon, Lynda M. 80
Thrale, Hester 22
Tickle, Tom 55
Tissot, Samuel-Auguste 140, 148
Tofts, Mary 155
Tomaselli, Sylvana 34
Tournefort, Joseph 169
trans activism 14
transvestism 26, *see also* cross-dressing

travel 159–60
travelogues 160, 171
tree of life 145, 148, 150, 156
trial reports 43–57, 64
tribadism 102–5, 143
*True History and Adventures of
 Catherine Vizzani, The* (Cleland,
 1755) 22
Trumbach, Randolph 12, 102–3,
 200 n.23

United States of America 8, 13
upper classes
 adultery trials 48–9
 arranged marriages 6
 and cross-dressing 26
 cross-dressing 25
 East Asia 11, 12
 and honour 42–3, 50
 Japan 12
 noble and royal women 114–15
 and pornography 28
 rarity of pre-marital sex (for
  women) 6
urbanization
 and bestiality 24
 East Asia 10–11
 effect on sex and marriage in
  Europe 6–7
 and homosexuality 15
 and prostitution 12

vaginal fluids 141, 142–3, 147, 153,
 164
venereal disease
 blamed on women 151, 152–3, 158
 botanical sexual metaphors 146
 Europe 7
 gonorrhoea (clap) 76
 medicine 63–4, 75, 76
 premium of virginity 76
 and prostitution 13, 76, 152–3
 sexual cures for 151–2
 syphilis (pox) 76, 151, 152–3, 158
Venette, Nicolas 106, 136, 139, 147
vengeful whore 97–9
Venus 56, 104, 163
Venus in the Cloister (1692 and 1725)
 104, 105, 108–9
Venus Schoolmistress, or Birchen Sports
 (1788) 111
victim-blaming 56
victims, prostitutes as 84, 87
violence 34–5, 96–7, 105, *see also* rape

virginity
    blood as proof of 106, 139
    checking of virginal status 107, 139
    courtesan's first sexual encounters 89–90
    defloration 74, 75–6, 102, 105–8, 139
    faking of 106–7
    and honour 91–2
    hymen, breaking of 106, 139
    in medical texts 139
    premium of 4, 76
    in rape trials 56
    seduction with force 34, 101
    society's view of chastity 74
    and the upper classes 6
virtuosi 146
Vizzani, Catherine 22
von Uffenbach, Baron 74
voyeurism 104–5, 108

Walpole, Horace 37, 118, 156, 162
Ward, Edward 170
Weeks, Jeffrey 13–14
Weir, Thomas 24
Welch, Saunders 74
West Wycombe estate 162–6
whipping, *see* flagellation
whore biographies 61–78
wildness 94–5, 161
Wilkes, John 32, 67, 69, 163, 165
Wilson, Amy 86, 89–90, 93–4, 95

Wilson, Fanny 86, 93, 97
Wilson, Harriette 27, 34, 82–4, 86–99
Wilson, Sophia 34, 86, 88, 93
Winckelmann, Johann Joachim 160
Winklin, William 22
Wisebourn, Elizabeth 63, 76, 78
witchcraft 23, 24, 56
women
    bestiality 21, 23
    botanical sexual metaphors 152–8
    cross-dressing 25
    double moral standards towards 75, 90–2
    female ejaculation 142–3
    female friendships 115
    as flagellators 32–3, 108, 110, 170
    and the humoral system 135
    masturbation 140–2
    objects of necrophilia 36
    power and authority 51
    rape 34–5
    readers of erotica 78
    as second-class citizens 79
    seen as inferior to men 4, 19, 22, 144, 152
    status of women and women's literature 81
    women's social place 22
Wood, Robert 160
wronged daughter 85–7
Wycliffe 19

Yeazell, Ruth 102

www.ingramcontent.com/pod-product-compliance
Lightning Source LLC
Chambersburg PA
CBHW050138240426
43673CB00043B/1709